# THE STORY OF
# LEICESTER

# THE STORY OF
# LEICESTER

## SIOBHAN BEGLEY

*For my husband Paul Winstone (1951–2006),*
*who loved Leicester*

First published 2013

The History Press
The Mill, Brimscombe Port
Stroud, Gloucestershire, GL5 2QG
www.thehistorypress.co.uk

British Library Cataloguing in Publication Data.
A catalogue record for this book is available from the British Library.

ISBN 978 1 86077 695 3

Typesetting and origination by The History Press
Printed in Great Britain

# CONTENTS

# ACKNOWLEDGEMENTS

I would like to acknowledge the help I received in locating and reproducing material from Evelyn Cornell, Margaret Maclean, Laura Unwin and Ben Wynne at the David Wilson Library, University of Leicester.

A special thank you also goes to Jenny Moran at the Record Office for Leicestershire, Leicester and Rutland for her help and patience.

Thanks are also due to Malcolm Noble for his support and his help with reproducing old photographs.

For those images provided courtesy of the University of Leicester Special Collections on pages 12, 13, 17, 25, 26, 27, 35, 36, 37, 45, 50, 51 ,61, 63, 65, 67, 76, 79, 83, 84, 90, 91, 92, 93, 107, 116 and 147 thanks must also be given for reproduction to the My Leicestershire History website www.myleicestershire.org.uk.

Finally I would like to thank all the other people who have encouraged or helped me while writing this book, including Lucy Byrne, John Booth, Eva Sitaram Booth, Margaret Crane, Gervase French, Loveday Hodson, Asaf Hussain, Gwen Jackson, Kath Longford, Aubrey Newman, Richard Rodger, Janet Smith, Sue Wale, Ben Webb, Caroline Wessel and especially Rob Colls, without whom I would not have written this book at all.

# FOREWORD

This version of the story of Leicester attempts a quick journey through the last 2,000 years, tracing both changes and continuities. The first episode belongs to the Romano-British town of Ratae that once stood on the site of Leicester and which thrived for more than 300 years before disappearing into obscurity. During the next six or so centuries we catch only brief glimpses of the town in various phases – as a Mercian bishopric, as a Danish borough, as an English town – until the Normans describe it fully for us in the Domesday Book. The story then moves on to Catholic, medieval Leicester, a busy market town under the control of the lord at the castle, though struggling and gradually gaining more independence. There follows change under the Tudors: stately buildings are destroyed, the town becomes a Protestant stronghold and poverty is widespread in the town for lack of a staple industry. During civil war, the townspeople suffer still more when the Royalists sack the town. More welcome change comes in the late seventeenth and eighteenth centuries when the town prospers as an agricultural centre, people in the town and county take to manufacturing stockings and better roads, and canals open up the town to the outside world. The hosiery industry, though, does not live up to its early promise, and poor working conditions and a fluctuating market make the life of the framework knitters hard. Improvements are made to the town and, for those with money, a round of entertainments are available. The story of nineteenth-century Leicester is a complex story of political reform, population expansion, public health issues the emergence of shoe manufacture, industrialisation, suburbanisation and the rebuilding of much of the town centre. Late Victorian Leicester is also a town with a vibrant organised social life. In the twentieth century, Leicester is a more democratic and inclusive place but the survival of the traditional industries into the late century maintains a strong continuity with the past. The latest episode of Leicester history is full of change, the city has been enriched by new cultures and the old occupations have largely gone. Many of the old buildings have gone too but there is still enough remaining to remind us of the past.

In writing this account of the story of Leicester I have drawn very extensively on existing literature. I have acknowledged the writers, I hope sufficiently, in my notes to the text and have greatly enjoyed reading their work. A special mention, however, must be made of the work of the late Professor Jack Simmons whose work has been drawn on in every chapter. His *Leicester Past and Present* is an absorbing and scholarly piece of work with which I would not have the audacity to compete.

*one*

# BEGINNINGS

### Romans, Anglo-Saxons and Danes

## Ratae Corieltavorum: the Settlement at the Crossroads

The twelfth-century chronicler Geoffrey of Monmouth created a myth that Leicester was named after King Lear, and that the legendary king was buried somewhere in the city or close by. Sadly for all of us who have enjoyed this story, there is no historical evidence to support it. All we know about the origins of Leicester is that there was an Iron Age settlement on the bank of the River Soar, and from this developed the Romano-British town of Ratae.[1] No contemporary historian recorded the history of Ratae, and therefore what we know about the town stems from archaeology, wider historical knowledge and speculation. Much is owed to an excavation of the Roman baths in the 1930s and later projects led by archaeologists based at the University of Leicester, including the recent excavations in the Highcross area.[2]

At the time of the Roman conquest, Iron Age Britain was inhabited by a variety of different tribes, each commanding certain geographical areas of land. Ratae was a settlement of the Corieltavi tribe, who were associated with a large swathe of territory in what is today's East Midlands, including the lands that would later become Leicestershire, Nottinghamshire and Lincolnshire. The tribe had trading links with Gaul as well as other parts of Britain and they minted their own coins. Their settlement by the Soar had been established for at least a hundred years before the Romans arrived, and although details of the life led here are obscure, excavations have unearthed pottery, jewellery and coins as well as revealing traces of roundhouses.[3]

When Julius Caesar invaded Britain in 54 BC, Britain was to the Romans a place beyond the boundaries of the known world, and the success of Caesar's adventure won him considerable prestige in Rome. Back in Britain, however, the Roman troops did not venture beyond the south, and it was not until nearly a hundred years later, after the second Roman invasion in AD 43, that the invaders advanced on the Midlands and arrived at Ratae. The name Ratae derives from a Celtic word meaning ramparts, a derivation shared by certain Irish place names such as Rathmines. Such a name might suggest that Ratae was a defended settlement, though no evidence has been found that local people put up any resistance to the Romans.[4]

The Roman Milestone at Belgrave Gate: a drawing by Leicester artist John Flower (1793–1861). This milestone was discovered in 1771 near Thurmaston. In 1783 it was moved to Belgrave Gate, and in 1844 to the Town Museum. In 2013 it is in the Jewry Wall museum. This image is taken from J. Flower, *Views of Ancient Buildings in the Town and County of Leicester* (Leicester, 1825), courtesy of the University of Leicester Special Collections.

The settlement at Ratae held a key geographical position near a crossroads and a river crossing. The Romans drove a main road, the Fosse Way, between Devon and Lincoln, and close to Ratae this road met a second route extending from east to west, later known as the Gartree Road. It is sometimes said of modern Leicester that it is a place that people go through to get to other destinations, and while this characterisation is annoyingly dismissive there is a certain geographical truth to it that dates back to the time of Ratae.

Early Roman development of the settlement was modest. It is uncertain whether the Romans established a garrison at Ratae, as the archaeological evidence is inconclusive. The geographical features of the site, however, made it a probable choice for military occupation: a river crossing, in particular, was always vulnerable. If there was a garrison, however, the troops would doubtless have left by around AD 80, when the Roman legions moved further north and west in a campaign to extend their territories.

These markings on the Roman milestone record a distance of two miles from Ratae. The inscription translated reads: 'To the Emperor and Caesar, the august Trajan Hadrian, surnamed Particus, grandson of the divine Nerva Pontifex Maximus, four times invested with tribunitial power, three times consul: from Ratae two miles.' This image is taken from J. Nichols, *The History and Antiquities of the County of Leicester, Vol. 1. Part I., The Town of Leicester* (London, 1795); courtesy of the University of Leicester Special Collections. The translation of the inscription is taken from www. Leicester.co.uk/roman/16/accessed 12 July 2013.

It was in the second century AD that Ratae began to develop into a sophisticated town. The Romans maintained control of it by making it a *civitas*, an administrative capital for the region run by the local tribal aristocracy but in accordance with Roman procedures. It was a well-used approach throughout the Empire and was applied in a variety of middle-sized settlements in Britain. At the top of the hierarchy of Romano-British towns were York, Lincoln, Colchester and Gloucester. These were the *coloniae*, centres where Romans, often veteran legionaries who had been given land, formed a large part of the local population. Less prestigious than the *coloniae*, the *civitas* capitals were also important towns on the urban network, and their development was planned so that they could perform their administrative responsibilities as well as fulfilling the commerce and leisure functions that Roman culture expected towns to provide. The *colonia* of Lincoln was in the northern part of the Corieltavi region, and therefore Ratae, in the south of the region, was a logical site for the administrative capital.

## Ratae Corieltavorum: Romano-British Town

In the early second century a street grid was laid out, with individual plots reserved for building, and in the early to mid-century two major stone public buildings, the public baths and the forum, were constructed at the heart of the town. The remains of the baths can still be seen in Leicester today at a site by St Nicholas Circle, flanked on one side by the Jewry Wall Museum and on the other by St Nicholas church. All that is left of the interior is the outline of the different chambers, which provided hot, cold and tepid baths as well as changing rooms and latrines. There was a hypocaust providing underfloor heating and furnaces to heat the hot baths, but it is uncertain how the water supply was organised. The buildings were enclosed by porticoes on the south side as well as on the north side, where there may also have been a row of shops.[5]

On the west side, by St Nicholas church, there still stands an impressive stretch of Roman wall with two arches, thought to have been an entrance into the baths from an adjacent 'exercise hall', the remains of which lie under the church. The wall has long been known locally as the Jewry Wall, and many suggestions have been made about the origins of the name. Most recent scholarship suggests that it dates from the late medieval or early modern period and that there was no connection between the wall and a Jewish community living in Leicester; rather the name derived from a tendency among Gentiles of the period to attribute unusual and mysterious things to the Jews.[6]

There was also a building close by the baths on the site of St Nicholas Circle, apparently constructed in the late second century. This was a basilica with a 20ft aisle and a 50ft nave that may have been a temple dedicated to Mithras.

The forum was situated just east of the baths and comprised an open piazza flanked by ranges of porticoes on the west, east and south sides, with a basilica at the north end. In the basilica, local officials and their staff would have conducted public business, while the open centre of the forum was for markets and meetings. There would most likely also have been shops in the forum porticoes looking inwards to the piazza and possibly also outwards to the street.

In the late second or early third century a large market hall, or *macellum*, was constructed directly north of the forum. Like the forum this also had an open court bounded by colonnades, in between which were individual shops. This provision for extra market space is testament to the fact that Ratae was a prosperous and growing commercial centre.

As well as public works, there were also private building projects in the town. These included workplace accommodation and simple dwellings as well as more elaborate houses. A luxurious private house was excavated in the late 1950s at Blue Boar Lane, on a site that now lies under Vaughan Way.

This was a courtyard house erected in the early second century and improved some decades later with decoration that included floor mosaics as well as elaborate wall frescos depicting mythological scenes. The quality of the wall paintings was outstanding in comparison with most of the fresco work in Roman Britain, and as a result it has been speculated that perhaps an Italian or Gaulish artist lived in Ratae at this time.[7]

Some attractive mosaic floors from other well-appointed houses have also been found. A geometric mosaic discovered at Blackfriars is considered to be an exceptionally fine example of Romano-British work, and another attractive floor, also of geometric design and with a centrepiece depicting a peacock spreading its feathers, was found in excavations at St Nicholas Street. A further mosaic pavement, first discovered near All Saints' church in the seventeenth century, is a representation of Cyparissus and the stag – recalling the story of a boy who, inconsolable after killing his pet deer by mistake, was turned into a cypress tree, a tree forever linked with sadness, by the god Apollo. This mosaic, intriguing but of lower quality than the others mentioned, is a later creation from a fourth-century house.

A detail from the mosaic depicting Cyparissus and the stag. This was discovered near All Saints' church in the seventeenth century. This image is taken from J. Throsby, *The History and Antiquities of the Ancient Town of Leicester* (Leicester, 1791), courtesy of the University of Leicester Special Collections.

The largest private Roman house excavated in Leicester so far is a villa discovered at Vine Street during the Highcross excavations in the early 2000s. This stone-built house, which had a central courtyard and twenty-six rooms, some with underfloor heating from a hypocaust, clearly belonged to a citizen of exceptional wealth.[8]

In addition to its central area of public buildings and houses, Ratae also had suburbs. Between the early and mid-second century, suburban building rapidly extended from the town centre in all directions. Just as now, some housing locations had more status than others: the wealthier suburban housing was predominantly found in the western part of the town and alongside the Fosse Way. A particularly fine suburban dwelling, long known in Leicester as Danett's Hill or Cherry Orchard Villa, was situated to the west, surrounded by farmland, on the opposite side of the river from the central public buildings.

In the third century, stone town walls were built for the first time, replacing earthworks that had been constructed in the previous century. It is believed that these walls, like those of many other towns, may have been reinforced in the fourth century when city defence would have seemed more urgent. Soldiers of Germanic origin from the Roman army were also stationed in some Romano-British towns to strengthen defence, and certain belt fittings found in Leicester suggest soldiers of this type may been in Ratae.[9]

## The People of Ratae

Unfortunately very little is known about individual inhabitants of the Romano-British town. It was a town of significant size at the heart of the road network, and therefore between the first and the fourth century it seems likely that, in addition to the descendants of the indigenous Corieltavi, the residents included some Latins, people from other parts of Britain and possibly a few residents from other parts of the Roman Empire.

Only fragments of more personal information remain. We know that one resident of the town was Adcobrovatus, whose son M. Ulpius Novanticus was a soldier in a British cohort of the Roman Army in AD 106. This information comes from an army discharge certificate that was found in Porolissum, in modern Romania. The certificate, awarded to Novanticus, gave the details of his origin as Ratae, where he must have enlisted in the early days of Roman occupation, and also reveals that while in the service of the army he was awarded Roman citizenship.[10]

The names of a few other townspeople are known to us from items found in Leicester. One of these is a piece of limestone bearing the name C. Pal Gracilis, engraved in the manner of a tradesman's stamp. A tile has also been found inscribed with the words *Primus X fecit* ('Primus has made ten'). It seems that Primus was a tile maker who at least on this occasion decided to record how many tiles he had made. A further evocative fragment left to us is a piece of Samian pottery linking two names, Verecunda Lydia and Lucius, a gladiator, suggesting a romantic attraction or attachment. Nothing further is known about the couple; one or both may have been a visitor to the town. The mention of a gladiator suggests that there may have been an amphitheatre at Ratae, although no remains have been found. It is possible that a temporary amphitheatre could have been constructed for special occasions and visiting entertainers.[11]

While we know little about the individuals who lived at Ratae, recent archaeological findings have provided us with new information about the diet of the townspeople. There were wells in the town for drinking water, and meat, fish, eggs, cereals, vegetables and fruit and dairy products were all consumed. In the early days of Roman Ratae it seems that mutton was popular, but beef later supplanted this as the most favoured type of meat. Poultry was also part of the diet, as well as freshwater fish, eel and seafood, including mussels, whelks and oysters, thought to have been imported from the Essex coast. The cereals enjoyed were for the most part wheat and barley, and the fruit and vegetables eaten included legumes, leaf beet, plums and apples. Items such as imported olive oil and dates added some luxury to the basics that were locally available, as did wines imported from Italy, Gaul and Rhodes.[12] Of course there were varying levels of wealth and status in the town, and this would have been reflected in diet, just as it was in housing.

A fragment of pottery bearing the names Verecunda Lydia and Lucius Gladiator, a possible romantic attachment. This image is taken from W. Kelly, *Royal Progresses and Visits to Leicester* (Leicester, 1884), courtesy of the University of Leicester Special Collections.

Although Ratae was clearly a significant commercial centre, very few details of the industry and crafts carried out in the town are known, although there are fragments of information that provide glimpses of working life. Activities included sand and gravel quarrying in the second and third centuries, and it is thought that these materials were used for metalling streets and yards. At the same period there were horners and possibly tanners working in the town, and other work included bronze/brass-casting, boneworking, ironworking, metalworking and glassmaking.[13]

The final years of Roman Ratae are obscure. For much of the fourth century it is believed that a settled and prosperous life continued, with renovations made at the forum and roads well maintained.[14] However, in the later years of the century the public buildings of the town were badly damaged by fire, and there was apparently no attempt to fully repair this damage, suggesting that the town was perhaps lacking in resources and on the decline.[15] During these later years, of course, the whole Roman Empire was severely threatened as barbarian peoples breached the imperial frontiers. This resulted in a series of troop withdrawals from Britain, as Rome sought to deal with the pressure in other parts of the Empire. Britain was under threat of attack from Saxons, Picts and Scots, but when British leaders appealed to Rome in 410 for military help this was not granted, and the cities of Britain were told that they were responsible for their own defence.

The links with Rome were crumbling, but the full implications of the change would only have gradually become evident, as villas and public buildings began to decay and barter replaced coinage. Up until the mid-fifth century it is likely that there was still some kind of central authority in Britain. There is evidence that at this time there was still a functioning town life in some larger towns, including Verulanium, Cirencester and Silchester, though it is not certain what was happening in Ratae.[16] By the end of the century, however, the urban life that had been such a significant feature of Roman Britain had collapsed.

## Saxon and Danish Leicester

A scarcity of written sources means that our knowledge of Britain in the fifth and sixth centuries is very limited. However, an account of the period written by the British cleric Gildas recorded that by 550 most of the island was under the sway of Germanic invaders.[17] These migrants, usually called Anglo-Saxons for convenience, comprised three main groups, Angles, Saxons and Jutes, and those who settled in the Midlands came to be known as the Middle Angles.[18]

It is difficult to reconstruct what happened locally during these early years, but archaeological evidence shows that the Angles formed settlements near to the Trent and Welland, the rivers by which they probably arrived, and that later settlements spread to the Soar Valley. To what extent the town that had been Ratae was inhabited at this time, or what happened to the native townspeople after the Roman departure, is unclear. Finds of fifth- to sixth-century Anglo-Saxon jewellery and traces of early Anglo-Saxon houses suggest that some of the migrants settled in the ruins of the town. There may have been conflict between the settlers and any native inhabitants who remained, but as yet there is no evidence of this, and it could be that if there were any townspeople left the newcomers were just absorbed into that population.[19]

A more personal trace of the period comes not from Leicester itself but from nearby Glen Parva, the remains of the so-called Glen Parva lady. This was a skeleton dating from around 600 that was accidentally uncovered at Rye Hill in 1866 and later identified as a young woman aged about 20. She had been buried fully clothed, and among the items found with her were the brooches that had fastened her tunic, and a girdle hanger shaped in the form of a Roman key; this indicated her identity as a married woman with authority in her household. Another item of interest buried with her was a necklace that included a Roman bead. It is thought that the new settlers may have found a superstitious meaning in such relics from the more sophisticated Roman past, and used them as charms. It is clear that the Glen Parva lady was relatively wealthy, but there are no clues pointing towards who she was or why she died. Even so, the story of her discovery and the reconstruction of her appearance presented at the Jewry Wall Museum in Leicester helps bring alive this largely unaccounted-for era in local history.[20]

Different groups of Anglo-Saxon settlers eventually became identified with three main kingdoms, Northumbria, Wessex and Mercia. These were formed through power struggles and warfare between a constellation of smaller kingdoms and tribal groupings, and in the seventh century the Middle Angles were brought under the control of Mercia by the warlord Penda. Since the late sixth century new links had been established with Rome, this time through the missionaries of the Christian Church, and by the mid-seventh century

# ETHELFLOEDA: LADY OF THE MERCIANS

In a corner of the Guildhall courtyard in Leicester is a small statue inscribed with the name Ethelfloeda. This is the image of a Mercian queen, a shadowy but nevertheless important figure in the history of Leicester – for she and her armies liberated the town from the Vikings in 918.

Ethelfloeda, whose name can be also found in the forms Ethelfleda or Aethelflaed, was the eldest child of Alfred the Great, King of the West Saxons. Like her father she was confronted with the need to defend home territory during the Viking wars. She also fought to recapture the lands that had been lost to the invaders, furthering Alfred's aim of uniting the kingdoms of Britain into one Christian kingdom.

As a young woman, Ethelfloeda had left the West Saxon kingdom to marry Ethelred, King of Mercia. The leading role that she came to play in government was, for a woman of her culture and period, highly unusual, and seems to have been encouraged by Ethelred's increasingly poor health.

After the death of her husband, Ethelfloeda succeeded him as ruler of Mercia and became known as Lady of the Mercians. She continued her husband's policy of building strategically placed fortified towns, which acted both as a defence and as a base for attack, and she led campaigns against the Vikings that were coordinated with those of her brother Edward, successor to King Alfred. In 917, Ethelfloeda's armies scored a significant victory when the Danish borough of Derby was recaptured, and in early 918 the Vikings peacefully surrendered Leicester.

Ethelfloeda died at Tamworth later in the same year and was buried in the minster in Gloucester. Her daughter succeeded her, but was soon supplanted and sent to a nunnery by her uncle, Edward of the West Saxons, who then took over the government of Mercia.

## Sources

M. Costambeys, 'Aethelflaed (d.918)' *Oxford Dictionary of National Biography* (Oxford, 2004), www.oxforddnb.com/view/article8907, accessed 28 October 2012; D. Stansbury, *The Lady Who Fought the Vikings* (Plymouth, 1993); F.T. Wainwright, 'Aethelflaed Lady of the Mercians' in (ed.) H.P.R. Finberg, *Scandinavian England: Collected Papers by F.T. Wainwright* (Chichester, 1975), pp.305–24; I.W. Walker, *Mercia and the Making of England* (Stroud, 2000).

Christianity was widespread in Britain. When the son of Penda was converted, missionaries were sent among the Middle Angles, and new monasteries were founded, including those at Peterborough and Breedon.[21]

Leicester remerged from obscurity as a place of importance on the Christian network when in 679 it was made a bishopric. There is little information about this besides the names of the bishops, but artifacts found at Breedon show that new contacts were made between the area and other parts of Britain, as well as with Ireland and the Continent, and we know that one eighth-century Leicester bishop, Torthelm, exchanged letters with St Boniface.[22] However, the bishopric of Leicester proved fragile and short lived. It lapsed in 679, and though it was revived in 737 it only lasted until the 870s, when the Danes invaded the region. The Mercian leaders, unable to withstand the Viking onslaught, surrendered their eastern territories to the invaders, and Danish Mercia became an important part of those occupied lands known collectively as the Danelaw.

Leicester, together with Stamford, Nottingham, Derby and Lincoln, all fell within the occupied territory, and while they were in the Danelaw they were recreated as five boroughs or fortified towns. Saxon Wessex remained independent of the Danes, and under the rule of King Alfred the idea of an English Christian kingdom began to develop, a kingdom that would unite the Angles of the Midlands and the Saxons of the south. Alfred's successors made this vision a reality between the years 911 and 918 when, with a combination of Wessex and Mercian military power they recovered the occupied lands of Danish Mercia and took control of East Anglia to gain an English victory. Leicester was recovered in 918 after a negotiated surrender.

It was after this victory that Leicestershire was created as an entity, when the districts surrounding the five boroughs each took on their borough's name. The Viking threat, however, had not permanently retreated, and during the tenth and eleventh century the region came under Scandanavian control twice more. In 939 Norwegian Vikings took the area for a two-year period and in 1013 the five boroughs fell again to the Danes, shortly before the whole of England was brought under the Danish rule of King Canute; a rule that lasted until the Anglo-Saxon lineage was restored in 1042 under Edward the Confessor. The legacy of Scandinavian rule in Leicestershire is reflected in the local place-names of Leicestershire, where the common Danish ending 'by', in names such as Oadby and Frisby, is particularly widespread.

Although little detail is known about Leicester and its hinterland in the years between the collapse of Roman Britain and the Norman Conquest, we know that the people who lived there gradually cleared the forest and developed the land for open field agriculture. Most of the Leicestershire villages that we know today have roots in the Mercian period, and so were founded long before the Normans arrived. By the time of the Conquest a small English town on the site of the Romano-British town of Ratae was well established. The origin of the name Leicester is surrounded in mystery, but it is believed to mean 'the fortified town of the folk called the Legore'.[23] It is not known when the name Ratae fell into disuse, but by 803 we find the Bishop of Leicester referred to as *Legorensis civitatis episcopus*. The name Ligore is thought to be derived from an ancient river-name Legra, related to the French river-name Loire, and it is thought this name is echoed in both the word Leicester and in the name of a village south of Leicester called Leire. It is not certain, though, that the Legra, rather than the Soar, was ever the name given to the part of the river that flowed past the town's site. The name of the town only gradually developed into its modern form, but after the Normans arrived in England they recorded the place-name as 'Ledecestre', not so different from the name we know today.[24]

*two*

# MEDIEVAL LEICESTER

## The Lords, the Townspeople and the Clerics

After the Norman Conquest of 1066, William the Conqueror set out to secure his authority, and for this purpose he built a string of castles throughout the country. There is no exact record, but it is likely that Leicester Castle had been built by 1068, situated in the south of the town on the bank of the River Soar. It was a typical Norman castle of the motte-and-bailey type. The motte was an earthen mound topped by a timber palisade, designed to tower above the town and provide a lookout over the river and surrounding countryside, and below this there was the court or bailey, encircled by a stockade and ditch.[1] This was to become the base of the new Norman overlord of Leicester, and in the centuries that followed, both the castle and local lands would come under the auspices of a series of Norman and then Plantagenet lords.

How the residents of Leicester reacted to the arrival of the Normans and the building of the castle is not recorded but there is no evidence of extended resistance. For those at the very bottom of the social structure, struggling to survive, this may not have seemed a change of great importance. For people with more to lose it may well have seemed expedient just to cooperate. Certainly, those who resisted in other parts of the country found they were ruthlessly brought to heel.

Another way in which William consolidated his victory was through the compilation of the Domesday Book. This was a thorough inventory of the lands and other assets that the new king had acquired, a survey that would help him extract the maximum revenue from his subjects. The section concerning Leicester was completed in 1086. A side-effect of this tax assessment exercise was that it has provided posterity with a detailed description of Leicester, revealing what had developed at the site since the collapse of the Roman town of Ratae. Leicester was now a town of around 2,000 inhabitants, approximately 378 houses, two mills and six churches.[2] The town was bordered in the north by woodland, and on the other sides lay three great open fields: South Field, West Field and East Field.

The story of Leicester in the four centuries following the Conquest has three major interweaving strands. The first strand belongs to the Norman and then Plantagenet lords, who wielded power locally and were also politicians of national importance. The second narrative concerns the townspeople, who struggled to build a prosperous trading town with a clear civic identity and a measure of independence from their rulers. Finally there is the story of a conventional, medieval Catholic town with many churches, friaries and a famed abbey, but also an early centre of religious dissent.

## Power and Ambition: the Castle and the Medieval Overlords of Leicester

### The Grandmesnils and the Beaumonts

The magnates who ruled from the castle in the centuries after the Conquest brought both benefits and disasters to Leicester. Some improved the environment and added stately buildings to the town, and this, combined with the national status of some of the lords, brought a certain prestige, even splendour, to Leicester during the medieval centuries. Less positively, the personal ambition of several magnates provoked royal retribution, and when punishment came it was the townspeople who were made to suffer for the misdemeanours of the lord.[3]

The first two Norman incumbents of the castle at Leicester, Hugh de Grandmesnil and his son Ivo, left a predominantly negative legacy. Hugh de Grandmesnil had fought alongside William the Conqueror at the Battle of Hastings and was rewarded with 'the honour' of Leicester, which meant that he held dominion over the castle and a group of estates in both Leicestershire and the wider Midlands. There were a number of landowners in Leicester, including the king himself, but the Domesday Book records Hugh de Grandmesnil as the largest landowner in the town, personally owning two churches and 110 houses, and sharing ownership of twenty-four more houses with the king.

Although Hugh de Grandmesnil derived considerable income from Leicester there is no evidence that he contributed anything significant to the welfare of the town. When Ivo succeeded his father the situation became worse. As well as engaging in private warfare in the Midlands, Ivo's ambition led him to join a rebellion against Henry I in 1101. Retaliation came quickly, and the royal forces attacked both the castle and the town of Leicester, causing severe damage. Ivo escaped retribution by going on a crusade, from which he never returned.

After the demise of the Grandmesnils the honour of Leicester was transferred to the Beaumont family, and in 1107 Robert de Beaumont was created the first Earl of Leicester. Beaumont is a name still remembered today in Leicester; examples include Beaumont Leys, a modern suburb, and Beaumont Hall, one of the university halls of residence. The Beaumonts deserve to be remembered

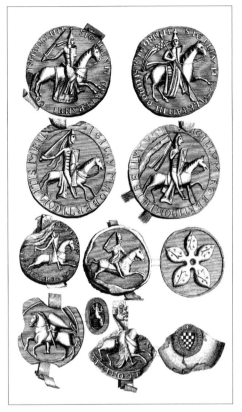

Coins from the period of Robert de Beaumont. This image is taken from J. Nichols, *The History and Antiquities of the County of Leicester, Vol. 1. Part I., The Town of Leicester* (London, 1795), courtesy of the University of Leicester Special Collections.

for the building work that they carried out. One local project completed during the period of Robert de Beaumont was the West Bridge over the River Soar. The first earl was also responsible for building the church of St Mary de Castro at Castle Mount and establishing with it a college of twelve canons and a dean. Robert de Beaumont built St Mary's to replace an earlier church that the Normans had destroyed when building the castle, and no doubt hoped to accrue grace for his soul by carrying out this project.

The second Beaumont earl, Robert le Bossu, continued in the same vein as his father and founded an Augustinian abbey and church where Abbey Park lies today, a site that was then outside the town. The fervour for monasticism in Europe was at its height in the eleventh and twelfth centuries, and the founding of Leicester Abbey should be seen against this backdrop. The abbey church was said to have been a magnificent stone structure, comparable in scale to Westminster Abbey, with a high square tower and a richly ornamented interior.[4] Robert le Bossu died before it was completed, but the building work was continued by his daughter-in-law Petronilla, who commissioned and paid for the church nave. A curious story tells that Petronilla had a rope made of her own hair and that the rope was used to suspend a lamp from the choir roof.[5] The abbey became one of the wealthiest monastic houses in England. Inevitably it did not survive the Reformation, when the abbey church was stripped of its riches and destroyed.

West Bridge: a drawing by Leicester artist John Flower. This image is taken from J. Flower, *Views of Ancient Buildings in the Town and County of Leicester* (Leicester, 1825), courtesy of the University of Leicester Special Collections.

The Beaumont family also developed the castle, replacing the wooden defences with stone, and in about 1150 Robert le Bossu also built the great hall, a large aisled hall divided into six bays situated in the castle bailey. From the thirteenth to the late twentieth century this was used to accommodate the local assizes and is still used for ceremonial occasions today. Unfortunately many medieval features of the hall were seriously damaged over the centuries, especially by an intensive renovation in 1821.

The more positive contributions of the Beaumonts ended with the rise to power of the third Earl of Leicester, Robert Blanchmains, who brought catastrophe to the town by taking part in a rebellion against Henry II in 1173. The rebellion failed and Robert Blanchmains was killed in battle. This did not stop the king's forces from wreaking revenge on Leicester, significantly damaging the castle and destroying large swathes of the town. Enormous suffering was inflicted on the townspeople: many were killed, imprisoned or

Leicester Castle: an eighteenth-century view. This image is taken from J. Throsby, *The History and Antiquities of the Ancient Town of Leicester* (Leicester, 1791), courtesy of the University of Leicester Special Collections.

punitively fined, while others escaped and sought refuge in towns as far away as St Albans and Bury St Edmunds. The population was sadly diminished, and the survivors were left among ruined buildings. It took several decades to recover, and some of the northern parts of the medieval town never did, being given over to alternative use such as the cultivation of orchards.[6]

The son of Robert Blanchmains, the fourth earl, took little interest in Leicester, and with him the family line ended. After his death the earldom passed to another family whose name remains well known in Leicester, the Montforts.

## The Montforts

Both the fifth and sixth Earls of Leicester, father and son, were called Simon de Montfort. They were nobles who belonged to a prominent French dynasty, and their claim to the earldom of Leicester originated from Amicia de Beaumont, the sister of the third Earl of Leicester, who married into the Montfort family. The younger Simon de Montfort has been celebrated as the creator of the first elected English Parliament, as we shall see, and for this reason, modern civic leaders have sought to represent him as part of Leicester's heritage. His image decorates the Victorian clock tower in the centre of the city, and the concert hall built in 1913 was named the De Montfort Hall as an expression of local pride. There are also roads and a square named after him. When Leicester Polytechnic gained university status in the 1990s it continued the tradition by taking the name De Montfort University. This continuing link between Leicester and the name Montfort justifies a closer look at the men behind the myth.[7]

The elder Simon de Montfort was only notionally the Earl of Leicester. He was a crusader and a general of international reputation, famous or, to modern thinking, notorious for his brutal suppression of the Cathars during the Albigensian crusade in the south of France. Montfort's claim to the earldom of Leicester was recognised by the English sovereign King John, but his status as a French subject was an obstacle to him actively taking up his inheritance. Moreover, this powerful figure who allegedly had a following among John's enemies in England would undoubtedly have seemed a threat, and John preferred to transfer responsibility for Leicester to a series of caretakers. Montfort, therefore, remained a distant figure who never took up his position among the English barons or lived in England. He was killed in battle at the Siege of Toulouse in 1218.

The younger Simon de Montfort, unlike his father, did establish himself in England, where he became a major player on the national stage. Little is known about his early life, but it is likely that after his father's death he was involved with his elder brother Amaury in the renewed crusade against the Cathars. By 1230 he was in his early twenties and had poor financial prospects; as a result, the possibility of exploiting his Leicester connection was attractive. Montfort himself tells us what he did next: 'I went to England and asked my lord the King to give me my father's inheritance.'[8] This mission was successfully accomplished, and he acquired the honour of Leicester with the permission of Henry III. Unlike his father he did not hold any land belonging to the French king, which meant that his claim was not automatically debarred. Even so it was still a notable achievement for Montfort to gain Henry's trust and cooperation, and it was the first of many achievements that resulted in his ascent to power.

Montfort displayed energy and political intelligence, and rapidly became a valued advisor to Henry III. At first the income he squeezed out of Leicester was absolutely essential to him, but his position and income were greatly enhanced when he married the king's sister in 1238. However, his relationship with Henry deteriorated, and in 1263 to 1264 he led a group of barons in rebellion against the king. This culminated in military success at the

Battle of Lewes in 1264. Henry and his son, the future Edward I, were held captive while Montfort became, in effect, the ruler of England for the next two years. The rebellion was a reaction to alleged mismanagement of government by Henry, and was the culmination of a radical reform movement that sought to constrain royal power with a Parliament that placed the sovereign under institutional control. The reforms also sought to address abuse of power more generally, checking not only the conduct of the king but also the conduct of barons toward their tenants. A reforming Parliament was held in 1264, and for the first time the principle of election was introduced, with shires and selected boroughs, including Leicester, asked to send two elected representatives. For this reason Simon de Montfort has frequently been credited as a pioneer of the modern Parliamentary system. His regime, however, was eroded by factionalism and soon collapsed. Montfort had a close circle of allies of his own rank, and he also looked for support to the Church and wider society. However, outside his inner circle he had many enemies among the barons, and because of these divisions he lost power. Prince Edward escaped captivity and was able to muster a royal force, which defeated Montfort and his followers at the Battle of Evesham in 1265. Montfort himself was killed during the fighting.

Unsurprisingly, there are differences between Simon de Montfort the historical figure and the heroic Simon de Montfort created by myth and tradition. His public cause was the reform of English government, and his actions showed commitment to this; however, his commitment was clearly not just to the common good. He was consistently quick to advance his own interests in terms of power and wealth, and he used the disorder caused by the rebellion to significantly enrich himself and his family. Montfort's relationship with Leicester was chiefly about the income that he derived from the estate, although he did secure a number of benefits for the town. These included a transfer of pastureland to the town as well as an exemption from the royal right to claim a share of the goods from any fair held in Leicester. Notoriously, Montfort expelled the Jews from Leicester, demonstrating the same militant and intolerant religious zeal that his father had shown before him. It is perhaps understandable, however, why Victorian civic leaders in Leicester were keen to publicise the connection with Montfort and play down the more unattractive aspects of his character. His successful takeover of the country for two years made him a towering figure of his time, and the connection was thought to add grandeur to the profile of the modern town.

## The Plantagenets

After Montfort's perceived treason and defeat, Henry III took back the earldom of Leicester and awarded it to his second son, Edmund Crouchback. In this way the castle and estates at Leicester fell into the hands of another famous medieval family, the Plantagenets. Unfortunately for the town, the fact that the Leicester Plantagenets were related to the king did not curb the recalcitrance of some of the earls. In 1324, Earl Thomas, the second Plantagenet earl, entered into hostilities with Edward II, which resulted in the town being sacked. A few years later it was plundered yet again, when under the control of the third Plantagenet lord, Earl Henry.

However, after the horrors of the 1320s the Plantagenets made a contribution to both the welfare and the built environment of Leicester. Having survived the early crises of his ascendancy, Earl Henry spent most of his years quietly at Leicester Castle, and during this time he built a hospital near the castle mound. This foundation had the capacity to care for fifty inmates, some temporary, some permanent, and was referred to as the New Work. The name The Newarke, as this area became known, is derived from this. After Henry's death in 1345 his son, the fourth earl and also named Henry, succeeded him and developed the project further.

This fourth Earl of Leicester achieved significant prestige both as a military leader in the Hundred Years War with France and as an advisor to Edward III. In recognition of his achievements he was created Duke of Lancaster in addition to his inherited status as Earl of Leicester. Under his rule, Leicester continued to enjoy peace and prosperity, and the town benefited from his talents when he planned and began an ambitious extension to his father's building works near the castle mound. The hospital was expanded and a college established at the same site. Work also began on the construction of a magnificent new collegiate church. While the fourth earl was in France in 1351 the French king, John II had presented him with a sacred relic, a thorn allegedly from Jesus' crown of thorns, and the plan was to build a church fit to house this precious gift. Earl Henry did not live to see his church, as he died in Leicester in 1361, a victim of the Black Death. The church, which became known as St Mary in the Newarke, took more than fifty years to build and was finally completed in 1415. The elaborate complex of buildings in the Newarke became a centre of learning and pilgrimage, but unfortunately little remains today. A part of the hospital was preserved, and some minimal traces of the church can be seen within the Fletcher building on the De Montfort University campus. Also remaining is the stone archway that formed the entrance to the Newarke. This archway later became known as the Magazine, after being used to store arms during the seventeenth century.

Earl Henry died in 1361 without a male heir, and as a result the earldom of Leicester passed to William of Bavaria, the husband of his elder daughter Maud. At his death a year later, in 1362, he was succeeded by John of Gaunt, the husband of his younger daughter Blanche.

## John of Gaunt

John of Gaunt, the second Duke of Lancaster and sixth Earl of Leicester, was the fourth son of Edward III and Queen Philippa of Hainault. The name John of Gaunt, like that of Simon de Montfort, is a name still commonly remembered today, although, as in the case of Montfort, those who remember the name have often forgotten the details of his career. For people interested in the history of Leicester a brief resumé of Gaunt's life may be helpful.[9]

John of Gaunt is perhaps most familiar to us as a character in Shakespeare's *Richard II*. Gaunt is portrayed as a patient and wise elder counsellor to his callow nephew Richard, who famously advises him not to abuse 'this royal throne of kings, this sceptred isle, this blessed plot, this earth, this realm, this England' (*Richard II*, Act II, Scene 1). Shakespeare's play has helped keep John of Gaunt in common memory, and has made his connection to Leicester a point of interest for civic leaders and the local community.

Gaunt was born in 1340 in the town of Ghent in the Low Countries, and the name Gaunt is derived from his birthplace. He became one of the wealthiest magnates of his time, with extensive estates especially in the north and Midlands of England, and a lavish palace outside the walls of London known as the Savoy. Gaunt's influence increased after the death of his father Edward III in 1377, when the young Richard II inherited the throne at the age of 10. As uncle and advisor to the young king, Gaunt became a prominent and influential figure. He was also the father of Henry Bolingbroke, the future Henry IV, who took the throne from Richard in 1399; the story of this usurpation is, of course, at the heart of the play *Richard II*. Shakespeare shows Gaunt as having no part in the usurpation of his nephew, and this is generally accepted as being true.

Gaunt favoured Leicester as a residence and spent considerable amounts of time living and entertaining there. During his ascendancy, repairs and improvements were made to the castle, and he also interacted with the townspeople in some important aspects of local governance. The major instance of this was his transfer of the management of the town fair to the town. However, while Gaunt maintained a positive working relationship locally, by the 1380s he had earned widespread unpopularity at a national level as a result of his part in implementing a poll tax. This culminated in the rebellion known as the Peasants Revolt. In 1381 rebels sacked his property at the Savoy, and it was believed that they intended to march on Leicester. When the message arrived that they had already reached Market Harborough, the duke was able to muster around 2,000 Leicester townsmen for the defence of the town. They assembled on what was then known as Gallowtree Hill, and is now where the University Gate at Victoria Park stands. The message, however, proved false, and the attack never materialised.

Gaunt was married first to Blanche of Lancaster and then to Constance of Castille, and was widowed twice. After the death of Constance he married his long-time mistress Katherine Swynford, familiar to many people as heroine of Anya Seyton's novel *Katherine*.[10] She was the daughter of Payn de Roet, a knight from the Low Countries, and was first a servant and then governess to the daughters of John of Gaunt's first wife Blanche. As depicted in the novel, Katherine's sister was married to the poet Geoffrey Chaucer, to whom Gaunt became a friend and patron. During the 1370s, and while Gaunt was still married to Constance of Castille, Katherine bore him four children, three boys and a girl. When he finally married her, the children were legitimised and given the romantic surname Beaufort. The first Tudor sovereign, Henry VII, was a descendant of Katherine's eldest child, John Beaufort.

In 1399, John of Gaunt died at the castle in Leicester, and in the same year his son Henry Bolingbroke was crowned Henry IV. The earldom of Leicester then passed to the Crown, and because of this there was no longer a lord in residence at Leicester. It was the end of an era that had lasted well over three centuries, from the early days of the Norman Conquest. The Norman and then the Plantagenet lords had sometimes brought disaster on the town but they had also brought grandeur and national status. For this reason the change that came in 1399 has been described as the close of an 'age of splendour' for Leicester.[11]

## The Fifteenth Century: the Castle and the Wars of the Roses

During the early fifteenth century money was regularly spent on the maintenance of the castle, but this was not enough to stop a decline in its condition. Now that the buildings lacked a lord in residence to take a personal interest, the general trend for the next century was decay. Despite this, it was during these years that two attractive parts of the castle complex were built, which still survive today and add interest to the modern city. The first was the Turret Gateway that leads from the Newarke to the castle, while the second was the timbered building that stands beside the entrance of St Mary de Castro.[12]

The heyday of the castle had passed by the fifteenth century but it was still used occasionally.[13] One such event occurred in 1426 when the 5-year-old Henry VI was knighted at St Mary de Castro. On this same occasion a full national Parliament was held in the great hall of the castle. Before this assembly there had been an ongoing violent feud between the followers of the Duke of Gloucester and the Bishop of Winchester. This unresolved dispute led to fears for the safety of the assembly, and those attending the Parliament were forbidden to carry weapons. To circumvent this restriction many carried clubs, commonly called bats. When these were also forbidden it was claimed that members of hostile factions resorted to hiding stones in their sleeves.[14] From these impromptu weapons the assembly earned the name the Parliament of Bats. A further Parliament was held at the castle in 1450, when Leicester was chosen as a venue in preference to London because of an outbreak of plague in the capital. This Parliament is portrayed in Shakespeare's *Henry VI*, and is memorably described as dissolving when news arrived of a popular revolt in the South East. This was Cade's Rebellion, in which a band of Kentish peasants marched on London, causing serious havoc. The Parliament did in fact dissolve as Shakespeare describes, and was the last Parliament to be held in Leicester.

Tensions between the House of Lancaster and the House of York increased in the mid-fifteenth century, as both claimed their right to the throne and this erupted into the Wars of the Roses. Despite the long connection between Leicester and Lancaster, there was considerable support for the Yorkist faction in Leicester. It has been suggested that this may partly have been because the influential Hastings family was based in Leicestershire at Kirby Muxloe. Sir William Hastings in particular had spent time in the service of Richard, Duke of York, the father of the future Edward IV and Richard III.[15] On the other hand, it has been pointed out that the mayor and town leaders of Leicester may have needed no persuading to support the House of York. They were quite likely dissatisfied with the weak government of Henry VI and may have been more than ready for change. There had been some very recent contact with the House of Lancaster when Margaret of Anjou, the mother of Henry VI, spent Christmas at Leicester in 1459. However, as one local historian wryly comments, Margaret was such a notoriously difficult person that this Christmas stay may have actually detracted from any local Lancastrian support.[16]

Whatever the reason, in 1461 a contingent from Leicester was involved in fighting the House of Lancaster at the Battle of Towton, a battle that resulted in the Yorkist Edward IV taking the Crown. In 1462, King Edward visited Leicester to thank the town for the supporting him, and during his reign he showed his gratitude by granting a number of favours. These included an annuity of 20 marks and permission to hold an extra annual fair. He also gave the town a charter that authorised the mayor and town leaders to appoint four magistrates from among their number each year. This brought welcome new independence from the county magistrates who had previously held jurisdiction over Leicester.

## Richard III

Richard III, Edward's successor, brother and the last Plantagenet king, also visited Leicester during his reign. In 1483 he stayed at the castle and wrote a letter there that he marked 'from my castle of Leicester'. This letter has been described as 'the last authentic record' of occupation at the castle apart from officials employed as caretakers at the site.[17] Two years later Richard returned to the Leicester again, but this time to a battlefield to play out the last chapter of the Wars of the Roses. This was of course the Battle of Bosworth Field, at which he was defeated and killed.

In Castle Park in Leicester there is a statue of Richard III, which is represented on many postcards of the city. Close by, an inscription on the Bow Bridge tells passers-by that the remains of Richard III lie close at hand, and a short distance away there is also a King Richard's Road. This positive commemoration of Richard III is a source of particular interest and fun to anyone who has enjoyed Shakespeare's Richard III. This play, of course, represents Richard as the embodiment of evil – a wicked yet compelling character who murders his way to the throne, most famously imprisoning and killing his two young royal nephews in the Tower of London. The

Richard III. This copy of Richard's portrait is taken from J. Thompson, *The History of Leicester from the Time of the Romans to the End of the Seventeenth Century* (Leicester, 1849), courtesy of the University of Leicester Special Collections.

commemoration of Richard in Leicester reminds us that he spent the night in the town on his way to the Battle of Bosworth Field, and that he was later buried in Leicester. It also reminds us that the long-standing debate over whether Richard III has been unfairly judged still continues. As in the case of Simon de Montfort and John of Gaunt, a brief outline of Richard's life may be a useful reminder.[18]

Richard was born in 1452 at the castle of Fotheringhay in Northampton-shire, the third surviving son of Richard, Duke of York, one of the most powerful of the English magnates. From childhood onwards political conflict and war were the backdrop to Richard's life, with his immediate relatives key players in the violent struggle for power between the houses of York and Lancaster. In his adolescence, Richard saw his 18-year-old elder brother successfully usurp the throne of the consecrated king, Henry VI, and become Edward IV, and by the age of 17 he himself had fully entered the world of adult politics. Richard's twenties, the 1470s and early 1480s, were years of cut-throat factionalism and competition between magnates. One particularly ambitious faction emerged around the relatives of Elizabeth Woodville, the wife of Edward IV. During this period Richard improved his standing by building a solid powerbase in the north of England, where he was a significant landowner. When Edward IV died in 1483, Richard became protector to his son, the 12-year-old Prince Edward, heir to the throne, and at the same time he set about securing his own power. He rapidly imprisoned and disposed of the members of the Woodville family who were competing against him for influence, and then imprisoned Prince Edward and his younger brother Richard in the Tower of London. The two young princes were never released from the Tower, and after the summer of 1483 were never seen again. Shortly afterwards Richard himself was crowned king, and the suspicion that he had murdered the young princes spread. Richard's reign lasted a mere twenty-six months, and when he died he was still only 32 years old. A rebellion against his rule in 1483 failed, but in 1485 a second rebellion led by Henry Tudor, Earl of Richmond and great-grandson of John of Gaunt, was successful, culminating in victory at the Battle of Bosworth Field.

Leicester and its hinterland were the backdrop against which Richard's defeat was played out. This was such a significant national event that naturally various stories about Richard's last days, his death and burial, lingered in Leicester for centuries. These are recorded in detail in Billson's account of medieval Leicester, and some of the main points are summarised here.[19]

Richard arrived in Leicester on the evening before the battle, having travelled from Nottingham Castle, and is believed to have stayed at the Blue Boar Inn. This was situated in the medieval High Street, today known as Highcross Street. The Blue Boar was a large and attractive gabled building, and it is thought that Richard stayed in the front chamber that overlooked the street. The symbol of King Richard was, of course, the white boar, and it has been suggested that the name of the inn may have been speedily changed from the White to the Blue Boar after Richard's downfall. The traditional story is that Richard left Leicester the next morning for the battlefield with full pomp and ceremony and wearing his crown. As he passed over Bow

The Blue Boar Inn: a drawing by Leicester artist John Flower. This is the inn where Richard III is said to have stayed before the Battle of Bosworth Field. This image is taken from J. Flower, *Views of Ancient Buildings in the Town and County of Leicester* (Leicester, 1825), courtesy of the University of Leicester Special Collections.

Bridge his spurs hit the parapet, and a crowd of spectators led by a local 'wise woman' prophesied that Richard's head would be broken in the same way. After the battle, Henry, the victor, reputedly slung Richard's dead body over his horse and brought it back to the town to parade through the streets. It was reported that as the procession passed over the bridge Richard's head struck the parapet in the way his spurs had done on the outward journey.

Richard's body was displayed naked for several days at the collegiate church of Our Lady in the Newarke, before being given to the Leicester Franciscan friars to bury at their church. This funeral was a quiet and impoverished affair, although ten years later Henry VII provided Richard with a marble tomb. The Franciscan church did not survive the Dissolution of the Monasteries and two stories emerged as to what happened to Richard's remains. According to one account the coffin was vandalised and the bones thrown into the River

The Battle of Bosworth Field, 1485: Richmond's army advancing on the eve of battle to meet Richard III. This image is taken from J. Throsby, *The History and Antiquities of the Ancient Town of Leicester* (Leicester, 1791), courtesy of the University of Leicester Special Collections.

Soar, and after this the coffin was used as a horse trough outside the White Horse Inn in Gallowtree Gate. In 1654, diarist John Evelyn visited Leicester and inspected this trough, which he took to be 'the tomb of the tyrant Richard III'.[20] It was said that later the coffin was broken up and used to make cellar steps at the White Horse. The other story was that after the destruction of the Franciscan church, Richard's burialplace fell within the private land of a local citizen. This was Robert Herrick, an ancestor of the poet of the same name and a well-known town leader, who at one point during his career was the Mayor of Leicester. Christopher Wren, father of the famous architect of the same name, was a tutor to Herrick's son. In his papers he recorded that in 1612 Herrick showed him the burialplace of King Richard in his Leicester garden, as well as a handsome memorial that he personally had erected over the grave. Recent research indicated that this second story was more credible.[21] The area in modern Leicester known as Grey Friars was where the Franciscan church and then Herrick's garden lay, and it was thought that Richard's remains might still lie buried here. This proved to be true, for in 2012 a team of archaeologists from the University of Leicester excavated part of the Franciscan church and located the remains of a body – in February 2013 it was confirmed that these were indeed the remains of Richard III.

The debate regarding Richard III's reputation shows no signs of being resolved, and the Richard III Society is active in Leicester as elsewhere. Supporters of Richard argue that he was an effective ruler who was defamed by Tudor propaganda, and that the negative representations of him by both Shakespeare and Thomas More were grossly unfair. The author of a modern scholarly biography of Richard takes a measured and moderate stance. The role of Tudor propaganda is acknowledged, and Richard is viewed less as an inhuman monster and more as a man of his time, an ambitious individual brought up in and operating in a violent and ruthless political culture. If he committed acts of inhumanity, so did the Tudor monarchs, and they are generally not demonised to the same extent. With regard to the fate of the princes, contemporary sources show that during Richard's reign the belief that he had ordered their murder was widespread both in England and Europe. Richard had the motive and means to get rid of them, and bones found in the Tower have been identified

A nineteenth-century drawing of the old Bow Bridge, with a plaque commemorating Richard III. This image is taken from R. Read, *Modern Leicester* (London, 1881).

as a likely match. However, the evidence does not exist for us to know exactly what happened, or the extent of Richard's involvement.[22]

## The Medieval Town of Leicester and its People

Medieval Leicester was a small, walled town on the site of the Roman town of Ratae. The walls enclosed an area of about 130 to 160 acres, and there were four gates and two main thoroughfares that crossed, dividing the town into four quarters. The ground plan remained fairly constant throughout the medieval period, although the town developed during the centuries. One terrible setback was the sack of Leicester in 1173, although by the early thirteenth century recovery was well underway. Billson gives a general description of the streets of medieval Leicester from the thirteenth century onwards. Obviously the town did not remain static during this time, but the description gives a useful overall impression and one that does not seem to have been much disputed by modern archaeological discovery. Some of the main points he makes are as follows.[23]

By the thirteenth century the four quarters of Leicester were treated officially as separate 'vils' or townships, to facilitate tax collection and the keeping of the peace. In the north quarter the most important street was the old High Street. Here was All Saints' church as well as the mayor's house and the homes of several leading citizens, the Hospital of St John and the main inns of the town. It was also the site of the town stocks and, from 1309, the county gaol. Another feature of High Street was Cordwainers Row, where shoemakers worked, and for several centuries there was also a bellfoundry. Further industry in the north quarter included soapmakers and parchment makers. By the fifteenth century the parchment makers had become associated with a street called Parchment Lane, a street that later became New Bond Street. A further important thoroughfare in the neighbourhood followed the path of the modern High Street, and this was named Swinesmarket on account of the regular pig market that took place there.

The east quarter of the medieval Leicester included the main market of the town. This was situated where it still is today, although at that time it covered a larger area and was bounded by the town wall. The monastery of Grey Friars was also in this neighbourhood, as well as several streets that retain their medieval names today. Friar Lane and Loseby Lane both existed at that time, as well as Cank Street, where the cank or public well stood. On the other side of the wall from the market were two other names also familiar to modern residents, Millstone and Horsefair Lane.

There were not many houses and streets in the south quarter of the town. In this district the castle and St Mary de Castro stood, and after the mid-fourteenth century the buildings of the Newarke, the whole complex encircled by walls. However, there were some signs of the bustle of town life in the neighbourhood. Public baking ovens were situated in a street called Hotgate, so called for obvious reasons. This was near the area called, as it still is, Holy Bones, and butchers' shambles were also close by in a street known as Shambles Lane. An extension of Hotgate was Applegate, which still exists today. The derivation of the name Applegate is uncertain, although one simple explanation is that apple trees grew there. However, it has also been suggested that the name may come from the French verb *appeller*, 'to call', a possible reference to the fact that the guards on the nearby castle wall used to call the hour during the night.

Finally there was the west quarter of the town. Here were the churches of St Nicholas and St Clement as well as the monastery of the Leicester Black Friars. The remains of the Roman baths, known by this time as the Jewry Wall, were next to St Nicholas church. The origins of this pre-Conquest church are obscure, but it seems that masonry from the Roman remains was incorporated into its structure. On the other side of the Roman site lay Talbot Street, where the Talbot Inn was situated. This west quarter of the town was bounded to the north by the town wall, and on the west side by the River Soar.

Outside the town wall there were also a north and an east suburb. In the north suburb was St Leonard's church and hospital, and beyond this lay the great Augustinian abbey. Some of the street names from this northern suburb have survived, including Woodgate and Sanvey Gate. Woodgate is said to have been so called because it was along this road that timber was brought from the neighbouring woodland into Leicester. Sanvey Gate was originally known as Senvey Gate, and the derivation of this name is more obscure. One possible explanation is that it originated from the words *Sancta Via*, or Holy Road, so called because it was the road to St Margaret's church, the route of many religious processions.

St Margaret's church itself lay in the east suburb, which was a busier and more important district than the area outside the north wall. Several of the main thoroughfares that are now in the heart of modern Leicester were here, including Churchgate, Humberstone Gate, Belgrave Gate and Gallowtree Gate, while on the site of the Victorian clock tower was another set of stocks. There was also a gallows at the top of the hill to the south, near to what is now Victoria Park.

The population level of Leicester would have fluctuated in the centuries after the Norman Conquest. The fate of the townspeople lay, to a great extent, in the power of the local lord. If the lord chose to involve himself in local feuds or set himself up in opposition to the king, it was likely that the town would be sacked, as we have seen. This violence naturally affected the level of population, with people killed or fleeing the town, as was the case after the sack of 1173. Although the town recovered, further setbacks occurred in the fourteenth century when there were two significant outbreaks of plague.

Public health in a medieval town, with its lack of sanitary facilities, was always precarious but the death tolls resulting from the Black Death in 1349 and 1361 were unprecedented. The disease spread to England from Europe, where it had already ravaged the population. From the south coast of England it moved through London, where it was said to have taken 50,000 lives. Henry of Knighton, an Austin canon and chronicler based at Leicester Abbey, recorded the effects of the epidemic in Leicester. There were terrible death tolls in every parish: in St Margaret's parish alone, Knighton claimed there were around 700 deaths.[24] In all it was estimated that about 2,000 people died, approximately a third of the population, leaving the town traumatised and the local economy severely disrupted. The outbreak that followed in 1361 was also severe, this time affecting the gentry and nobility more harshly. The victims included several canons at the abbey as well as Henry, the fourth Earl of Leicester.

The townspeople of medieval Leicester built their economy by producing the basic commodities for everyday life, by manufacture and by trading in the markets and fairs.[25] Although part of an urban community, they also engaged in individual agricultural activity, and cultivated the strips of land that had been allocated to them in the common open fields outside the walls. They also collected timber from the wood that bounded the town to the north.

The traders of Leicester identified and protected themselves by banding together in an association called the Guild Merchant. This association was in existence from the early years after the Conquest, and by the first decades of the thirteenth century it was thoroughly institutionalised, with procedures, officials and a special meeting house. The general meeting of the association was referred to as the Morningspeech. Two very important issues that the traders had to deal with were their relationship with the local lord and regulation of trade in the town. With the lord, the major issue was the tight control imposed from above on all trading and town activities, and the numerous rents and tolls extracted to supplement the lord's income. As regards regulation, the aim of the Guild was to ensure that, in those tight financial circumstances, no individual and especially no outsiders gained unfair advantage.

An early concession came from Robert de Beaumont, the first Earl of Leicester. Sometime before his death in 1118 the earl granted the Guild Merchant a charter, which referred to the traders as his 'merchants' and gave them the official right to trade in Leicester, as well as ratifying various privileges and customs that had been held and observed by the group since the Norman Conquest. No doubt it also benefited the earl to encourage the guild. A group working together would be more likely to produce a good income, and a cooperative relationship would reduce difficulties in collecting tolls.

In terms of local trade regulation, the Guild Merchant established strict rules. Guild members were the only people allowed to conduct business in the town, and they were also exempt from certain tolls. The only exceptions to this were certain stallholders with a special licence to trade in the market. All individuals had to pay to join, though natives of Leicester were charged less than outsiders. The Guild seems to have had some of the qualities of a brotherhood. Women were barred, members took an oath of loyalty and there were demanding rules of honour. For example, if a Leicester guildsman made a bargain in the presence of another guildsman, that guildsman was entitled to share in the profit, even if he was miles away from Leicester. There was some resistance among local tradesmen to the total control of the Guild Merchant. During the thirteenth and fourteenth centuries the fullers and weavers, and finally the watermen, all made small bids for independence. Their efforts, however, were unsuccessful, and they were forced to conform. By the mid-fifteenth century, however, certain subgroups had organised themselves into unions known as occupations, which were officially recognised, although in no way independent of the Guild Merchant.

Among the most prominent industries and trades in medieval Leicester were food supply, woollen cloth, wool and leather. Food supply, as might be expected, was important throughout the period and at the forefront were the bakers. In an early roll of the Guild Merchant dated 1196 they comprised nearly an eighth of guild membership.[26] One disadvantage that bakers faced was that they were compelled to use the lord's ovens in Hotgate, from which the lord, of course, extracted a rent. In addition to this, their trade was subject to particularly close scrutiny. Because bread was such an important commodity, legal regulation of the price and quality was introduced under the Assize of Bread in 1236, and offending tradesmen could be fined and put in the pillory if they did not comply. Butchers were also important to the food supply of the town. In 1196 two butchers were recorded as members of the Guild Merchant, but in 1376 it was recorded that there were thirteen renting shops at the shambles in the north quarter near St Nicholas church. The butchers were also subject to some regulation in order to protect both their reputation and customers' health. One rule was that the same meat could not be put on sale for three days running. There were fishermen in the Guild as well. Although there was some limited fishing in the River Soar, most of the supplies, including salmon, cod, turbot and seafood, came from the East Coast ports such as Scarborough, Yarmouth and Lynn. The fish traders were regulated as to when and where they could sell their goods, but there seems to have been less scrutiny over the quality. It has been speculated that this may have been because keeping a check on the quality of imported fish was considered a hopeless cause.[27]

The heyday of the woollen cloth industry in Leicester was in the early thirteenth century. Good-quality coloured cloth was produced, and Leicester established an excellent reputation. So much so that in 1254 the king's tailor ordered £50-worth of cloth in colours of russet and blue.[28] The Guild Merchant had to monitor all those involved in the production of cloth, including weavers, fullers, dyers and drapers, or mercers as they were often known. At the heart of the process were the weavers, and in 1260 the Guild made them take an oath that they would maintain the expected standards of work. Certain practices, such as weaving with two shuttles instead of three and working at night, were outlawed. They were also forbidden to hide any flaws the cloth from the customer, and prices were officially fixed.[29]

However, despite these precautions, by the end of the century the Leicester cloth industry was in decline, and more emphasis was gradually placed on the sale of wool not only in English markets and fairs but overseas as well. During the later medieval period Leicester played an important role in the English wool trade and produced some exceptionally talented and wealthy businessmen. In the early fifteenth century, a Leicester merchant called Roger Devet was shipping large consignments of wool to continental Europe, and by 1470 there were at least sixteen wool exporters based in Leicester. In Calais, France, then under English control, was the official or staple port designated to receive English exports of wool. The port was commonly known as The Staple and the exporters as woolstaplers.[30]

The most outstanding staplers from Leicester came from the Wyggeston family. At least five members of this family, over two generations, were wool merchants. From the older generation these included Roger Wyggeston, who was born in about 1430 and lived until 1513. He built an impressive fortune from his trade, which included property in Swinesmarket and five manors in the county. He was also active outside his trade, serving as Mayor of Leicester more than once and representing the town as a Member of Parliament. He also gained distinction in Calais when he was elected lieutenant of The Staple in 1483. William Wyggeston, the famous Leicester benefactor, was from the

Wyggeston's Hospital: chapel and almshouses, an eighteenth-century view. The hospital was originally established by William Wyggeston in 1513 and was demolished in 1875. This image is taken from J. Nichols, *The History and Antiquities of the County of Leicester, Vol. 1. Part I., The Town of Leicester* (London, 1795), courtesy of the University of Leicester Special Collections.

next generation; born in about 1470, he died in 1536, and during his life he built up the Wyggeston fortune to spectacular heights. Following the family tradition, William involved himself in public life, served as a Member of Parliament for Leicester, was Mayor of Leicester twice and Mayor of Calais four times. Although he married twice he did not have children, and chose to let the town of Leicester benefit from his wealth. Through his generosity the Wyggeston charitable hospital was established in 1513, and some of the remaining buildings, as well as a chantry house that he built in the same year, still stand today. His image is another of the four figures that decorate the Victorian clock tower in the centre of modern Leicester.[31]

The leather industry was also important in Leicester, although not nearly as prominent as cloth and wool. Various branches of the industry, including skinners, tanners, barkers, shoemakers and dealers in hides, worked in the town. One early large-scale dealer in hides was a leading townsman called Simon Curlevache. In 1239, for unknown reasons, Curlevache aroused the anger of Simon de Montfort, who fined him the very large sum of 500 marks, approximately £330. This sum was so punitive that Bishop Grosseteste intervened and wrote a critical letter to Montfort, suggesting that the fine was seriously out of proportion to the offence. Montfort, however, refused to relent, and Curlevache had to pay. The story is interesting for two reasons: first because it apparently highlights a vindictive and grasping attitude on the part of Montfort; secondly because Curlevache was able to pay such a large amount and still remain a public figure.[32] Dealing in leather had clearly brought in a good profit. It has been observed, however, that there is no record of Curlevache after 1242, so it is possible that even if he survived in the short term, the loss of his money eventually ruined him.[33] Apart from the story of Simon Curlevache there is no further information about the hide-dealing trade at this time, but it seems that the leather industry in general may have risen to greater prominence in later medieval Leicester. During the fifteenth century the position of mayor was held seven times by leather dealers named as saddlers, glovers and skinners. This was a new departure, suggesting that both the financial means and prestige of the leather industry had increased in the town.

Markets and fairs were of the utmost importance to everyone in the medieval centuries, because this was where the bulk of buying and selling went on.[34] Leicester was no exception to this. In the early centuries after the Conquest all such events were tightly controlled by the local lord, who extracted his tolls accordingly. Markets were regular events, which generally involved only local people from the town and hinterland; in Leicester they were held on Wednesdays, Fridays and Saturdays. Fairs, however, were more elaborate and infrequent, were held only at set times of the year and were usually associated with a holiday. Leicester traders visited the fairs held in other towns and outsiders came to Leicester.

The Wednesday market is thought to have been the oldest Leicester market. There is no surviving document recording its establishment, but it was certainly a weekly event in the twelfth century, and its origins may be much earlier than this. It was held at the High Cross, where the two main roads of the town formed a crossroads and where by the thirteenth century a stone cross had been erected to mark the spot. In the sixteenth century a shelter was also built here to protect the traders and their wares. The market was particularly associated with butter and eggs, which people from the surrounding countryside brought to sell in the town. By the time of Henry VIII, however, a Friday market had also been established at the High Cross; this specialised in bread.

The Saturday market, which came to be the main market of the town, was held in the same place as the modern Leicester market, although at that time the site was larger and trading spilled over into the surrounding lanes. The first recorded mention of this market is in 1298, but like the Wednesday market it may date back, albeit in a different form, to a much earlier time. One of the roads leading to the modern marketplace is still called Cheapside, derived from the Danish word *chepe,* meaning sell, suggesting that some kind of trading went on in this area when Leicester was part of the Danelaw.[35] The market had a number of specialised sections including ones for corn, grain and beans. By the fourteenth century a fish market was also operating, and at some point a specialist 'housewives' or women's market was established. There was also horse trading, a cattle market, a sheep market held in Silver Street and the swine market nearby, held on the site of modern High Street. By the early fifteenth century a covered hall had been built in the marketplace, in which traders could rent a stall. Those who took advantage of this included butchers, who established slaughterhouses (shambles) there. As previously described, there were also butchers shambles near St Nicholas church, but the shambles in the market hall must have been thought better placed to take in the busy Saturday trade. Another part of the market hall was given over to tradesmen selling cloth, a section that became known as 'le draperie'. As well as the market hall, there were shops and booths to let in the marketplace, and among the traders that rented these were ironmongers, glovers, shoemakers and cobblers. The rents collected from them went to the Earl of Leicester, who in return was meant to keep the market buildings in good repair.

In medieval Leicester there were several regular annual fairs, although the dates of these changed a number of times over the centuries. Fair days were also chosen to coincide with significant feast days in the Christian calendar, and following this pattern the earliest fair originally took place over fourteen days in June around the feast of St Peter ad Vincula. It is not known when this was established, but it was an annual event by the thirteenth century. In 1229 Henry III granted permission for the fair date to be changed to February, and in 1235 it was altered again, to May. By this time it must have been regarded as a town institution, for when the king gave leave for the date to change he granted it not to the earl but to 'the good men of Leicester'. The earl was granted his own fair in 1307, but in about 1360 the two fairs amalgamated, becoming a Michaelmas fair. For the next century, Leicester had just this one annual fair, and it has been speculated that this reduction may have reflected less positive economic trends in the town.[36] When the amalgamation was implemented in 1360 the cloth industry was badly in decline and the town was between the two savage outbreaks of the Black Death in 1349 and 1361.

The next change came when Edward IV granted Leicester a new fair in 1473, for which a May date was chosen. This May fair and the Michaelmas fair in later centuries became the Leicester May and October pleasure fairs, long celebrated in Humberstone Gate and part of the local calendar until the twentieth century.

The centuries after the Conquest were marked not only by economic development and change but also by a gradual change in the relationship between earl and townspeople, the trend in later centuries being towards an increased role for leading citizens in the management of the town.[37] The relation between Leicester and its earl was slightly unusual in that it was not, unlike the majority of boroughs, directly under royal control but under the direction of the earl. This meant that a closer than average relationship between the townspeople and the local lord had to be developed. With some notable exceptions, and despite the financial burdens imposed on the town, a reasonably good relationship was maintained. Possibly for this reason the townspeople did not press for concessions with the singlemindedness of some other towns, including those in the same region such as Northampton and Lincoln. What many towns strived for and gained was a system known as *firma burgi*. This meant that town leaders took an active part in town management by agreeing to collect and pay a single set payment annually to cover the numerous dues that were owed. Such participation encouraged town leaders to develop a corporate identity. Although Leicester did not press for full *firma burgi*, the associational life of the town created channels of communication and systems that allowed a civic leadership to emerge. These leaders were able to involve themselves in town affairs and to negotiate effectively with the earl. This was apparent at the end of the fourteenth century when John of Gaunt agreed to hand over all management of the annual Leicester fair to the town, and to give up most of the income he derived from the fair in exchange for a yearly payment of £80.

Two long-standing town institutions lay at the heart of citizen participation in medieval Leicester: the Guild Merchant and the Portmanmoot. The Guild Merchant, as previously described, was originally just an interest group for traders, but in the late medieval centuries it became associated with the common good of the town as a whole. The Portmanmoot was the town court, and although the earl had control over this, twenty-four townsmen who acted as jurors and passed judgement in the various cases were essential to proceedings. In addition to the jurors, a townsman took on the role of presiding officer, and by the mid-thirteenth century this officer was referred to as the mayor. Although the Guild Merchant and the Portmanmoot were separate in origin, it is likely that the same townspeople were at the heart of both. Certainly the distinction between the two institutions diminished, and by the end of the thirteenth century they had more or less become one, assuming a municipal role. After 1399, when there was no longer a lord at the castle, this group had more space and freedom, and gained increased prestige when Edward IV appointed the mayor and four other leading citizens as justices of the peace. Finally, a law passed in 1467 authorised the representation of popular opinion by a local body, and in Leicester the twenty-four members of the Portmanmoot and the Guild Merchant took on this role. An early form of official local government had been created.

# Religious Life

The influence of the Church in medieval society was all-pervasive, and medieval Leicester illustrates this as much as anywhere else in the Christian world.[38] To modern perceptions, for instance, it is striking that Leicester is described in the Domesday Book as having six churches, although the population of the town was only around 2,000, and by the mid-fourteenth century there were considerably more, including nine parish churches, and various churches and chapels attached to religious houses. However, it was not only the number of church buildings that demonstrated the importance of the Church at the time. These churches varied in wealth, but the grandeur and architectural merit of some of them must have made a startling contrast with the houses of the town, especially the squalid dwellings of the poorest.

Seven of the nine parish churches of medieval Leicester were inside the walls of the town. Four of them, St Mary de Castro, All Saints', St Martin's and St Nicholas, still stand in modern Leicester, although all have been subject to alterations over the centuries, of course. The three other churches within the walls, St Peter's, St Clement's and St Michael's, did not survive. St Michael's and St Clement's were in the northern part of the town, which was badly damaged during the sack of Leicester in 1173; after this disaster the two church buildings deteriorated, and were eventually lost. Likewise, St Peter's, which was near the old High Street, was also lost to decay. The parish churches of St Margaret's and St Leonard's stood outside the walls. The original St Margaret's has survived, but St Leonard's is a late nineteenth-century construction built as a replacement for the medieval building.

Inside St Mary de Castro church: a nineteenth-century drawing. This image is taken from Mrs T. Fielding Johnson, *Glimpses of Ancient Leicester* (Leicester, 1891), courtesy of the University of Leicester Special Collections.

After 1143 all the parish churches of Leicester were put under the jurisdiction of the newly built abbey, which was built on the meadows outside the town. The full dedication of this religious house was the Abbey of the Assumption of St Mary, though it was sometimes referred to as St Mary in the Meadows or just Leicester Abbey. The community that lived here were canons of the Order of St Augustine. They can be more accurately described as priests rather than monks, and as such they were not restricted by their vows from working with the laity in the town. In practice, however, the running of the churches was generally left to the parish priests while the Augustinian canons lived a more enclosed life at the abbey. They based their lives around prayer, and built up a library of more than a thousand manuscript books. They also administered their buildings and land, raised sheep and marketed the wool in the town.

An Augustinian canon of Leicester Abbey. This image is taken from J. Nichols, *The History and Antiquities of the County of Leicester, Vol. 1. Part I., The Town of Leicester* (London,1795), courtesy of the University of Leicester Special Collections.

The life of the abbey in the twelfth and thirteenth centuries is obscure because of a lack of surviving records. However, in the mid- to late fourteenth century, Henry of Knighton, who was a member of the community, described an exceptionally successful period of abbey life under Abbot William Clowne, who headed the community between 1345 and 1378.[39] Clowne was a talented administrator who also had prestigious friends. Among these were Henry, the first Duke of Lancaster, and Edward II, the friendship with whom was apparently based on a shared love of hunting. Through his abilities and contacts Clowne secured both the finances and reputation of the abbey. Another notable abbot at St Mary's was Philip Repyngdon, who was appointed in 1393 and by 1404 had risen to become the Bishop of Lincoln. By mid-century, however, things had deteriorated. In 1440 there was an episcopal inspection of the abbey, and complaints made against Abbot John Sadyngton, who was allegedly terrorising the community and practising sorcery. After this time standards fluctuated. In the late fifteenth century the environment was

Friars of Leicester. This image is taken from J. Nichols, *The History and Antiquities of the County of Leicester, Vol. 1. Part I., The Town of Leicester* (London, 1795), courtesy of the University of Leicester Special Collections.

productive enough for William Charyte to produce a catalogue of the books in the abbey library, and from 1496 to 1505 the house was under the rule of Abbot John Penny, who was distinguished enough to be later appointed Bishop of Bangor. However, further inspections in 1518 and 1525 revealed that the number of canons had dropped and that their way of life had become undisciplined. Despite its decline the abbey was still at the time of the Reformation one of the wealthiest religious houses in England, and provided rich pickings for the looters.

The friars based in medieval Leicester comprised another sector of local religious life. Unlike the abbey brethren they worked primarily with the people of the town, supporting the poor and the sick as well as reinforcing the Christian message. Many friars were also skilled clerks, and likely contributed to the administration of local affairs. The Franciscans were in Leicester by the 1230s, the Dominicans by the 1280s, and from the early fourteenth century there was also a house of Augustinian friars west of the River Soar. Little detail is known about them, although the names Grey Friars and Blackfriars Street in modern Leicester are a reminder of where their houses were situated and indicate that they were once an important social force in the town. The only exceptions to this dearth of information are two incidents involving the Franciscans. One was their involvement in the burial of Richard III, related above. The other occurred earlier, after Henry Bolingbroke had deposed Richard II and taken the crown as Henry IV. A group of Leicester Franciscans denounced the king and refused to accept that Richard was dead. For this protest they were tried, and eleven of them were hanged.

## Religious Dissent

Despite the power and influence of the Church throughout the medieval period, by the late fourteenth century religious dissent had become a significant issue both nationally and locally.[40] The response to these new ideas was patchy, but in parts of the Midlands, including Leicester, there was significant interest. A dissenting movement emerged, the adherents of which were known as Lollards. These dissenters should be seen in the context of the many different sects that emerged in Europe at this time, and also against the backdrop of an increased circulation of ideas encouraged by the invention of the printing press and growing rates of literacy among laypeople.

There were two strands to Lollardy: one was academic, and focused on the unorthodox teachings of the theologian John Wycliffe, long associated with the university at Oxford; the other was a popular, non-academic form of dissent. Lollardy did not comprise a consistent body of ideas, and the term Lollard was often just used as a general word to describe heretics. Despite this, there were two central and recurring themes that characterised the Lollard point of view: criticism of clergy who did not live in a simple and spiritual manner, and a call for less emphasis on the external ritual of religion. Both these themes foreshadowed the Reformation. Wycliffe's theology both underpinned and reflected these criticisms, although he himself did not take part in the popular movement. There is, of course, a direct connection between Wycliffe and Leicestershire, as he spent the latter part of his life as the rector of Lutterworth.

One Leicester cleric briefly associated with Lollard ideas in their more academic form was Philip Repyngdon, Abbot of Leicester Abbey. As a young man he was sent to study at Oxford, where a large part of the academic community was sympathetic to Wycliffite thought. Repyngdon became a champion of Wycliffe's teaching, and in 1382, after he had preached a controversial sermon, he found himself in serious trouble with the Church authorities. Following allegations that he had denied the eucharistic dogma of transubstantiation, he was excommunicated. Within the same year he repented, however, and was returned to the Church. From then on he remained orthodox in his views, and embarked on a successful Church career. In later life, after he had been appointed Bishop of Lincoln, Repyngdon was responsible for disciplining dissenters within his jurisdiction, and in 1414 and 1415 he was forced to deal with individuals who had been identified as Lollards. This he did, but appears to have been fair and humane, displaying no desire to persecute. In 1415, when the Council of Constance ordered that the bones of Wycliffe, laid to rest in Lutterworth, should be exhumed and burnt, Repyngdon showed similar restraint by ignoring the order. Eventually, in 1428, his successor Richard Fleming was forced under papal pressure to carry out the exhumation.

The popular non-academic strand of Lollardy had a significant impact in Leicester and in Leicestershire, and in the surrounding counties there were also networks of sympathisers. Henry of Knighton perceived the movement as having wide support in the town, and strongly disapproved. While he refrained from commenting on the early Lollard sympathies of his colleague Philip Repyngdon, he left a record of some of the humbler characters involved locally in the movement.[41] One of these was a young priest named William Swinderby, who arrived in Leicester under the name of William the Hermit. He gained a reputation as a holy man and for his puritanical preaching, which frequently focused on the decadent morals of women and the vice of moneymaking. For a while he lived in the woodland that bordered Leicester, but was then given living space adjoining the abbey; he used this as a base for preaching tours around the county. When he left the abbey he became part of a Lollard school that met at the chapel of St John the Baptist outside the town walls. Two other dissenting preachers in this group were another young priest called Richard Waytestathe and a layman named William Smyth, who, Knighton claimed, took to dissent after a rejection in love. These two were alleged to have shown their contempt for religious images by desecrating a figure of St Catherine.

In future centuries Leicester became a well-known centre of dissent, which makes the popularity of Lollard preachers in an earlier period particularly interesting. Knighton suggested that half the residents had Lollard sympathies, although this may be an exaggeration. Swinderby, in particular, acquired a significant local following, so much so that when Bishop Buckingham of Lincoln had him arrested in 1382 for expounding heretical beliefs, a number of local burgesses, including the mayor, offered their support. John of Gaunt also showed an interest, and he and his son Henry Bolingbroke attended Swinderby's hearing with the bishop. Swinderby crumbled under pressure, however, and having recanted was forced to travel around the county forswearing his views. Unsurprisingly this diminished his popularity; but even so, in that same year, Thomas Beeby, a local mercer and a previous mayor of the town, left him a bequest of 40s in his will. Shortly afterwards, Swinderby left Leicester for good.

In 1389 Smith and Waytestathe were among a group of local Lollards called before Archbishop Courtenay and charged with heresy. Although at first the accused ignored this call, eventually they were forced to comply; they renounced their beliefs and did public penance in Leicester. In this way the Church tried to contain the Lollard movement, though its popularity persisted. When Philip Repyngdon, as Bishop of Lincoln, visited Leicester in 1413 to review the situation, eight cases of Lollardy were found in the county. Wigston especially was a noted centre for Lollards, all the more significant because the individuals involved were from leading burghal families.

The movement eventually overreached itself when, in 1414, Lollards led by Sir John Oldcastle made an abortive attempt to seize King Henry V, as a prelude to imposing Lollard beliefs in England. In the aftermath two Leicestershire Lollards were hanged, and after a visit from the king's commissioners eight parishioners of St Martin's church in Leicester, identified as Lollards, were arrested and sent to Marshalsea Prison, although they were later sent back to Leicester and dealt with by Philip Repyngdon. Their number included members of leading local families and a well-known malcontent named John Belgrave, who, embarrassingly for Repyngdon, had made it his business to remind people of the Bishop of Lincoln's youthful Lollard sympathies. The Oldcastle rebellion doused the popularity and impact of the Lollard movement, because from then on it became associated with dangerous political sedition rather than religious dissent.

It has been suggested that while Lollard activities became less apparent in Leicester after the Oldcastle rebellion, criticism of orthodox religious ideas likely continued but in a more discreet way. Religious guilds became a prominent form of associational life in Leicester from the mid-fourteenth century until the mid-sixteenth, and it may be that dissent was kept alive in these groups.[42] The religious guilds were separate from the Guild Merchant and the fraternities centred on particular occupations, although their

In 1417 a visionary called Margery Kempe visited Leicester and came into conflict with the mayor. The story of her life, including this unfortunate visit, is recorded in *The Book of Margery Kempe*, widely considered to be the first English autobiography. Although Kempe was illiterate, she recounted the details of her life to a scribe. A mid-fifteenth-century copy of this original text was discovered and brought to public attention in 1934 by the American scholar Hope Emily Allen.

Kempe (*c*.1373–*c*.1438) was from Bishop's Lynn, an earlier name for King's Lynn, and was the daughter of a prominent burgess who had been the mayor of that town on several occasions. When young she married a local townsman, and they had a family of fourteen children. In middle age, however, religious visions led her to renounce material life, take a vow of chastity and travel as a pilgrim, expressing her insights. She dressed in white and frequently gave way to fits of loud weeping that were linked to her mystical visions. Kempe had her supporters, including the famous mystic Dame Julian of Norwich, but her loud and unusual behaviour often stimulated hostility in those she met.

When Kempe arrived in Leicester she soon annoyed the mayor, who accused her of Lollardy, confiscated her belongings and detained her. She only escaped prison because the local gaoler took pity on her and offered to keep her locked up in his own house. Shortly after this she was brought before the town steward, who also took against her, allegedly intimidated her and generally treated her without respect.

Eventually Kempe received a more favourable audience when she was taken to All Hallows' church, and was cross-examined by an assembly of local clergy, including the abbot and dean of the town. They judged Kempe, correctly, to be orthodox in her religious views and therefore innocent of Lollardy. The Mayor of Leicester only reluctantly accepted this, and ordered Kempe to get a letter justifying her conduct from Philip Repyngdon, the Bishop of Lincoln. This she succeeded in doing. The hostility shown towards Kempe in Leicester should no doubt be seen in relation to upheavals that the town had been through after the Lollard rebellion of 1414.

## Sources

C. Ellis, *History in Leicester* (Leicester, 1976), M. Gallyon, *Margery Kempe of Lynn and Medieval England* (Norwich, 1995); A. Goodman, *Margery Kempe and Her World* (Harlow, 2002; F. Riddy., 'Kempe, Margery (b.c.1373, d.in or after 1438)' in *Oxford Dictionary of National Biography* (Oxford, 2004), www.oxforddnb.com/view/article/15337, accessed 18 October 2012; Windeatt, B.A. (ed.), *The Book of Margery Kempe* (London, 1985).

Leicester Castle in the fifteenth century. This image is taken from R. Read, *Modern Leicester* (London, 1881) where it is attributed to the eighteenth-century antiquarian John Throsby.

memberships would have overlapped. There were six important religious guilds in Leicester, five of which were attached to parish churches, as well as other minor groups. In terms of religious activity, one major function of a guild was to maintain a priest to say chantry masses for the souls of its members. Beyond this the guild functioned as a mutual support group, a cushion against sickness and misfortune. It was also a social club to which both men and women could belong and would likely hold an annual feast and a procession. One particularly well-known annual procession was the 'Riding of the George', held in April on the feast of St George by the Guild of St George, a group linked to St Martin's church.[43]

The parishioners of St Martin's who were identified as Lollards and arrested after the Oldcastle rebellion were also associated with a religious guild known as the Corpus Christi Guild, attached to St Martin's church. This guild was by far the most prominent and it became associated with the mayor and corporation. Frequently the guild master and the mayor were the same person, and at the annual procession of the guild the mayor and corporation paraded in their official robes. By the end of the fifteenth century the Corpus Christi Guildhall was being used for corporation meetings and an extension, known as the Mayor's Parlour, was added to the building in 1489. In this way this building gradually became the Town Hall, and in fact remained so until 1876. The building, much altered over the centuries, still stands in the centre of Leicester today.

We leave this chapter in the early years of the sixteenth century. The castle was empty and the local lords had been gone for over a hundred years. Their absence brought some obvious advantages, but also brought a certain decline in Leicester's prestige. Tudor rule was now well established, and a more centralised approach to national government helped to curb the ambitions of powerful subjects. At the same time, the extent to which citizens locally ran town affairs increased considerably, and the Guild Merchant and the Portmanmoot combined to become a civic institution. A wider associational life also developed in the town, most notably in the religious guilds, where residents could meet and discuss all aspects of town business. There were some major setbacks in Leicester over these centuries, such as the devastation caused by the sack of 1173 and the outbreaks of plague in 1349 and 1361. The townspeople, however, weathered these difficulties in the long term, with Leicester being sustained by its trade and industry, among which were the development of the cloth industry in the thirteenth century and the successful wool trade later. However, despite the successes of the woolstaplers a general economic decline was apparent in Leicester in the fifteenth century, continuing in the sixteenth. The formal religious life of the town was remarkable owing to the multitude of churches, the abbey and the magnificent religious centre in the Newarke. Less formally, religious dissent made a significant impact during the late fourteenth and early fifteenth centuries. At the beginning of the sixteenth century all was relatively calm in the religious life of the town, but a cataclysm was on its way. Things would soon change irrevocably.

# three

# TUDOR AND EARLY STUART LEICESTER

## Religious Change, Economic Struggle and Civil War

O n 26 November 1530, Cardinal Thomas Wolsey rode into Leicester Abbey in the custody of Thomas Kingston and guards of the Tower of London. Until a short time before, Wolsey had been the Chancellor of England and right-hand man of Henry VIII, but now he was disgraced, under arrest and on his way from the north to the Tower of London. He was also dying.[1]

Wolsey, the son of an Ipswich butcher, had risen to prominence by means of a scholarship to Oxford and a successful Church career, aided by his exceptional shrewdness and organisational talents. He was chaplain to the Archbishop of Canterbury and then to Henry VII, and by the time Henry VIII came to the throne in 1509 he was Royal Almoner, charged with responsibility for the king's charities. The young king recognised Wolsey's abilities, and he was soon promoted to high office in both Church and State. In 1515 he was named Archbishop of York, and the following year the pope made him a cardinal, while Henry appointed him Lord Chancellor.

As Henry's advisor and friend, Wolsey became a public figure of immense power and influence. The king relied heavily on his judgement and the administrative apparatus of both Church and State was dominated by Wolsey's appointees. He became outstandingly wealthy, accumulating in addition to his main offices a string of other lucrative positions. He is thought to have had a personal income of about £35,000 a year, at a time when a magnate might expect to have an income of around £8,000, and the king's income for governing the entire country was about £100,000.[2] A good part of this was spent on an ostentatious lifestyle, Wolsey's Hampton Court being especially renowned for its magnificence. This combination of power and wealth made him seem invulnerable, and for the first twenty years of Henry's reign his luck held.

In 1529, however, Wolsey fell from favour over the issue of Henry's proposed separation from Catherine of Aragon and his remarriage to Anne Boleyn. He was under pressure from Henry to use his influence as a cardinal to obtain a papal annulment of the king's marriage to Catherine, and when he failed to secure this, his career in the service of the state was destroyed; he was dismissed and his property was confiscated. The following year, after Wolsey was found to have been in unauthorised contact with Spanish and French agents, as well as the pope and Queen Catherine, he was arrested for treason. This was his situation when he arrived in Leicester in November 1529.

Wolsey never reached the Tower of London: he was too ill to leave Leicester Abbey, and a few days after his arrival he died. His personal servant and biographer George Cavendish had been allowed to accompany him on the journey to London, and it is from his eyewitness account that we know what happened during those few days in Leicester.[3] The party arrived on a Saturday night at the gate of the abbey, where Abbot Peixall and all the canons came out with lighted torches to meet them. Wolsey's fall from grace clearly did not dampen the awe of the abbey community at receiving such a famous visitor, for they greeted him with 'great reverence'. Cavendish tells us that Wolsey was so ill that he had been barely able to keep his seat on horseback during the journey from Nottingham to Leicester, and that he returned the abbot's greeting with: 'Father Abbot I am come to lay my bones among you.'

While he lay ill at Leicester Abbey, Wolsey was disturbed by demanding messages from the king, and according to Cavendish it was in this context that he famously lamented: 'Had I but served God as diligently as I have served the King, he would not have given me over in my grey hairs.'

Wolsey's condition worsened, and after the abbot had administered the last rites he died at eight o'clock on 29 November in the presence of the Tower guards, who had assembled as witnesses. News of this was immediately sent to London, and to prevent any 'false reports' that Wolsey was still alive, Abbot Peixall and Thomas Kingston decided to call 'the Mayor of Leicester and his brethren' to view the body. After this had been done, Wolsey was laid in an open coffin in the lady chapel of the abbey for anyone who wished to view the body, following which he was buried with much ceremony in the same chapel.

One aspect of Leicester in the sixteenth and early seventeenth centuries concerns the interaction of the town with figures of national importance and the local impact of this. By the early sixteenth century it was a market town of only moderate rather than outstanding significance, having lost some of the kudos it had gained by being a residence of the Plantagenets. However, some of the actors on the national stage still came into contact with the town. Occasionally this happened almost by accident: Leicester was geographically in the heart of England, a convenient stopping-off point between the north and London. This was how Cardinal Wolsey came to spend his last days at Leicester Abbey. A more regular contact with individuals of political importance came from the county. In Leicestershire, two prominent noble families, the Greys and the Hastings, dominated, and both made their influence felt in the town. When choosing representatives to send to Parliament it was in the best interests of the town to consider the wishes of the Greys

The funeral of Cardinal Wolsey at Leicester Abbey. Wolsey died at the abbey in 1530 on his way to London. This image is taken from J. Nichols, *The History and Antiquities of the County of Leicester, Vol. 1. Part I., The Town of Leicester* (London, 1795), courtesy of the University of Leicester Special Collections.

and the Hastings, as it was dangerous to cause offence and difficult for bodies of humbler status to function effectively without the patronage of those at the top of the social scale. The fortunes of the two families fluctuated. In the mid-sixteenth century the Greys made an unsuccessful bid for the throne, which diminished their influence for some time. In contrast this was a particularly bright time for the Hastings family, and in the second half of the century Henry Hastings, the fifth Earl of Huntingdon, wielded a strong influence in Leicester for nearly fifty years.

Although the leadership of Leicester still continued to be beholden to the aristocratic families of the county, it was during the reign of Elizabeth I that

Leicester received its first charter of incorporation, and with it the potential for a more independent future. Powerful neighbours aside, the corporation had many other challenges to deal with. In terms of the local economy these years were not especially good. There was widespread poverty: despite the range of trades in the town there was not enough employment to go round.

An important part of Leicester's story during these years concerns the religious changes brought by the Reformation, and how these affected the lives of local people. Wolsey's downfall heralded Henry's decision to break with Rome over the question of his divorce, and in 1534 the Act of Supremacy declared Henry sole head of the English Church. This was soon followed by the first legislation to dissolve the monasteries and confiscate their land and property for the Crown, a move that strengthened Henry's position and substantially increased his wealth and income. The decision to destroy the monasteries, as elsewhere, changed the physical environment in which Leicester people lived, and the introduction of Protestantism saw the end of many traditions associated with the Catholicism. A more austere form of worship was introduced countrywide, and this was particularly enforced in places like Leicester where the Puritans got the upper hand. However, in spite of the religious upheavals of the times, and the great changes they brought to Leicester, many aspects of everyday life continued without major disruption, and carried on unchanged into the new century.

## Religious Revolution and the Birth of Protestant Leicester

The Dissolution of the Monasteries led to the destruction of Leicester's most beautiful medieval buildings. After only token resistance, Leicester Abbey was handed over to the king's commissioners in August 1537 by the last Abbot of Leicester, John Bourchier. The monastery and church were stripped of their treasures; it was recorded that the lead alone from the roof of the abbey church was worth £1,000. After they had been defaced, the abbey church and most of the monastic buildings were dismantled and left to decay. The land and what remained of the buildings were leased to Dr Francis Cave, a member of the local Leicestershire gentry and one of the royal commissioners who had directed the operation. All that remains of the abbey complex today is the enclosing brick wall built by Abbot Penny in the early years of the sixteenth century.[4]

The ruins of Leicester Abbey: a drawing by Leicester artist John Flower. This image is taken from J. Flower, *Views of Ancient Buildings in the Town and County of Leicester* (Leicester, 1825), courtesy of the University of Leicester Special Collections.

In the town itself there was further destruction. The friaries were suppressed in 1538 and the buildings were stripped; then in 1547 colleges, chantries, religious guilds and certain chapels were also dissolved. As well as being looted, the religious buildings were either demolished or severely damaged and left to decay. The most notable loss was that of the Church of the Annunciation of Our Lady of the Newarke, the collegiate church built near the castle by the Plantagenet earls and completed in 1415.[5] When John Leland, the Tudor antiquarian and traveller, visited Leicester in about 1540 he expressed his particular admiration for this church, referring to it as 'not very large but exceptionally fine', bounded on the south-west side by 'a large and attractive cloister'. He added that 'all the prebendal houses within the college precinct are very pleasant' and that 'the walls and gateways of the college are imposing'. Inside the church were the graves and images of members of the local nobility and gentry. Those referred to by Leland included Henry, the third Plantagenet Earl of Leicester, who built the hospital in the Newarke, and his son Henry, the fourth Plantagenet Earl of Leicester and first Duke of Lancaster, who commissioned the collegiate church but died of the Black Death in 1361 before it was completed. Also buried there were Constance, the wife of John of Gaunt, members of the Brokesby and Shirley family and three of the Wigstons.[6] For a while there was a chance that this church would be saved. Following the Bishoprics Act of 1539 it was planned that Leicester would be one of twelve new bishoprics, and that the collegiate church in the Newarke would become the cathedral. However, the plan was deemed too expensive and the number of new bishoprics was reduced to six. Leicester was omitted from the list, and as a result the church in the Newarke did not survive.[7]

Other losses in the town included the chapels of St Sepulchre and St John, which were left to decay, and the Hospital of St John, which was first converted into a woolhall and then later demolished to make way for new almshouses. There were a few survivors, though. The Corpus Christi chantry houses and Guildhall were bought by the town from the Crown, and as a result escaped demolition. The Guildhall, which still stands in Guildhall Lane today, was used as the Town Hall until the 1870s.[8]

The loss of so many medieval buildings must have detracted greatly from the appearance of Leicester. The abbey and the collegiate church in the Newarke were stone-built structures of some grandeur, and they would have contrasted magnificently with the poorer timber buildings of the town. Moreover, Leicester Castle, once another great focal point of the town, offered no counterbalance to this loss. The fabric of the castle had deteriorated, and Leland found it to be 'badly damaged' and a building of 'no great significance'. Henry VIII's commissioners also reported that it was in a state of decay: the great hall was still in good condition, but the castle yard was used to enclose stray cattle and other beasts. The destruction that had taken place meant that by the mid-sixteenth century Leicester's townscape was clearly diminished, and far less visually appealing than it had once been.[9]

The destruction of buildings was, of course, only one change that followed the dissolution of the monasteries. The break-up of the religious houses meant that the men and women who had lived there were dispersed, losing their role and livelihood. In Leicester the abbot and canons were awarded pensions, but the trauma of losing their way of life would have been substantial. The dispersal of these communities also affected the life of the town. Religious houses had provided a spiritual backdrop for townspeople, who might call upon them to pray for special intentions, and in more practical terms the everyday work of the friars had been to minister to the sick and the poor. Although the abbey had led a more separate life, it had also been a source of welfare and some schooling, and had been responsible for the local parish churches.

The lodge and gateway as seen from the Castle Yard. This image is taken from Mrs T. Fielding Johnson, *Glimpses of Ancient Leicester* (Leicester, 1891), courtesy of the University of Leicester Special Collections.

The Act of Supremacy and the Dissolution of the Monasteries did not mean that Catholic England became Protestant with immediate effect. Indeed, Henry VIII continued to regard himself as a Catholic, although he no longer accepted the authority of the pope. However, Henry's legislation permitted Protestant attitudes to spread and take root. After his death in 1547, the short reign of Edward VI unleashed a much more aggressive and evangelical Protestantism. It was in the early period of Edward's reign that chantries and religious guilds were suppressed. Any traditional processions that still continued did not survive these years, and wall paintings inside parish churches were systematically whitewashed out. In Leicester, the sale at St Martin's church of plate, vestments and altar hangings in 1547 demonstrated the arrival of this more austere religious culture.[10]

It is not possible to know what local people thought of these changes, but there must have been some who were sorry to see the old traditions disappear from their religious life. The feasts and saints' days had blended with the rhythms of the seasons to make a calendar that belonged to the whole town. Moreover, the religious guilds had been a source of social life that brought men and women together on a regular basis. On the surface at least, though, the people of Leicester seemed to take all these changes in their stride. There was, presumably, just enough to hold things together. The new calendar was still a Christian calendar after all, and the really important markers, such as Christmas and Easter, were still there. Before the changes set in, however, it seemed for a short while that everything might be reversed.

## Lady Jane Grey, Mary Tudor and the Aftermath

When Edward died prematurely in 1553 at the age of 15, a struggle for the Crown began between Henry's daughter, Mary, and Lady Jane Grey, Henry's great-niece. Although Mary was in direct line to the throne, Edward had chosen to will the succession to Jane shortly before his death.

The struggle was of particular local interest because of the Grey family's involvement. Jane was brought up at their house in Bradgate, 3 miles

The ruins of Bradgate House at Bradgate Park. This was the home of the Grey family, and was built in about 1520. The image is an Edwardian postcard taken from the author's own collection.

from Leicester. John Leland, on leaving Leicester, rode through the surrounding woodland and passed by the house. He commented on the lodge built there by the Greys and admired the 'fine park' in which it stood. Today, Bradgate Park belongs to the City of Leicester, and is still admired for its craggy landscape, its deer, and the romantic ruins of the Grey family house. Because of the connection between Leicester and Bradgate Park, and because the Grey bid for the throne was of such national importance, a brief reminder of the story is given here.[11]

Lady Jane Grey was also 15 at the time of Edward's death, and was described by contemporaries as a scholarly young woman. She had enjoyed a classical education,

Lady Jane Grey. This image is taken from W. Kelly, *Royal Progresses and Visits to Leicester* (Leicester, 1884), courtesy of the University of Leicester Special Collections.

and when Roger Ascham, tutor to Princess Elizabeth, visited Bradgate in the early 1550s he famously recorded that he found her alone in the house reading Plato while the rest of the household was out hunting.[12] Jane had been solidly grounded in Protestantism, and this was all-important.

The bid of Lady Jane Grey for the throne was an attempt to keep England Protestant; it was clear that Mary intended to restore Catholicism. The power behind Jane was John Dudley, the Duke of Northumberland, who by the time of Edward's death was the king's chief adviser. Religious concerns apart, Dudley was clearly trying to consolidate his own power. Not only did he prevail on the young King Edward, who was fervent in his Protestantism, to will the succession to Jane, but he manipulated the Greys and prevailed on them to force Jane to marry his son Guildford. As soon as Edward died, Dudley pre-empted Mary, and Jane was declared queen. A visiting Genoese merchant called Battista Spinola observed the new queen in procession in London, and recorded his impressions of her in a letter: he described her as an attractive figure, small and graceful with freckled skin and reddish-brown hair. He also observed that although she had been declared queen she did not have popular support.[13] He was right: she had some support, but not enough. The followers of both Mary and Jane mustered opposing armies, but when Mary's army reached London the privy council and Parliament rejected Jane and accepted Mary as queen. John Dudley was executed and Jane was sent with her husband to the Tower. Her reign had lasted only nine days.

As soon as Mary became queen she began the expected restoration of Catholicism. This was agreed to by Parliament only after it was ensured that the change would not reverse the Dissolution of the Monasteries, a guarantee that was important to the many individuals who had profited from the sale of monastic lands. Throughout the country, parish churches began to revert to their previous appearance and practices, and in Leicester the traditional Whit Monday processions were revived. Many of the items that had been sold off from St Martin's church were either retrieved or replaced.

Some of Mary's support evaporated when she declared her intention to marry her cousin Philip, King of Naples and heir to the Spanish empire. Opposition to this marriage largely took a nationalist form, as it was thought that the queen was handing over interests to a foreign power. A group of some 3,000 rebels under the leadership of Thomas Wyatt, son of the famous poet, formed and prepared to march on London. One supporter of the cause was Henry Grey of Bradgate. When news of his involvement was leaked he and his brothers fled back to the Midlands, and on 29 January 1554 they entered Leicester and proclaimed their cause. About 400 townspeople assembled to hear them, though this group did not include the mayor – who pointedly kept out of it.[14] As Leicester people had accepted the religious changes imposed by Henry VIII and Edward VII without complaint, and had equally passively proclaimed Mary's accession, it is uncertain why 400 people gathered in the town to hear Henry Grey preach rebellion against Mary. There may have been religious and anti-Spanish sentiments expressed, but it has been suggested that the main motive for assembly was probably deference to the Greys as a prominent local family.[15] After Leicester, the Greys rode to Coventry, where they received a negative reception and the townspeople barred the gates against them. The rebellion failed, and Lady Jane Grey and her husband, languishing in prison, were executed, for fear that they could become the focus of future discontent.

The Mayor of London at the time of Lady Jane Grey's bid for the throne was a merchant called Thomas White, who firmly supported Mary and was involved in the trials of both Lady Jane Grey and those who took part in Wyatt's rebellion. White was later knighted, and became known in Leicester as a benefactor who, on his death, favoured the Midland towns of Leicester, Coventry, Northampton, Nottingham and Warwick with a bequest.[16] He left land, the profits of which were intended to help needy young men start out in life. In Leicester the first loan from the Sir Thomas White charity was paid out in 1613, and the charity is still providing loans to aspiring young businesspeople today. White was phenomenally rich at certain periods during his life, wealthy enough in the 1520s to lend Henry VIII over £20,000 to finance his wars. He was also a famous patron: the founding of St John's College in Oxford being one of his most famous projects. It is not known whether White ever visited Leicester, but by the nineteenth century he had become a venerated historical figure in the town, and his statue is one of the four figures commemorated on the Victorian clock tower in the city centre. It is perhaps ironic, in view of Leicester's generally Protestant sympathies, that White played such a major role in helping Mary to the throne and punishing the Grey faction.

The long reign of Elizabeth I began in 1558 after Mary's premature death. England was far from stable, with a poor economic situation, hostile relations with France and an increasingly difficult relationship with Scotland. In addition to this, religious divisions in the country had been aggravated by the zeal with which Mary had persecuted dissidents. During her reign, over 300 people, many of them of humble origin, had been burned at the stake for deviating from orthodox Catholic belief. The borough records of Leicester reported just one burning: a local man called Thomas Moor, who publicly denied that the real presence of God was in the consecrated host.[17]

In 1559 Elizabeth restored the Act of Supremacy, and a religious settlement was made that attempted to follow a middle way. The Anglican Church, established in the same year, adopted Protestant doctrine but retained much of the Catholic ritual as well as a hierarchical structure. In Leicester the churches again fell obediently into line, and for the second and last time St Martin's disposed of those church items linked to the old religion. By the end of the century Leicester had become a firmly Protestant town.

# Living in the Town

What was it like to live in Tudor Leicester? In the early sixteenth century it was a town of around 3,000 residents. Although it had lost the political prestige that had distinguished it when the castle had been the favoured residence for the Dukes of Lancaster, it was still a significant place, 'the largest and wealthiest town between the Trent and the Thames'.[18] At this time Leicester still more or less retained its medieval boundaries, covering approximately 100 acres with suburbs to the east, south and north. It was very much a country town, surrounded by farmland that the residents used both for pasturing animals and for cultivating individual smallholdings, while within the town walls there were also gardens and orchards. Quality of life as a Leicester resident unsurprisingly depended on income. In terms of population distribution, the pattern of a wealthy centre and poorer suburbs was a general characteristic of towns throughout the country at this time, and Leicester was no exception. The most heavily populated districts were in the suburbs, and this was where most, though not all, of the poorest people lived. Within the walls there were poor enclaves, but there was also a wealthy central district around Swinesmarket, the modern High Street and Highcross Street area, where there were larger and smarter houses.[19]

The richest people in the town during the early decades of the century were the wool merchants, and foremost among these was the younger William Wyggeston. When a special tax was raised by the king in 1523–24, Wyggeston personally paid £600, over a quarter of the gross tax raised in Leicester. At the other end of the social scale were a large group of poor people who lived at purely subsistence level. In between were craftsmen and traders of varying income levels.

The wool export trade was on the decline by the sixteenth century, and William Wyggeston was the last of the great Leicester wool exporters, although the wool trade continued in the town at a more local level. There was now no major industry in Leicester, just a range of trades and occupations, some more lucrative than others. The most prosperous townspeople at the beginning of Elizabeth's reign in 1559 were those in the clothing and the food and drinks trade, and those involved in the processing of hides and the crafting and sale of leather goods. The leading occupations at this time included butchers, tanners, shoemakers, clothiers, bakers and mercers, and there were also townspeople, such as wheelwrights and smiths, involved in supplying essential goods to the population of the nearby countryside. Goods were sold at the Wednesday and Saturday markets, as well as the four annual fairs, two of which were in the spring and two in the autumn.

Most people in Leicester lived in one-storey houses with two or three rooms, the basic two rooms being a living room and a parlour that was used as a bedroom. Where there was a third room this was generally a buttery. A bigger house might include a loft, where children could sleep, while a poorer option was a cheaply built one-room cottage. In contrast, at the top of the social pyramid William Wyggeston lived in an impressive house

Nineteenth-century view of the High Street, showing the tower of Lord's Place, the third Lord Huntingdon's Leicester House. Lord's Place was demolished in 1902. This image is reproduced courtesy of the Record Office for Leicestershire, Leicester and Rutland.

with seventeen rooms. The larger houses sported courtyards and gardens, and because there was plenty of open land in the city even quite a humble cottage often had a small garden, which gave a poor family an added means of support.[20]

Poverty made the lives of some townspeople a constant struggle. In England, generally, levels of poverty rose in the sixteenth century, spurred on by growth in population, rising prices and extensive unemployment, and it was during this century that the first English poor laws were passed. Widespread poverty was considered a threat to public order, and the new legislation was seen as a way of dealing with this. The drive to pass the new poor laws came from central government, and local governing bodies were given orders to follow.[21] From the beginning there was a strong emphasis on punishing vagrancy and idleness. In Leicester a cuckstool and stocks were in use, and by the first years of the seventeenth century there was also a Leicester house of correction. However, the Poor Law legislation also resulted in some organised poor relief. In 1536 weekly collections for the poor where introduced, and in 1572 justices of the peace were commissioned to survey the local poor so as to assess the cost of their needs. This cost was passed to the parish and overseers, and tax collectors were appointed to ensure that money was collected from parishioners.

Responsibility for managing day-to-day town affairs fell to the mayor and burgesses, and during the Tudor period this body gained new powers and prestige. Since the Act of Parliament in 1489, Leicester's local governing body had comprised the mayor, a group of twenty-four leading burgesses and another forty-eight burgesses who represented the other freemen of the town. This body, as previously discussed, evolved from a combination of the Guild Merchant and the Portmanmoot. The old names died out, and by the sixteenth century the body was often referred to as the corporation, even though it was not until 1589 that Queen Elizabeth I awarded a charter of incorporation to the town and the name corporation became legally accurate. The charter described the composition of Leicester's local governing body, as had been laid down in 1489, although now the twenty-four were referred to as aldermen and the forty-eight as councillors. In addition to this, the legal right of the corporation to hold land was confirmed. This new right was of particular importance to the town leaders, as they had bought local land and property after the Dissolution of the monasteries, guilds and chantries. These acquisitions included both the Corpus Christi Guildhall and the Newarke Grange estate, which had previously belonged to Newarke College.

The 1589 charter was followed by a second in 1599, which gave a wider description of the corporation and its powers. It was declared that all areas of the Leicester suburbs came under town jurisdiction, and the right of the corporation to impose by-laws was confirmed. Further to this, specific descriptions were given of the principal offices of the borough: these were to include a town clerk, steward, two bailiffs and five sergeants at mace. Altogether the two charters bestowed on the town government what the name corporation suggests: a legal corporate personality that officially represented the town and its people.[22]

The corporation managed all those aspects of life that were thought to concern the common good of the town. The regulation of trade and commerce was held to be of vital importance and, just as the Guild Merchant had before, the corporation ensured that trade in Leicester was restricted to the freemen of the town. They also attempted to regulate prices and the quality of goods that were traded. Further major responsibilities included maintaining the streets, monitoring sanitation, taking fire protection measures and promoting law and order. Regulations were imposed on the local populace to further these goals, including rules about the management of animal dung, penalties for blocking the street and a curfew, which made it an offence to be out at night after nine o'clock.

Certain new practices and rituals helped to underline the growing prestige of the mayor and corporation during these years. The corporation meetings were known as common halls, and towards the end of the sixteenth century more formal written attendance records were kept. Special caps and gowns were introduced for aldermen and councillors, and these were worn on important annual civic occasions, such as the assizes and the town fairs. Town Waits were established and, dressed in livery, they played in the town twice daily, as well as enlivening important civic events with their music. The election day for the mayor was St Matthew's Day, 21 September, and the mayor was required to take an oath in the presence of the steward shortly after Martinmas Day, 11 November. From the borough records we know that by the early years of the seventeenth century the mayor went in procession to the castle to perform this duty. This type of observance stressed the authority of the mayor and corporation, and became part of the rhythms that shaped the local year.

## The Earl of Huntingdon and the Leicester Free Grammar School

In Leicestershire at the outset of Elizabeth's reign, the star of a young Protestant noble, Henry Hastings, third Earl of Huntingdon was on the rise. Huntingdon came to dominate Leicester as well as the county; he involved himself extensively in town affairs and left his mark on the religious orientation of the town.[23]

The Greys and the Hastings were the foremost families in the county, but after the Lady Jane Grey affair the Hastings family became the more influential. This branch of the Hastings family had been connected with Leicestershire since the thirteenth century, their property including a manor at Wistow and a castle at Ashby-de-la-Zouch. Among their ancestors was the Hastings who was executed by Richard III in an incident made famous by the Shakespeare play of the same name. The third Earl of Huntingdon was made the Lord Lieutenant of Leicestershire, a position his father, the second earl, had also held.

In addition to this, Queen Elizabeth awarded him further local offices, including Steward of the town of Leicester, a position that justified intervention in town affairs. Huntingdon took this seriously, and involved himself extensively with the town. He advised and guided the mayor and burgesses, and to maintain a visible presence in Leicester he kept a townhouse on High Street, known as the Lord's Place, and a personal pew in St Martin's church. Huntingdon was an ardent Protestant who had been educated by Protestant tutors alongside the young Edward VI. He had emerged from this experience with zealous religious convictions that never faltered, regardless of the pressures of Mary Tudor's reign and despite the fact that there were Catholics in his own family. Elizabeth I had chosen a middle way to settle the religious divisions that racked the country, but there were many who believed that English Protestantism had been diluted too far; it was from this group that the Puritan movement developed within the Church of England. Cross refers to Huntingdon as 'The Puritan Earl', and this conveys the flavour of his religious stance – although his loyalty to Elizabeth remained steadfast.[24]

It was Huntingdon's intention to shape religious beliefs in both Leicestershire and Leicester that coincided with his own. After the Elizabethan religious settlement, many of the Puritan preachers, who found themselves part of the Anglican Church but at odds with the establishment, found it either difficult or unappealing to seek Church office or preferment. For this group, freelance preaching, which allowed them greater freedom to expound their ideas, became an attractive option. Before long, some provincial towns had acquired a salaried Puritan preacher who delivered sermons, or lectures as they were known, in parish churches. In the 1560s, under the influence of Huntingdon, Leicester became one of the first towns to engage a preacher of this type.[25] He delivered his lectures each Wednesday and Friday at St Martin's church, and it was compulsory for at least one member of every Leicester household to attend, with a 4d fine as a penalty for absence. The general population, of course, had very little guidance in what to think, apart from what they heard from the pulpit, and regular preaching was used to secure the Elizabethan settlement at popular level. By installing a Puritan lecturer Huntingdon ensured that Leicester townspeople were guided to the more solidly Protestant wing of the Church.

Huntingdon treated Leicester as though he were a feudal lord, and the town was his borough.[26] There had been no lord in residence since 1399, when the honour of Leicester passed to the Crown, and this change had given town leaders the opportunity to gain much more control over local business. It might be thought, therefore, that the mayor and burgesses would resent Huntingdon's interference, but it seems that the town was generally willing to fall in with him. He was conscientious and capable, as well as being an individual of standing who had some influence with the queen, and because of this it is likely that many town leaders saw his help as beneficial. It is also likely that many of them shared his religious attitudes. In general, Leicester seems to have adapted very easily to Protestantism.

Huntingdon also intervened in the affairs of the local grammar school for boys.[27] This school was one of many founded in England during the sixteenth century. Throughout the country, from the late fourteenth century onwards, there had been an expansion in the number of schools, and this investment in education continued during and after Queen Elizabeth's reign. A nineteenth-century schools enquiry commission found that at least 435 endowed schools were founded in the years between 1500 and 1660, in addition to many private fee-paying schools.[28] Improved schooling benefited the Elizabethan state because it was an opportunity to indoctrinate young minds with Protestantism. Moreover, the emphasis that Protestantism placed on the written word, and the ability of the individual to read the Bible for himself, made more sense to people who had received some education. For Huntingdon, intervening in the school was another opportunity to ensure that his religious stance was promulgated.

The grammar school in Leicester was founded when the town was especially badly in need of a school. It is thought that a grammar school was maintained by the abbey in the late thirteenth and fourteenth century, but at some point this collapsed. There was also an almonry or charity school at the abbey, but this was also lost either before or when the abbey was closed in 1538. A further attempt to provide a school was made in the first half of the sixteenth century, when the Bishop of Carlisle donated a piece of land to found a school in St Margaret's parish. It is thought likely that this bishop was none other than John Penny, former Abbot of Leicester, famous for building the enclosing wall at the abbey. The school never materialised, however, because of the fraudulent dealings of John Beaumont, the Recorder of Leicester, who took the land for himself and sold it.

The sixteenth-century grammar school had no connection with any of these previous projects. The idea of a school for local boys originally came from

Thomas Wyggeston, who was a trustee of his late brother William's estate and proposed that the estate should provide an endowment. In 1545, land was bought to fund this endowment and was placed unofficially under the control of the Hospital of St Ursula, the hospital that had been founded at the direction of William Wyggeston. The arrangement was that £7 per annum would be provided for a schoolmaster. The first appointed was an Oxford graduate named John Hopkins; it is thought likely that this was the same John Hopkins who, together with Thomas Sternhold, produced well-known translations of the psalms in metrical verse in the 1550s. The link between the hospital and the school was legalised, and the

The Old Grammar School: a nineteenth-century drawing. This image is taken from Mrs T. Fielding Johnson, *Glimpses of Ancient Leicester* (Leicester, 1891), courtesy of the University of Leicester Special Collections.

schoolmaster's salary was raised to £10 per annum. Meanwhile, further funds for the school were provided from the estate of William Gillot, who before his death had been another trustee of the Wyggeston estate. This money was used to buy property that would generate enough income to pay an assistant master.

The Earl of Huntingdon began to take an active interest in the school during the early years of Elizabeth's reign, and he sought to build it up as well as mould it to his own way of thinking. As a result of his intervention the school, now known as the Free Grammar School of Leicester, was re-established on a new basis. Huntingdon's first step was to apply to the queen for a grant. This application was successful, and it was laid down that £10 be paid yearly from the Duchy of Lancaster to finance a schoolmaster who would be appointed by the mayor and burgesses. This was a break from the past, when the appointment of the schoolmaster was purely the responsibility of the hospital. Money from the Wyggeston and Gillot estates was still forthcoming, and the close link to the Wyggeston hospital was retained, but the town now had an important say in the running of the school.

The town leaders undertook to find the school a proper home. St Peter's church had fallen into disuse, and this was re-equipped as a schoolroom, with the costs covered by selling one of the church bells. By 1562 a new schoolmaster had been appointed and installed, and the new school was established and working. This new teacher was a scholar from Merton College, Oxford, called John Pott, and he turned out to be the very opposite of what Huntingdon wanted.[29] Pott was a scholar of repute but he was also a closet Catholic, who had been forced to leave Merton because of his views. It seems highly unlikely that either Huntingdon or the town leaders knew this when they consented to his appointment. As well as taking on the role of schoolmaster, Pott was made a confrator (or fellow) at the hospital. At the time, the master of the hospital was Nicholas Harwar, and under his regime the institution provided an environment where Catholic sympathisers could discreetly blend in. This situation was not allowed to last, and Harwar was the first victim. Allegations were made that his appointment to the mastership was invalid and that his administration had been irregular. In the midst of the campaign to oust him from office, Harwar helped his enemies by dying from natural causes. He was replaced by a well-known cleric called Thomas Sampson, who was famed for his Protestant fervour.

With Sampson in charge, John Pott was in a very difficult position, as his Catholic sympathies would clearly not be tolerated. Soon he too was under investigation, for allegedly misusing money. Pott quietly disappeared from Leicester, leaving just over £8 for his persecutors to find.[30] He also took with him one of his pupils, a boy called Arthur Faunt, who was the third son of the Squire of Foston in Leicestershire. Apparently this was with the permission of Faunt's parents, who were also Catholic sympathisers. At first they went to Oxford, where they stayed for about a year, and then they crossed the Channel and went to the Jesuit monastery of Louvain. Faunt's abilities caught the attention of Pope Gregory XIII, and as a result he had a distinguished Church career. This took him to Poland, where he rose to be the head of a Jesuit college at Posen, becoming a well-known and well-respected public figure. Pott travelled to Ireland, but did not escape Sampson, who continued to pursue him for money until a legal financial settlement was made.

In the years that followed Pott's departure the school received a further makeover. A new and apparently uncontroversial schoolmaster was appointed, and he held the post for the next decade. In 1573 the corporation applied to the queen for permission to pull St Peter's church down, their intention being to use the stone and other materials to build a schoolhouse 'meet and fitt for childarne to be taught in'.[31] Permission was granted, for a small fee, and the new school building was erected on the corner of High Street and Dead Lane, now known respectively as Highcross Street and Freeschool Lane. The master and pupils raised money for school equipment, and Thomas Sampson of the hospital and a benefactor by the name of Sir Ralph Rowlett, who lived in St Albans but had family connections with Leicestershire, both made personal donations to the school. The solid stone school building with its Swithland slate roof has survived. At the time of writing it has been converted into a restaurant called 1573, recalling the year in which it was built.

The guiding hand of the Earl of Huntingdon was very evident in the reorganisation of the school, and when new school statutes were produced his signature was at the bottom of every page. A strict timetable was observed, with pupils attending six days a week; there was a possible half-holiday on Thursdays at the discretion of the authorities. In summer, lessons started at five o'clock in the morning and finished at five o'clock in the evening, with a two-hour break in the middle of the day. A similar pattern was followed in winter, with the concession that lessons began at seven rather than five. The curriculum required the older pupils to become proficient in Latin and Greek and to be familiar with a range of Classical writings; all, of course, were thoroughly grounded in Protestant religious teaching. On Sundays there was no real break, as all the boys were required to attend their parish church and take notes from the sermon, while older boys were also expected to attend sermons and additional religious services during the week. Huntingdon provided some scholarships for poor boys, and special funding was also put aside for suitable candidates who wished to move on from the school to university, and become preachers.

As well as intervening in the affairs of the school, Huntingdon also participated in further changes at the hospital and laid down new hospital statutes. With Sampson at the helm, he already had a master on whose Puritan views he could rely. It was, therefore, not too difficult to smoke out the last traces of popery. It was with this intention that the hospital's dedication to St Ursula was removed. To the Puritan mind the dedication was superstitious, and the new statutes stated that the hospital would no longer carry the name of any 'fancied saint', and from then on the institution was known simply as William Wyggeston's Hospital in the town of Leicester.[32]

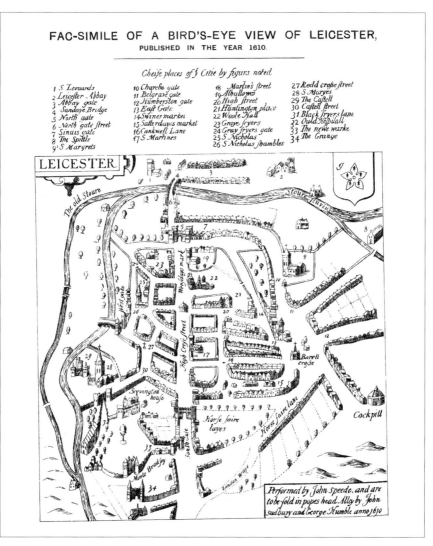

# FAC-SIMILE OF A BIRD'S-EYE VIEW OF LEICESTER,
## PUBLISHED IN THE YEAR 1610.

*Cheife places of y Citie by figurs noted.*

| | | | |
|---|---|---|---|
| 1 S. Leouards | 10 Churche yate | 18 Martin's ftreet | 27 Redd croffe ftreet |
| 2 Leicefter Abbay | 11 Belgraue gate | 19 Alhallowes | 28 S. Maryes |
| 3 Abbay gate | 12 Humberfton gate | 20 High ftreet | 29 The Caftell |
| 4 Sundaye Bridge | 13 Eaft Gate | 21 Huntington place | 30 Caftell ftreet |
| 5 North gate | 14 Swines market | 22 Woole Hall | 31 Black fryers lane |
| 6 North gate ftreet | 15 Satterdayes market | 23 Graye fryers | 32 Ould Hofpitall |
| 7 Sinuis gate | 16 Cankwell Lane | 24 Gray fryers gate | 33 The newe marke |
| 8 The Spittle | 17 S. Martines | 25 S. Nicholas | 34 The Grange |
| 9 S. Margrets | | 26 S. Nicholas fhambles | |

LEICESTER

The old Stoure

Stoure fluuius

Weftgate

Wenfdayes market

High Croffe ftreet

Bareli croffe

Seuington houfe

South gate

Horse faire layes

Horse faire lane

Cockpitl

Mire Bradley

Landon Woy

Performed by John Speede, and are to be fold in popes head Alley by John Sudbury and George Humble anno 1610

'Bird's eye view of Leicester', published in 1610. This image is courtesy of the University of Leicester Special Collections.

A further aspect of Leicester life in which Huntingdon took a special interest was the welfare of the poor. A project to set up local clothing workshops to provide extra employment failed, but a less ambitious plan to supply the poor with inexpensive coal was more successful. Huntingdon gave the mayor and burgesses money to buy the coal; this was then transported free of charge by Huntingdon's own servants and supplied at low cost to the poor. His generosity did not stretch as far as giving the coal to poor residents free of charge.[33]

Paradoxically, although Huntingdon was such a dominating character, in the last years of his life he used his influence with Queen Elizabeth to help the town gain a important marker of independence. This was a charter of incorporation, granted in February 1589. By welcoming Huntingdon's interference in the short term, it turned out that the town had gained a potentially more independent future. Huntingdon died in 1595, and although his successors expected support from the town they did not take the same level of interest in its everyday affairs. Because of this the corporation, its rights now enshrined in the charter, was able to govern with slightly more autonomy.

In the early seventeenth century, Leicester remained a sizeable, quiet and not very prosperous town, and the Puritan influence so encouraged by Huntingdon continued to dominate. However, as Simmons has observed, there was still some entertainment and enjoyment to be had, and the corporation played a part in helping to provide this. On the other hand, the leadership of the town strongly disapproved of dancing, and by the turn of the century they were taking steps to suppress maypoles, which they saw as an unseemly reminder of a less virtuous era. Despite this, in the early decades of the century Leicester folk were allowed to enjoy the visits of travelling entertainers and companies of players, who performed at the Town Hall; the corporation contributed to the cost of this. Leicester people also entertained themselves with a range of sports, including horseracing, cock-fighting and football.[34]

More soberly, Leicester corporation also helped establish one of the first town libraries in England. This grew from a store of books, mainly about Protestantism, which had been collected and kept in St Martin's church until moved to the Town Hall in about 1633. John Angel, a public lecturer in the town, master at the Free Grammar School and the future library-keeper, was at the heart of this initiative, which also received support from Bishop Williams of Lincoln. The corporation financed the move, and paid for new furnishings and even some more books. It was just the sort of project that the third Earl of Huntingdon would have approved of: educational, and with a view to encouraging a Protestant way of life through appropriate reading.[35]

# Catastrophe: Civil War and the Storming of Leicester

The conflicts that erupted into war during the reign of Charles I led to horrific trauma for people throughout the British Isles. War with Scotland, war in Ireland and the civil wars in England claimed an immense death toll: it has been claimed that more people died in proportion to the total population than during the First World War.[36] In addition to the deaths in battles, sieges, rioting or other direct violence, many people were killed by disease, and there was also great damage to property, with innumerable homes and livelihoods lost. In England the power struggle between king and Parliament badly damaged the social fabric, dividing communities and families. Some followed their own ideals and consciences, but many others were forced to take sides because of circumstances. Through it all religious differences shaped the rhetoric, encouraged bigotry and generally served to poison and aggravate hostilities. Catastrophe came upon Leicester on 29 May 1645 when Royalist forces stormed and sacked the town. There was widespread damage and looting, and hundreds of people, including many civilians, were killed.

Charles I had come to the throne in 1625, and from early on in his reign the tensions that led to war began to grow. From the beginning, Charles chafed against the restrictions placed on him by Parliament, so much so that he decided to rule without it. He caused widespread outrage by failing to call Parliament at all between 1629 and 1640, and by financing this personal rule with a range of questionable taxes, the most famous of which was ship money. Previously raised in coastal towns as a contribution to the defence of the coastline, it was extended by Charles, with no apparent justification, to inland towns. It was raised several times in Leicester during the 1630s, removing substantial sums from the local budget. Ruling without the counsel of Parliament and arbitrarily extorting taxes undermined the sense of reciprocity by which government in England had worked, and helped lead to a countrywide breakdown of trust.[37] This was further exacerbated by Charles's religious preferences, which were perceived by some, especially by the Puritans, as dangerously popish.

Typically, in the shires and provincial towns, grievances and controversy entwined with local affairs. In Leicestershire the argument between king and Parliament fed into the long-standing rivalry between the Grey and Hastings families: the Greys associated with the Parliamentary cause and the Hastings militant Royalists. The local gentry also took sides, with a concentration of Royalist supporters to the north and west of the Fosse Way and a greater number of Parliamentarians in the south of the county.[38]

By 1642 the conflict was edging towards war, and both king and Parliament struggled for power over local militia and munitions around the country. It was customary for the king to appoint the county lord lieutenants, but in March of that year, Parliament defied the custom and appointed Thomas Grey, Earl of Stamford as Lord Lieutenant of Leicestershire, giving him the power to raise troops for possible war and supplanting the Royalist incumbent Henry Hastings, son of the fifth Earl of Huntingdon.[39] Grey started to raise troops, and also removed arms from the town magazine at the Newarke, taking them to his home at Bradgate – although shortly afterwards he thought better of this and replaced them. Charles refused to accept Parliament's decision, and sent his own men around the country to raise troops, starting in Leicestershire, where Hastings was still championing his cause. The Mayor of Leicester, Thomas Rudyard, and the corporation were caught in the crossfire, and made every effort to commit to neither side. As Simmons observed, local desire to sit on the fence was perhaps reflected in the fact that one of Leicester's two MPs at the time was Royalist while the other was Parliamentarian.[40]

In the months that followed, the king visited Leicester on two occasions. On 22 July 1642 he came to the town with his son, Prince Charles, and his nephew, Prince Rupert of the Rhine, the son of his elder sister Elizabeth, who had married Frederick V of Bohemia. The mayor and corporation welcomed the royal party and accommodated them at Lord's Place, the house that had been built by the third Earl of Huntingdon. As the assizes were taking place at Leicester Castle at the time, the king took the opportunity to address all those assembled, assuring them that he was relying on their loyalty to his cause. He was listened to politely, but after his speeches he was given a petition suggesting that it would be better if he were reconciled with Parliament. On Sunday the king attended St Martin's, and went in procession to the church accompanied by the mayor and councillors, who were formally dressed for the occasion in their ceremonial robes. This implied a positive and reciprocal relationship between the king and the town, but in fact the support Charles received in Leicester was muted and conditional. The king returned to Leicester briefly for a second time on 18 August, after the people of Coventry had shut their town gates to him. He stayed one night in the town before travelling to Nottingham, where he raised his standard. The war had officially begun.

It was shortly after this that Prince Rupert, who was garrisoned at Queniborough, caused great alarm in Leicester by sending a menacing letter to the town leadership demanding £2,000. The horror and indignation with which this demand was met is reflected in a local ghost story that is sometimes still heard in Leicester today, in which a councillor in seventeenth-century dress is seen hurrying down Guildhall Lane to the old Town Hall, frantic with anxiety at Rupert's demand. The corporation borrowed £500 from a local citizen, Hugh Watts, a bellfounder, and sent it to Rupert to mollify him, while at the same time writing to the king to complain about what had happened. On this occasion Charles took the side of the town, and apologised. There was no demand from Rupert for the remainder of the money, but he never returned the £500.

Between 1642 and 1643 the people of Leicester quietly allowed Grey to take control of the town for the Parliamentary side, and all remained relatively quiet until 1645, when the king made the decision to attack Leicester. The Royalists were losing the war, and in order to stem the tide, Rupert and Charles joined forces to consolidate their strength in the Midlands. The Royalist army arrived in the town on 29 May. The main focuses of attack were the south gate and the south wall of the Newarke, and in readiness Rupert positioned troops near the Raw Dykes and set his cannons to face the wall. Meanwhile,

A note from Prince Rupert acknowledging receipt of £500 from the Mayor of Leicester. This image is taken from J. Throsby, *The History and Antiquities of the Ancient Town of Leicester* (Leicester, 1791), courtesy of the University of Leicester Special Collections.

Prince Rupert summoning the garrison of Leicester to surrender to the army of Charles I, 30 May 1645. This image is taken from J. Throsby, *The History and Antiquities of the Ancient Town of Leicester* (Leicester, 1791), courtesy of the University of Leicester Special Collections

other troops were positioned at strategic points around the perimeter to attack the town from various angles. From the outset, Leicester was at a great disadvantage because of its inadequate defences. Efforts had been made to construct a line of defence works around the town, but there were breaks and weaknesses in these, and the defenders of the town were far outnumbered. The Leicester garrison of approximately 2,000 was a mix of trained soldiers, Leicester citizens thought capable of fighting and some helpers from the county. Appeals had been made to Parliament for reinforcements, but no help had come. This hopelessly inadequate band faced probably around 5,000 to 6,000 Royalist troops.

At midday on 30 May, Rupert sent messages offering terms of surrender to the Mayor of Leicester, William Billers, and the corporation, who had gathered in the Town Hall to discuss the crisis. The town leaders fatally failed to come to a decision, and Rupert began the attack. A good defence was put up at the

Newarke, and even when the town wall was breached after a few hours the townspeople, including women and children, tried to barricade the opening with woolpacks and other materials. The barricades were not strong enough to keep the soldiers outside the wall, however; Royalist troops had penetrated the town elsewhere and were overrunning it. The defence of the Newarke continued, and in the streets there was hand-to-hand fighting, while town residents threw down roof tiles and other missiles on the heads of the invading soldiers. The fighting continued late into the night, but eventually the Newarke was surrendered and the town was plundered.

There is no doubt that many atrocities took place, but it is unlikely this brutality was supported by the king. There were conflicting reports: one account said that Charles rode through the streets of Leicester urging people to surrender so that they would not be killed, but another witness famously said that King Charles was seen in 'bright armour' in the Leicester streets allowing prisoners to be abused and saying, 'I do not care if you cut them three times more, for they are mine enemy.' Simmons argues that this level of cruelty was not typical of Charles, and suggests that the witness may either have lied or mistaken Rupert for Charles.[41] Whatever the truth, the suffering inflicted on Leicester people was immense. The storming and sack of the town resulted in serious damage to property, and left approximately 700 people dead, around 200 of whom were Royalist soldiers. In all, 140 wagons of loot were taken from the town, including the corporation seals, mace and the town archives. In addition to this the king imposed a £2,000 fine on the devastated town, and before departing the Royalist soldiers burned down what remained of Leicester Abbey. Charles left the town under the control of Henry Hastings, now known as Lord Loughborough, a title with which Charles had recently rewarded him.

Within a fortnight all had changed again: on 14 June 1645 the Battle of Naseby was fought in neighbouring Northamptonshire, and was an overwhelming victory for the Parliamentary forces. It was the decisive battle of the war: Parliament had won and the king had lost. Thomas Fairfax, the Parliamentary commander in chief, and Oliver Cromwell advanced on Leicester with their troops, and when Hastings seemed unready to comply with them they started another attack on the town. Fortunately for the townspeople it did not take long for Hastings to realise his mistake and surrender, thus saving the town from another bloodbath. When news of the surrender reached London a day of thanksgiving was proclaimed, and church collections were organised

# GEORGE FOX

George Fox (1624–91), a founder of the Quakers or Religious Society of Friends, was born in Leicestershire at the village of Drayton-in-the-Clay, now known as Fenny Drayton. In this village there was a strong tradition of Puritanism, and Fox's father, a weaver, was respected locally for his piety, while his mother was a descendant of a Protestant martyr, executed during the reign of Mary. Fox was apprenticed to a local shoemaker, but at the age of 19 he left his apprenticeship to concentrate on his spiritual life.

Fox broke with his parish church and spent much of his life travelling around proclaiming his beliefs. His religious approach placed an emphasis on equality – both social and spiritual. He believed that the inner light of Christ was within each individual and that clergy were unnecessary, as each person could find spiritual guidance within him- or herself. He also advocated less formal religious practice, rejected the need for special church buildings and held that all men, women and children had a right to contribute to religious gatherings and discussion.

Fox's journal tells how in 1648, early in his career, he forcefully communicated his views during a meeting in Leicester. This gathering of Protestant sects was held in a local church. A woman asked a question only to be told by the priest, 'I permit not a woman to speak in the church.' He was immediately challenged by Fox, who demanded to know if the priest believed the church was the building or the people in it. The dispute did not end there; as Fox remarked, 'This set them all on fire.'

The trauma of civil war resulted in a widespread questioning of religious beliefs and Fox and his associates attracted many followers. They were, however, regarded with suspicion by the authorities, and Fox had many spells in prison. The group first called themselves Children of the Light, or Friends of Truth, before settling on the Religious Society of Friends. The name Quaker, which became widely used, is thought to have been coined by a Derby magistrate, who claimed that members of the group trembled when they worshipped.

## Sources

'George Fox and the Quakers', *In Our Time* with Melvyn Bragg, Justin Chapman, John Coffey and Kate Peters, BBC Radio 4, 5 April 2012; W. Armistead (Ed.), *Journal of George Fox*, vols 1 and 2 (London, 1852), www.archive.org, accessed 29 October 2012; R.H. Evans, 'The Truth Sprang up in Leicestershire', *Transactions of the Leicestershire Archaeological Society*, vol.66, pp.121–155; H.L. Ingle, 'Fox George (1624–1691)' in *Oxford Dictionary of National Biography* (Oxford, 2004), www.oxforddnb.com/view/article10031, accessed 28 October 2012; H.L. Ingle, *First Among Friends and the Creation of Quakerism* (Oxford, 1984).

to help the people of Leicester. In the period that followed, Parliament made a financial grant to the town to help with the process of reconstruction, and further money, raised by confiscating Royalist assets, was also awarded to Leicester.

The town was not significantly involved in the second bout of civil war, between the years of 1648 and 1649, which culminated in the execution of Charles I. The interregnum years that followed were also quiet, made even more so by the fact that the more extreme Puritan attitudes gained a firmer hold, with most forms of entertainment and opportunities for celebration, including Christmas, abolished.

Between the onset of the sixteenth century and the Restoration there had been many changes in Leicester. A religious revolution had altered the face of the town and destroyed the grandeur of medieval Leicester, and by the end of the sixteenth century Protestantism had firmly taken root. The years of Tudor and early Stuart rule were not especially prosperous, although on the brighter side the town gained its charter of incorporation, which promised greater autonomy in the future. The crisis of civil war, however, put these hopes at least temporarily in the shade. Caught unwillingly in the argument between Parliament and the king, and between the Hastings and the Greys, Leicester paid a terrible price.

# four

# EARLY MODERN LEICESTER

New Industry, Communications, Repression and Reform

John Evelyn, the diarist, witnessed the triumphant return of Charles II to London on 29 May 1660. Charles rode into the city accompanied by 20,000 supporters on horse and foot, 'brandishing their swords and shouting with inexpressible joy, the ways strewn with flowers, the bells ringing, the streets hung with tapestry, fountains flowing with wine'. This was a mass celebration, and 'myriads of people' flocked to take part: the king's procession took seven full hours to pass through the city.[1] To show their support for the new king the corporation of Leicester sent a silk brocade purse containing £300 of gold to London.[2]

The Parliamentarians told the people that civil war had brought them liberty from the despotic rule of kings, but now Charles Stuart had returned and celebration was the order of the day. The Leicester corporation was anxious to curry favour with the new regime. The reflections of John Throsby, the eighteenth-century Leicester antiquarian, capture the irony of this sudden official turn-around. He wrote: 'They, who had been the foremost to rob him of his dignity and lay his sceptre at the feet of usurpers, now presented him with £300. What a change, in the passing of a few years, was wrought in the minds of the inhabitants of this place! Was it from conviction or necessity? Perhaps from both.'[3]

Whatever the answer, Leicester adapted to the change and local life continued – and for most people in the late seventeenth and early eighteenth centuries life was indeed a very local affair. Road communications were extremely poor, and were deteriorating because of the increased use of wheeled vehicles. If a rainstorm soaked the clay earth of the Midlands the roads became unusable until the mud had dried. Despite these obstacles several dedicated travellers made tours of the country, and their diaries give us their impressions of Leicester.

One visitor was John Evelyn, mentioned earlier. His home was in Deptford, and he moved in an elite social circle that numbered many leading figures of the day, including King Charles II. On his travels through the Midlands in 1654 he approached Leicester from the west. He had found Worcester an agreeable and clean place with 'neatly paved' streets; he also thought Warwick a fine town and had admired the castle. Even more extravagant was his praise for Coventry, where he had seen 'handsome' churches, a 'beautiful' town wall and 'streets full of great shops'. He was less impressed by Leicester, both town and county. He commented on the 'wretched' and 'impoverished' life that people were living in the rural parts of south-east Leicestershire and Rutland, and he declared Leicester an 'old and ragged city … large and pleasantly situated but despicably built'. It was less than a decade, of course, since Leicester had been sacked by the Royalist forces, and the century before that had not been one of prosperity. One thing Evelyn enjoyed enough to record was a dish of fruit he was given; he commented especially on the delicious melons and his surprise at finding them so far north. He soon exhausted his interest in Leicester, however, and passed on to other nearby towns, including Nottingham, where he found much more to admire.[4]

In 1698 the traveller Celia Fiennes visited Leicester, and her remarks, though not over-enthusiastic, are less dismissive than those of John Evelyn, suggesting that by this time the appearance of the town had begun to improve. Fiennes was from Wiltshire, the daughter of a family of committed dissenters, although her grandfather had been a member of Charles II's Privy Council. Fiennes travelled quite independently through England, with only a few servants for company, and recorded her impressions in her journal.[5] She approached Leicester from the east, passing through Peterborough, which she described as a handsomely built town with a magnificent cathedral. Arriving at Leicester, Fiennes was not particularly impressed by the architecture of the churches, none of which could compare with Peterborough Cathedral, of course. She observed, however, that although the houses were still mostly built from timber there were also some good-quality stone and brick-built houses in the Newarke, and that Leicester Castle had a smart brick frontage.[6] Towards the end of the seventeenth century, clay beds near the town were excavated to make bricks, and the new brick buildings that Celia Fiennes observed were some of the first results of

Leicester and the abbey ruins, eighteenth-century view. This image is taken from J. Throsby, *The History and Antiquities of the Ancient Town of Leicester* (Leicester, 1791), courtesy of the University of Leicester Special Collections.

this initiative, helping to give the town a more substantial and modern look. Although building with brick was introduced slowly, many houses in the centre of town were rebuilt in brick during the following century.[7]

Not only was the town beginning to look more modern, the population was increasing. Between 1670 and 1730 the number of inhabitants rose from about 5,000 to 8,000, and after a more static period numbers picked up again in about 1760, rising to approximately 17,000 by the time of the first census in 1801.[8] Despite these changes Leicester retained the appearance and life of a country town throughout the eighteenth century. Although there had been development to both the south and the east, the town had not in fact extended much beyond its medieval limits. Leicester had been exceptionally widely spaced in its layout, so even with significant growth in population there was still space for many trees and open spaces. Many houses had gardens, and all this green helped to give a rural aspect to the town.[9]

The open fields bordering Leicester also contributed to this country atmosphere. Two of the great fields, the East Field and South Field, remained unenclosed at the beginning of the eighteenth century. The use of the East Field by this time was generally considered to be the business of St Margaret's parish, and was relatively uncontroversial. However, many townspeople still pastured their animals in the South Field, and in the years that followed there was tension when the corporation made various attempts to fence in the land.[10] The attraction of enclosure was that large farms could be established on the land that, if run efficiently, would create substantial profits. This, though, was in direct contravention of the ancient rights of Leicester freemen to use the common land of the town. A plan to enclose was favoured by the corporation as early as 1708, but this failed to materialise. Half a century later the corporation tried to lease a large area of the field to three of their members, with the intention that they should create three large farms. This provoked such an uproar, including violent attacks on the property of the individuals concerned, that the plan had to be dropped. Eventually enclosure of the South Field arrived in 1804. The corporation took full possession of the majority of the land and the business was settled reasonably calmly, with 125 acres of the field set aside in compensation for the freemen of the town.[11]

In terms of the local agricultural economy, Leicester was able to develop its long-held role as the most important market town in the county. Horse trading, sheep breeding and cheese making were all successful, and this was reflected in and encouraged by the introduction of new fairs. In addition to the traditional May and Michaelmas fairs a new spring fair was introduced in 1684, and by 1759 there was also a specialist cheese fair. The weekly Wednesday and Saturday markets continued, but were supplemented by a new Wednesday cattle market in 1763.[12]

Another visitor to Leicester, Daniel Defoe, commented on major new developments in the Leicester economy when he published his *Tour Through the Whole Island of Great Britain* in the 1720s. Defoe, like Fiennes, was from a dissenting background and was keenly interested in new developments in trade and industry, having started out as a tradesman. Britain had acquired a new unified identity since the crowns of Scotland and England were joined in 1707, and this new Britain was now growing rapidly richer through the development of commerce. The motor of this growing prosperity was London,

A couple leaving St Mary de Castro, eighteenth-century view. This image is taken from J. Throsby, *The History and Antiquities of the Ancient Town of Leicester* (Leicester, 1791), courtesy of the University of Leicester Special Collections.

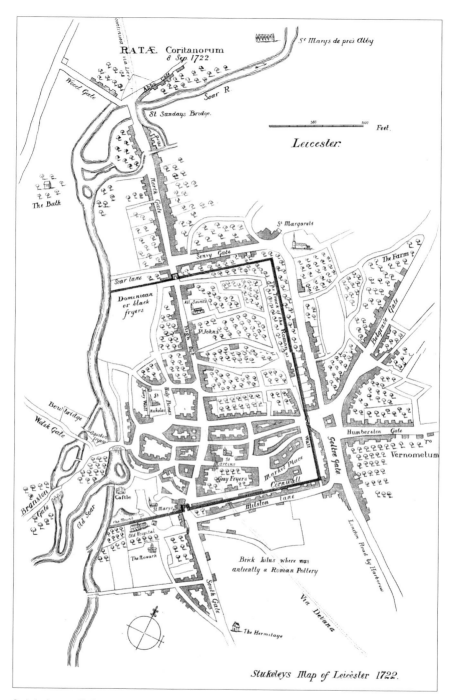

Stukeley's map of Leicester, 1722. This image is reproduced courtesy of the University of Leicester Special Collections.

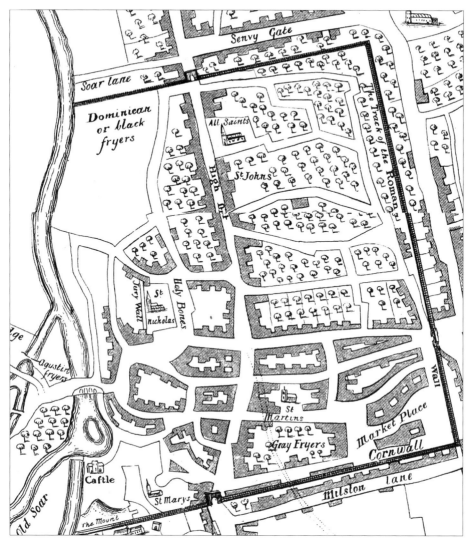

The central town: a detail of Stukeley's 1722 map. This image is reproduced courtesy of the University of Leicester Special Collections.

now an outstandingly large city of around half a million people. It was a huge wealth-making machine, a powerful financial centre and an extensive market supplied by provincial towns, which were themselves expanding as a result of manufacturing and trade. Defoe was intensely excited by this, and his intention was to write about the social improvements he observed while on his travels.[13]

In Leicester and its hinterland, Defoe was impressed by the successful 'country business' that was going on. He commented on the cattle breeding and marvelled at the Leicester sheep, which he found outstanding in quality with exceptionally luxuriant fleeces. These, he declared, provided 'a vast magazine of wool for the rest of the nation'. He also praised the horses he saw traded in Leicester, which he said were 'the largest in England and were generally the great black coach horses and dray horses of which so great a number are continually brought up to London'.[14] These new country trades widened the reputation of Leicester's fairs and markets, and brought prosperity to the town.[15]

## The Beginnings and Growth of the Hosiery Industry

Defoe also recorded another highly significant development. He observed that 'multitudes' of local people in Leicester and in the smaller neighbouring market towns were involved in the manufacture of stockings on frames, an industry and trade that was also flourishing in Nottingham and Derby.[16]

The manufacture of hosiery was providing what Leicester had previously lacked – a staple industry.[17] By the mid-seventeenth century the manufacture of hand-knitted stockings was already a popular and widespread occupation in the town. Sometime in the mid- to late seventeenth century the knitting frame was introduced, it is generally thought by Leicester hosier Nicholas Alsop. The local hosiery industry and also the textile trade went through a very rapid expansion in the first half of the eighteenth century because of this, bringing new wealth to the merchants and employment opportunities to the town. By mid-century there was so much work available that there was a shortage of operatives. Unfortunately, in the following years the situation began to deteriorate. From the beginning one disadvantage for stocking makers was that the knitting frames were expensive, and many were forced to hire their frame from a merchant; this practice, of course, detracted both from their independence and the money they earned. By the 1770s the fluctuations of the market and a sharp rise in food prices, combined with the deduction for frame rent and other related costs, left many in a desperate situation. A further problem was that entry to the industry had been unregulated, and the large reserve of operatives available meant that it was difficult for the workforce to protect their work conditions. Very long hours and low incomes now characterised the life of the framework knitter.

Old-style hosiery making. This image is taken from T. Blandford and G. Newell, *History of the Leicester Cooperative Manufacturing Society* (Leicester, 1898).

With these hard times upon them, the hosiery workers were in no mood to tolerate any innovations that they perceived as a further threat to their livelihood, and when new machinery was introduced into the town it was seen as just such a threat. Against this backdrop a riot broke out in Leicester in March 1773. A newspaper called the *Leicester and Nottingham Journal* had been operating locally since 1757, and the details of the disturbance were related to the readers.

It was reported that on this Monday morning in March the town had been 'alarmed' to hear that a 'great number of stocking makers from the county' were on their way into Leicester 'for the avowed purpose of destroying a stocking frame'. This particular frame was new technology, which had been invented by an 'ingenious mechanic in Scotland' and was being offered to some of the hosiery masters in Leicester. The machine, it seemed, would speed up production, but wild rumours travelled around the neighbourhood greatly exaggerating its powers: 'It was said that one man upon this frame could perform as much work in the same time as sixty men could upon a common frame', and 'it was capable of making a dozen stockings at once, with other reports equally extravagant, all tending to make the stocking maker believe that his labour would no longer be of value.'

When the county stocking makers arrived in Leicester they joined with a 'great mob of townspeople' and assembled in the marketplace. It wasn't long before things got out of hand: a football was kicked in the air and rioting started. To try and calm things down, the mayor, Robert Peach, and one of the hosiery masters, who had been viewing the new frame, came out and addressed the crowd. The hosier assured the men that 'he understood their fears' but that they were wrong to reject the new machine because it would not undermine them; it would merely help them in their work. The new frame was brought out so that it could be demonstrated, but before the hosiers had got the machine working, the mob 'carried it into the Market Place and after parading it round the town, pulled it in pieces and threw the parts among the rabble'. Faced with this violence, the hosiery masters assured the stocking makers that they would not introduce this or any similar machine into the local industry.[18]

A further violent incident took place in 1787, when there was an attempt to bring in a new machine for spinning worsted. This had been invented by a Leicester man named Joseph Brookhouse, who joined with two local businessmen, John Coltman, a hosier, and Joseph Whetstone, a spinner, to introduce the new machinery. When this became known, angry mobs attacked both the houses of Whetstone and Coltman, and Whetstone was forced to escape by means of a rope lowered from his back window. Not only was there extensive damage done to property, but the mayor was hit by a stone as he was reading the Riot Act and subsequently died as a result of his injuries. After this, worsted spinning lost momentum in Leicester and the initiative moved to other Midland towns, including Warwick and Nottingham, where the new machinery was established successfully.

Hosiery production brought new opportunities to Leicester, and was to have a lasting effect on the character and development of the town. However, the volatility of the market and the poor working conditions and low earnings with which the industry came to be associated meant that framework knitters often endured hardship. The London-based livery company of framework knitters proved little support to workers in the Midlands, and when petitioners from Leicester requested Parliament in 1778 and 1779 to legislate for basic work conditions and earnings this was rejected. Under these difficult conditions the frustration that led to breaking machinery was unsurprising, although the violence led to further negative effects on the prospects of the industry and its workers.

## The Development of Roads, Canals and the Railway

In addition to economic change, the eighteenth century also brought a drastic improvement to transport communications. The increase in population and the number of people living in towns, together with the growth in trade and industry and an expanding consumer market, all helped to drive the demand for this. Roads were improved beyond recognition after the introduction of turnpike trusts. Before this, roads throughout Britain had depended unsuccessfully on local parish rates for repair and maintenance, but tolls were charged on turnpike roads, and this money was used to keep the roads in good order.[19]

The new turnpike network reached the border of south Leicestershire in the mid-1720s, and local town and county leaders made a successful application to Parliament to create a turnpike road between Harborough and Loughborough, on the route of the modern A6 road, thus creating a link that extended down to London. Later, in the 1750s and 1760s, further turnpikes were established for other roads. These developments, by enabling cheaper and more effective transportation of goods, supported current initiatives in commerce and industry and promoted further expansion.

The turnpike system also led the way to improvements in passenger transport. The first public passenger vehicles started running from Leicester to London in 1753, and in 1759 a coach service to Leicester, Derby and Nottingham was established, running three times weekly. The coaches became better and more regular, and travelling times were reduced. By the mid-1760s there was a daily service, and by the end of the century the coach service also catered for passengers travelling on to Manchester, Birmingham, Sheffield and Carlisle. There were advances made in mail delivery as well, including a regular Royal Mail service from London to Leicester, which was set up in 1784.

The town gates of Leicester were not demolished until the early 1770s, and were an obstruction to large wheeled vehicles. So as to avoid these gates and the narrow streets inside the town, coaches stopped outside, usually near the East Gates where the Clock Tower stands today, and there were several inns close by to accommodate passengers. The East Gates were the most obvious stopping-off point for coaches coming along the turnpike from Harborough. Traditionally most vehicles coming from the south had approached and entered Leicester from the Welford Road, but now the Harborough Road became the more important route. This encouraged a shift in focus from the streets around the High Cross to the East Gates and Gallowtree Gate, the area that would eventually become the centre of the modern town.

In addition to the improvements to the roads, an extensive canal system was built in Britain during the eighteenth century, with a concentration of waterways in the Midlands and the North. This network enabled heavy goods to be transported far more cheaply and easily. By 1798 a stretch of the Soar linking the Trent and Loughborough had been made into a canal. A year later this was linked to the newly opened Erewash Canal, a development that gave Loughborough ready access to Derbyshire coal; and, as transportation was now easy, coal prices dropped.

Leicester, however, to the frustration of many of its residents, did not become part of the network until the 1790s. It was clear that the town would benefit from cheap coal prices if the canal could be extended, for although there was a Leicestershire coalfield it was cut off from the town of Leicester by Charnwood Forest. By 1780 there were calls for subscribers to a local canal project, the Leicester Navigation. While the project attracted supporters, there were also many opponents, including Leicestershire landowners whose property would be affected, mill owners who already had watermills on the Soar, county colliery owners who feared the competition from Derbyshire coal, and the Loughborough Navigation, who wished to retain their privileged position. It took many years to overcome this opposition but eventually, in 1790, the Leicester Navigation Act was passed. Work then began on canal extensions that would serve both Leicester and Melton Mowbray. The canal, as expected, led to a drop in coal prices, and the new transport opportunities benefited the hosiery industry.

Fifty years later there was an even more important breakthrough with the arrival of the railway. A line between Leicester and Bagworth was opened in 1830, and extended to Swannington in 1832. The line connected Leicester with the Leicestershire coalfield, and again helped to bring down the price of coal. The Midland Counties Railway was followed in 1836, with the Midland

Counties Company based in Campbell Street, close to an impressive new station on London Road, and four years later the North Midlands Railway was also launched. The use of the railway for the transportation of materials was soon playing a key role in supporting the local economy and building development in the town, as well as improving passenger travel and mail delivery.[20]

## Politics and Religion

From 1661 the new Cavalier Parliament was intent on securing its own position by marginalising dissenters, and the Anglican Church was re-established, while new criminal laws placed severe restrictions on the participation of dissenters in public life. These included the Corporation Act of 1661, which barred dissenters from taking municipal office, and in Leicester resulted in the removal of fifteen aldermen and twenty-five common council men from their posts.

In 1684 further steps were taken to shore up the political authority of the monarchy in the provinces, when towns throughout the country, including Leicester, were asked to hand over their charters for amendment. A town such as Leicester, which had been associated with dissent and the Parliamentary cause, had reason to be apprehensive. The new Leicester charter deflated some illusions of local independence, for it reduced the number of council members from forty-eight to thirty-six, and underlined the right of the monarch to purge the corporation of any alderman, officer or common council man thought to be unsuitable.[21]

Not only were dissenters barred from public employment, their religious activity was also significantly curtailed.[22] The Act of Uniformity of 1662 required all clergy to fully accept and use the Anglican Book of Common Prayer, and ministers who did not fall into line were deprived of their position, as well as the house and income that went with it. Soon afterwards it was also made an offence for those who did not comply with the Act to organise or attend their own religious services. The term Nonconformist emerged, to describe those who did not conform to the Act of Uniformity. Originally, dissenters who wished to separate themselves entirely from Anglicanism were distinguished from Nonconformists, who were in partial disagreement, though later the word Nonconformist became widely used to describe all the free Protestant churches.

These new restrictions forced Leicester dissenters to become more subdued. The town had long been a stronghold of dissent, however, and there remained a significant number who continued the tradition. At the time of the Restoration there were Quakers, Baptists, Presbyterians and Independents in the town, and all these denominations kept up their religious meetings – though this had to be done discreetly. Many local ministers chose to leave their position rather than obey the new rules, but some continued to conduct services in Leicester in private houses and barns that offered makeshift accommodation.

As might be expected, ill will festered between Leicester Anglicans and dissenters during these years. In October 1671 this erupted into violence, when fighting broke out between the two sides near the north wall of the town, and local guards were called to separate the brawlers. This tense situation was somewhat alleviated in 1672, when permission was given to dissenting ministers to preach under licence. The dissenters started to re-establish themselves, and by the 1680s both the Quakers and Independents had permanent meeting houses in Leicester. The Presbyterians also had a chapel on the site of the modern Infirmary Square, a place that was called the Paradise Meeting, on account of its attractive garden setting.

By the late 1680s another momentous political change was imminent. The events of 1688–89 have traditionally been referred to as the Glorious Revolution, and what emerged was the beginning of modern Parliamentary sovereignty. The Glorious Revolution was the backdrop to eighteenth-century politics, and a brief reminder of what happened may be useful in understanding the religious and political situation both nationally and locally.[23]

While tension between the Established Church and Protestant dissent was one feature of Charles II's reign, a further aspect of religious conflict during these years was a widespread anti Catholic feeling nourished by fear of an increased renewal of Catholicism in Europe and of the ambitions of the King's French brother-in-law, Louis XIV. The popular notion exacerbated by Protestant propaganda was that Catholicism equated tyranny and that English liberty, as embodied in Protestantism, was under threat. Some suspected Charles of being too close to Louis, and there was also the suspicion that he harboured closet Catholics in his government. To make matters worse Charles had no legitimate heir, and his brother James, the next in line to the throne, was an open, practising Catholic.

When James II became king after Charles's death in 1685 there was severe disquiet when he tried to reverse anti-Catholic laws, and anxiety increased when James's queen, Mary of Modena, produced a son and heir. At this point fear of Catholicism led a group of leading politicians to invite the staunchly Protestant Prince William of the Netherlands, married to James's daughter Mary, to invade England. William landed in England, accompanied by an armada, in November 1688, and James took flight. In February 1689 William and Mary were crowned, and this was accompanied by a Parliamentary declaration of rights that comprised firm conditions under which the monarch would be allowed to rule.

In the same year, the situation of dissenting Protestants improved when the Act of Toleration was passed. This recognised the right of dissenters to worship freely, to establish their own academies, and to vote if they fulfilled the necessary property qualifications. The Act did not extend to Catholics, and the Corporation Act barring dissenters from public employment was retained, but now at least the existence of Protestant denominations outside Anglicanism was recognised. Dissenters were exempted from attendance at the services of the Established Church, and their places of worship were legally protected. This was by no means full emancipation, but it paved the way for Protestant dissenters to re-establish themselves more securely during the eighteenth century.

A drawing of the Market Place, 1847. This image is taken from R. Read, *Modern Leicester* (London, 1881).

A drawing of Gallowtree Gate, 1847. This image is taken from R. Read, *Modern Leicester* (London, 1881).

In Leicester, during the following years, dissenters became more visible. Presbyterians and Independents formed a substantial proportion of Leicester dissent. In addition to their doctrinal differences, these two groups had fallen out politically during the mid-century over the execution of Charles I, which the Independents had supported but the Presbyterians had not. By the 1690s, however, they were seeking to resolve their differences and were on the road to amalgamation. This partnership led to the birth of an important religious body in Leicester known as the Great Meeting, and in 1708 the community established itself at a substantial new chapel at Leicester Butts.

In the last decades of the century, the congregation of the Great Meeting moved away from Presbyterianism to Unitarianism. An important aspect of the Unitarian outlook was the emphasis placed on citizen participation, and this had consequences for the town. Many of the leading local manufacturers attended the Great Meeting, and the chapel was associated with well-known Leicester names such as Paget, Biggs, Brewin and Coltman. When the Leicester Corporation was reformed in 1835, the first seven elected mayors of Leicester were members of the Great Meeting congregation.

Another noteworthy member of the Great Meeting was William Gardiner. Born in 1770, Gardiner was both a hosier and a musician, and he has been accredited with being the first musician in England to appreciate and play

Beethoven's music. Gardiner kept a journal recording both his life in Leicester and his travels in Britain and abroad, and this, published under the title *Music and Friends*, gives glimpses of Leicester life in the last decades of the eighteenth century and the early decades of the nineteenth.[24]

By 1719, the Baptists also had a permanent chapel, situated in Harvey Lane, and later in the mid-eighteenth century there was a chapel built at Friar Lane to house a congregation of Particular or Strict Baptists, who held to more traditionally Calvinistic views. The congregation at Harvey Lane was associated with the eminent Baptist William Carey, founder of the Baptist Missionary Society, who became the pastor in 1789. Seventeen years later another well-known Baptist, Robert Hall, renowned for his oratory, accepted the ministry at Harvey Lane. Hall was a native of Leicestershire, born at Wigston, who returned to Leicester after a prolonged period in Cambridge. William Gardiner described Hall's eloquence as that of a man inspired, and he judged that his sermons showed 'a display of intellect no words can describe'.[25] Hall is commemorated in Leicester today by a statue in De Montfort Square, off New Walk.

The Great Meeting chapel was built in 1708. Here it is seen in the 1960s. This image is reproduced courtesy of the Record Office for Leicestershire, Leicester and Rutland.

Methodism had also arrived in Leicester by the mid-century, and in 1753 John Wesley preached in Butt Close, near the site of the Great Meeting, to a 'serious and attentive' body of listeners.[26] A decade later Leicester Methodists, a congregation composed mainly of poor people, had set up a church in an old barn in Millstone Lane, and despite their rough surroundings the group flourished. Leicester was eventually made the head of a Midlands Methodist circuit. A new central chapel was opened in Bishop Street in 1818, and many other chapels were built throughout the town in the following years. The first Primitive Methodist chapel was built in York Street in 1827.

The cottage of William Carey (1761–1834), minister at Harvey Lane Baptist Chapel, seen here in the 1960s. This image is reproduced courtesy of the Record Office for Leicestershire, Leicester and Rutland.

The struggle for power that resulted in the Glorious Revolution not only affected religious freedoms; it also reshaped politics, both national and local, in a recognisably more modern mode. Two loose-knit political groups had come to the forefront: the Whigs and the Tories. The Tories were associated with support for the traditional role of monarchy, whereas the Whigs were associated with reform and constitutional monarchy.[27] Among the members of Leicester's corporation there was a mix of political opinion in the wake of the Glorious Revolution, with some more enthusiastic about the installation of King William than others. During the first half of the eighteenth century, however, the corporation became Tory-dominated, and remained that way until 1835.[28]

For several decades the usurpation of James II continued to be an issue. The Jacobite cause, the mission to restore the Stuart dynasty to the throne, had support in Scotland, and in England there had been Tory sympathy for the Jacobites, prompting accusations of disloyalty from the Whigs. In Leicester, accusations of Jacobitism were a prominent feature of local politics, and became particularly heated in the election of 1738. When the same accusations lingered into the 1740s the Tory corporation felt compelled to send an address to George II, expressing their loyalty and their intention to root out any treasonous elements in the town.[29]

In July 1745, however, a much greater crisis came perilously near to Leicester. Jacobitism gained fresh impetus when Charles Edward Stuart, Bonnie Prince Charlie, the grandson of James II, sailed from France to Scotland to claim the crown of Britain for his father. Rebellion broke out and, having gained ground in Scotland, the rebel army marched south into England, reaching Derby in December. Within days officers were sent ahead to Leicester to arrange quarters for the troops.[30]

With the Jacobites so near, there was considerable apprehension in the town. Although earlier in the year the corporation of Leicester had assured George II of its loyalty, the only show of resistance to the rebels was from some Nonconformists who had turned out for military drill in Leicester Castle Yard. According to Throsby, these men melted away to neighbouring villages, along with many other residents, when the threat became more immediate. The mayor and corporation, meanwhile, kept a low profile, trying to find out the intentions of the rebels. Throsby's account describes the townspeople's actions as they waited: 'Those who were left at home were some of them busied

House where Bunyan and Wesley lodged.

An Edwardian postcard of the house in St Nicholas Street where both John Bunyan and John Wesley are said to have lodged. The postcard is taken from the author's own collection.

A view of the Market Place in 1745, the same year the Jacobite army reached Derby. This image is taken from R. Read, *Modern Leicester* (London, 1881).

in depositing their valuables in the earth, and others in roasting and boiling to accommodate the unwelcome guests on their hourly expected arrival.' He added that some of the servants who had been kept in Leicester by their masters were overwhelmed by fear, and 'were in convulsions at the idea of being defiled and murdered by the rebel army'. Throsby's claim is that there were some in the corporation who 'prayed fervently' that the rebels would be successful.[31] Simmons suggests, however, that while there were Jacobite sympathies among some in the corporation this did not run deep, and was more of a resentful posturing, intended to assert that the town still took pride in its independence.[32]

As it was, the corporation of Leicester was never forced to make a stand, because the Jacobite army, while quartered in Derby, took the decision to return to Scotland. Charles Edward Stuart had set out to invade England, confident that there would be an English uprising, and assuring his followers that the French would give military support – but it now seemed increasingly unlikely that this support would materialise and it was this that caused the rebels to retreat. It was the beginning of the end of Jacobitism. When the Hanoverian forces fought the Jacobite army at Culloden near Inverness in April 1746, the rebels were decisively and brutally crushed. In Leicester, as elsewhere, the victory was officially celebrated.[33]

# Town Improvements and Social Life

During the late seventeenth to the mid-eighteenth century provincial towns generally became more pleasant places to live. Architecture was more attractive and substantial, sometimes with pretensions to grandeur, while leisure facilities and an organised social life for the middling to wealthier town residents also emerged and developed as the century progressed.[34]

In Leicester, urban renewal was rather slow in coming, but in the late 1740s the corporation authorised significant improvements to the Saturday marketplace. An old building known as the Gainsborough, previously used as a prison, was pulled down and a new corn exchange erected. By this time there were also shops around the perimeter of the marketplace, with glass windows to display wares.[35]

Shortly after this there was another important addition to the town, when private investor John Bass leased land in the Haymarket from the corporation and built assembly rooms, with theatre facilities and ground-floor space for shops. This provision was later improved on in 1800 when a new theatre, designed by local architect John Johnson, was opened in Horsefair Street. In the same year a hotel and ballroom, also designed by Johnson, were completed. They came to be used as assembly rooms, and still stand today in Hotel Street, near Leicester marketplace.[36]

'Companions in simplicity and probably also in chastity.' A sketch of two Leicester people, late eighteenth century. This image is taken from J. Throsby, *The History and Antiquities of the Ancient Town of Leicester* (Leicester, 1791), courtesy of the University of Leicester Special Collections.

Pedestrian promenades were popular additions to eighteenth-century provincial towns, and in 1785 the corporation of Leicester authorised the laying out of Queen's Walk, a promenade that led out of the town and up the hill on the south side of Leicester. The name of this promenade was later changed to Ladies' Walk and then to New Walk, the name it bears today. In the early nineteenth century the roads around New Walk were developed, including King's Street at the bottom of the hill, where the elegant terrace known as the Crescent was built in 1824.[37]

Public squares were also a feature of eighteenth-century urban architecture, and in the 1790s there was a project to create a grand formal square of stone buildings, called Brunswick Square, in the centre of Leicester on the site of the horse fair. John Johnson again provided an architectural design, but sadly the project came to nothing. Another ambitious plan to promote Leicester as a spa resort also failed, although a short terrace of buildings in Humberstone Road, known as Spa Place, remains today as a memento of this plan.[38]

Alongside the provision of new facilities, Leicester, like other provincial towns of the period, developed a more sophisticated social and cultural life for its wealthier residents. One highlight of the social calendar, which took place every September, was the Leicester Races. By the end of the eighteenth century this had become a momentous social occasion, which drew in the gentry from the county. The races had been held at Abbey Meadows from the early seventeenth century, but from the 1740s they were run at St Mary's Fields, part of the common land on the south side of the town. In 1804 they were moved again to the ground that is now Victoria Park. The races themselves were only one aspect of the entertainment, which was marked by a constellation of events, including balls, concerts, dramatic performances and firework displays.[39]

There was also regular entertainment during the winter months. By the late eighteenth century Leicester had a thriving musical society that gave concerts once a fortnight, and a company of players put on a theatrical season for two to three months around December.[40] One more unusual event, arranged in 1784 when the River Soar froze over, was a frost fair held on the ice.[41]

When spring brought the opportunity for more outdoor activity, bowling was popular, and as the season progressed there was some cricket as well. Town residents could also relax and socialise at the Vauxhall tea gardens, which had been created near the West Bridge.[42] For those with a comfortable income and leisure time these pursuits became part of the rhythm and shape of each year.

Highcross Street: a drawing by Leicester artist John Flower. This image is taken from J. Flower, *Views of Ancient Buildings in the Town and County of Leicester* (Leicester, 1825), courtesy of the University of Leicester Special Collections.

Despite the new facilities and activities that Leicester offered, the more basic aspects of cleanliness and safety did not keep pace. Street cleaning, drainage, lighting and paving all remained poor throughout the century, and the minimal policing that existed was ineffective. Walking in the town at night was unpleasant, so much so that when social functions took place organisers favoured times when the moon was full – so that those attending could at least see where they were going and where they were stepping.[43]

One important addition to public health, however, was the founding of Leicester Infirmary in 1771. This was part of a more general hospital movement that took place countrywide. By the mid-century, twelve provincial town hospitals had already been established, including one in neighbouring Northampton. The initiative for a hospital in Leicester came from William Watts, father of Susanna Watts who wrote a well-known guide to Leicester. William Watts had been a physician at Northampton Infirmary and had latterly given up medicine to become a clergyman. It was argued that hospitalisation would help patients who lived in poor housing, where conditions made treatment ineffective and recovery unlikely.

Daniel Lambert (1770–1809) of Leicester was well known locally and nationally for his immense size. According to his gravestone, by the time he died he weighed 52st 11lb. Lambert was featured in various contemporary cartoons, including several where he was represented as the substantial image of John Bull dwarfing a puny Napoleon. Literary allusions to him include references by Thackeray in *Vanity Fair* as well as by Dickens in *Nicholas Nickleby*.

Lambert was born in Blue Boar Lane in St Margaret's parish. He was a contemporary of William Gardiner, who remembered him as a child of a 'very quiet disposition' and a 'fine open countenance' who began 'to thicken rapidly' after the age of 14. It is thought that Lambert's obesity stemmed from a medical condition, as he did not appear to eat excessively and throughout his life he did not drink alcohol. Despite his size, as a young man he kept good health, engaged in field sports and particularly enjoyed bathing in the River Soar.

At the age of 21, Lambert succeeded his father as the keeper of Leicester gaol, but in 1805 the prison was closed and he was pensioned off. Although he was sensitive about his size, financial necessity drove him to exhibiting himself for money. For this purpose he moved to London in 1806, taking up residence in Piccadilly where he was viewed by all types of people, including visitors from abroad. William Gardiner saw him there and reported that 'he was distressed at being seen in a situation so degrading'. However, it seems that despite Lambert's reluctance to follow this path he showed himself capable of dealing with the situation, defending himself against any offensive customers in a courteous but witty manner that left his dignity intact.

Lambert returned from London later in 1806, but on a visit to Stamford a few years later he suddenly collapsed and died. He was buried in the town, in St Martin's churchyard.

## *Sources*

Anon., *The Life of That Wonderful and Extraordinary Heavy Man, Daniel Lambert, from His Birth to the Moment of his Dissolution, with an Account of Men Known for Their Corpulency, and Other Interesting Matter* (New York, 1818), www.archive.org, accessed 29 October 2012; J. Bondeson, *Freaks* (Stroud, 2006); D.T.D. Clarke, *Daniel Lambert 1770–1809* (Leicester, 1964); W.Gardiner, *Music and Friends or Pleasant Recollections of a Dilettante* vol.1 (London, 1838); T. Secombe, 'Lambert, Daniel (1770–1809)', Revd E.L. O'Brien in *Oxford Dictionary of National Biography* (Oxford, 2004), www.oxforddnb.com/view/article/15932, accessed 18 October 2012.

Watts's proposals were successful, and the plans for a voluntarily run hospital were developed. The Infirmary was to be financed by private subscription, and patients were to be admitted for treatment only on the recommendation of a subscriber. A building designed by Leicestershire architect William Henderson was erected, and the Infirmary was opened with one patient, Sarah Groce. The opening was accompanied by ceremony and celebration, including a grand concert held at the assembly rooms.[44]

Although the hospital was based in the town, initial financial support came from wealthy individuals in the county. However, before long, the Infirmary became both a town and county affair, and by the first decade of the nineteenth century, some of the first Friendly societies in Leicester, groups organised by ordinary working people and meeting mostly in public houses, were subscribing regularly to the Infirmary.[45]

## Repression and Reform

In the 1780s, the corporation was still a Tory, Anglican clique focused on preserving its own power. Although the Corporation Act excluding Nonconformists from public office was still nominally in force, it was possible to relax the rules if the individual paid lip-service to the establishment. In Leicester, however, no compromise of this sort was put into practice. A substantial number of the town's leading employers were Nonconformists and Whigs, and their resentment ran deep at their exclusion from the official governing of the town.[46]

The Tory corporation, intent on keeping the town independent from the county, was also at odds with powerful Whigs in Leicestershire, among whom were the Duke of Rutland and the Earl of Stamford. In order to express their solidarity, the Whig aristocrats and gentry from the county joined forces with town Whigs in the Revolution Club, which met at the Lion and Lamb tavern in Leicester. Not to be outdone, the Tories in Leicester formed a competing club called the Constitutional Society, which also met to dine, toast and generally boost morale.

So great was the appetite for reform among British liberals that when the French Revolution erupted in 1789 many reacted positively – but much of this support collapsed when the extent of the bloodshed in France became known.

The aristocratic Whigs in particular were so frightened that they rapidly dropped any radical pretensions. Fears of insurrection were stoked up by any tension or conflict with the lower orders. In Leicester there was mob violence accompanying the election of 1790, and upper-class anxiety was further provoked two years later, when acute food shortages again caused violent protest.

It was not only the hungry poor that the upper classes feared; it was also the thinkers and writers whose ideas, they believed, might inspire revolution. By 1792 the Whig Revolution Club and the competing Tory Constitutional Society in Leicester had both collapsed, and local aristocratic Whigs, as in other counties, had joined with Tories to form a Loyal Association, one aim of which was to root out seditious writing. Not all those who had held out hopes for reform were willing to keep quiet, however. Two new liberal newspapers, the *Leicester Chronicle* and the *Leicester Herald*, were founded in the town during these years. Richard Phillips, local bookseller and editor of the *Leicester Herald*, commented that the greater number of newspapers that were published the better, as 'men are made wiser and better as they are brought nearer by knowledge of each other's motives, pursuits and progress'.[47] This was typical of the liberal thought emerging in towns, which valued an active civil society in the belief that the free interaction of citizens benefited the common good.

In Leicester, while the Tory and Whig elite had their Loyal Association, local liberals founded a group named the Constitutional Society, for promoting equal representation in Parliament. Phillips himself also started two new societies in the town for the purpose of intellectual discovery and the sharing of ideas. One was a literary society and the other an association for scientific investigation, the Adelphi Society. These views and activities were hardly seditious, but such was the growing anxiety created by the situation in France that anything with even a slightly radical tinge could be regarded with suspicion.

When war broke out between Britain and France in 1793 suspicion turned to repression, and any person deemed to be a radical was at risk of being accused of treason. The new Constitutional Society soon collapsed, as did the *Leicester Chronicle* – although the *Leicester Herald* survived for a while. Phillips was arrested and sentenced to eighteen months in Leicester gaol for selling *The Rights of Man* by Tom Paine. William Gardiner, who had been involved in the Adelphi Society, regularly visited Phillips in prison and described his situation. Treated like a criminal, he was put into 'a vile apartment at the bottom of the

An Edwardian postcard of Leicester Prison, built in 1828. This postcard is taken from the author's own collection.

felons' ward' and locked up early every evening. His visitors were also given a hard time; Gardiner recorded how 'in these visits I was annoyed by many incivilities and sometimes locked up between two grated doors' while the gaolers sang threatening songs. Finally, when sitting with Phillips, 'the wretch that was set over him would sit down and say he was ordered to remain, that we might not talk treason'.[48] On leaving gaol, Phillips continued for a short while to run a bookselling business in Leicester, although the *Leicester Herald* was closed and his shop was destroyed by fire. Eventually he left Leicester for London in 1795. In that same year the Seditious Meetings and Assemblies Act was passed, which made it all but impossible to hold public meetings.

## Schools

During the eighteenth century, educational opportunities for most people throughout the country remained limited or non-existent, although the establishment of charity day schools helped to alleviate the situation a little. Early examples of these in Leicester were a school for poor boys at

St Margaret's church, which was up and running by 1716, a school opened by the Great Meeting and, towards the end of the century, two Anglican schools at St Mary's and at St Martin's.[49] Many children in the town had to work, and so were not available for a day school education. It was in an effort to reach this group that the Sunday School movement emerged. The Nonconformists were the pioneers in this, but the Anglicans quickly took up the idea, and by the 1790s it was common for churches and chapels in Leicester to have a Sunday School.

Secondary education was, of course, even more restricted, and what there was strongly reflected the split between Anglicanism and Nonconformity that dominated Leicester. The Free Grammar School of Leicester continued under the management of the civic authorities, and because Anglicans dominated local government from the Restoration period onwards, an Anglican outlook pervaded the school. The school went into a decline in the second half of the century, and though it continued to function it never regained its former confidence. Not only was it difficult to find a suitable master, but the rigidly Classical curriculum, which statute required the school to teach, seemed increasingly outdated. The last headmaster died in 1841, and after this the school was closed to pupils. In 1877, however, the school was re-established by the Wyggeston trustees under the name of Wyggeston Hospital Boys School, in a new building on the site of the original hospital.

An important eighteenth-century addition to Anglican schooling in Leicester was Alderman Newton's School, financed by the wealth of leading Leicester citizen Gabriel Newton. According to Greaves's biography,[50] Newton was born in 1683 and started out as a woolcomber, although he later became the landlord of the Horse and Trumpet, a local inn rumoured to be a meeting place for Jacobites. He gained the freedom of the borough at the age of 19 in 1702, which gave him the chance both to trade in Leicester and make money, as well as put himself forward for civic office. Newton grasped both these opportunities, accumulating a significant fortune and rising to be a magistrate and an alderman, finally becoming Mayor of Leicester in 1732.

When his son George died in 1742, leaving him without an heir, Newton dedicated his wealth to local education. A school was soon established, which comprised thirty-five boys, uniformly dressed in green, who were taught at St Martin's church. The boys were imbued with an Anglican outlook, instructed in reading, writing and accounts, and were apprenticed with a bond of £5. This first school only lasted a few years, and it has been suggested that this was partly because Newton was not easy to work with. After his death in 1762 plans to launch a school in accordance with his wishes were held up by complications in dealing with his estate. Eventually, in 1784, the civic authorities were able to take action, and by the end of the year Leicester Greencoat School was opened. This proved so successful that a second school was founded in the early years of the nineteenth century.

The provision of secondary school education still remained very limited, though, and in the 1830s Anglicans and Nonconformists both opened denominational schools in an effort to improve local opportunity. The Anglican school, known as the Leicester and Leicestershire Collegiate School, was the first, and in 1835 it opened in specially built premises in College Street. A company was formed to finance the project, the shareholders of which had a right to enrol their children in the school, one child per share. The school ran for nearly thirty years, finally closing in 1863. In 1836 local Nonconformists also opened a school, financed by a local company. This was named the Proprietary School, and it was housed in a striking building on New Walk designed by Joseph Hansom, architect and inventor of the hansom cab. The school was less successful than the Anglican project, lasting only until 1847, shortly after which the building became the town museum.[51]

A further addition to Leicester in the early 1830s was a mechanics' institute, a social and cultural centre for workmen, providing a library and reading room, educational classes and lectures, based at New Hall in Wellington Street. Mechanics' institutes had been springing up in towns around the country since the 1820s, inspired by the adult educational work of George Birkbeck in London and Glasgow. In Leicester the initiative came from a group of local artisans, though the need to seek middle-class financial help seriously detracted from their independence. After an initial burst of enthusiasm, most of the working-class students drifted away from the institute, as a policy of avoiding any contentious discussion proved unpopular and the quality of the programmes became patchy. Although the institute still attracted lower middle-class students, by the 1850s it had started to go into serious decline. It eventually closed in 1870.[52]

# The Reform of Leicester Corporation

At the beginning of the nineteenth century, the corporation of Leicester was still solidly Tory and Anglican. However, a sign of future change came at the 1818 General Election, when one of the Leicester candidates returned was Thomas Pares, a liberal local banker who favoured Parliamentary reform. The reaction of the corporation to this was both defensive and corrupt. In the years running up to the next General Election in 1826 they made hundreds of their political sympathisers honorary freemen of Leicester, a status that carried with it the right to vote. A very large amount of corporation money was set aside to use for election purposes and a secret committee was set up to plot tactics, in which bribery played an important part. These tactics succeeded, and the corporation managed to get two Tories returned.[53]

This was a temporary victory, however, for change was on its way. In 1832 a Whig government passed the first of the major Parliamentary reform acts of the nineteenth century, intended to reduce corruption in the electoral system

The Old Town Hall: a drawing by Leicester artist John Flower. This image is taken from J. Flower, *Views of Ancient Buildings in the Town and County of Leicester* (Leicester, 1825), courtesy of the University of Leicester Special Collections.

and provide a fairer level of political representation. The Act gave the vote in town boroughs to all adult males who occupied a house with a value of at least £10. This made it far more difficult to rig elections, and in 1833 the General Election returned two radical candidates in Leicester.

The days of the Tory corporation were now numbered. In the wake of the Reform Act a commission was set up to investigate the business of town boroughs. The Town Clerk of Leicester, Thomas Burbidge, fought his corner with the inspectors, but the ensuing report condemned the way the town had been run and accused the civic authorities of significant financial mismanagement. There was much to criticise, and the liberal reformers in control of the inspection did not hold back in destroying their political enemies. The corporation of Leicester was left with its reputation in ruins.

In 1835 the Municipal Corporations Act abolished the old model of corporation, which co-opted its members, and introduced in towns throughout the country elected town councils accountable to ratepayers. In the same year, the first town council election in Leicester was an overwhelming victory for the Whigs and Radicals. So anxious were they to throw off the past that one of their first actions was to sell off the insignia and plate of the old corporation, including the great mace. This was bought back later in the century.

Thomas Paget was the first mayor of the reformed corporation, and among the most prominent mayors in the first decades of the new regime were the hosiers John and William Biggs, who both served as mayor three times. John Biggs was particularly popular in the town, and a statue of him, paid for by local working men, still stands in Welford Place.

A negative image of the old unreformed corporation lingered on, and the liberals dominated Leicester for the greater part of the nineteenth century. It has been said that the reform resulted in the exchange of one political clique for another, albeit one that was less corrupt and more accountable.

## Chartism

The Chartist movement arose from the dissatisfaction of working men with the Great Reform Act of 1832. Having supported the middle-class struggle for reform, the working classes found that it had not addressed their interests. In view of this they created a charter proposing six changes to the electoral system:

votes for all men over the age of 21, the end of the property qualification for voting, equal size of constituencies, payment for MPs, annual Parliaments and the secret ballot. Other triggers of the movement were fluctuations in the economy as well as changes to the Poor Law in 1834, which introduced more punitive measures of relief that condemned the able-bodied unemployed to the workhouse.

In Leicester the desperate situation of hosiery workers drove local Chartism. The 1830s had been a decade of hardship, in which record numbers had sought poor relief, and in 1838 the charter was published. In 1840, Thomas Cooper, a journalist for the *Leicestershire Mercury*, newly arrived in Leicester, reported on a local Chartist meeting, and was appalled to discover the paltry earnings on which whole families were trying to survive. He admitted that this revealed to him 'the real state of suffering in which thousands in England were living'.[54] Soon Cooper left his job, become involved in a Chartist publication called the *Midlands Intelligencer* and quickly rose to become a leader of the movement. Within Chartism there was a division between those who favoured physical force to convey their views and those who believed that the moral force of the message was enough to carry it. Chartism in Leicester originally fell into the moral force camp, and because of this gained the sympathy of middle-class radicals in the town. Under Cooper's leadership, however, the approach became more militant. In August 1843, during a particularly difficult time in the hosiery industry, the yeomanry came face-to-face with rioting workers on Mowmacre Hill. Cooper was in Staffordshire at the time, involved in another fracas. In his biography he wrote: 'The police I was told had charged the people in the streets as well as upon Momecker Hill and smitten and injured many with their staves.'[55] The riot seems in fact to have been dispersed with relatively little damage, but in local legend the incident became known as the Battle of Mowmacre Hill. Cooper was arrested and imprisoned shortly afterwards, and was not active in Leicester again.

By the end of the decade Chartism was a spent force. This became clear in 1848 when a national rally, organised to present a petition to Parliament, proved a dismal failure. In the 1850s, however, although widespread poverty continued, a growing new industry of boot and shoe manufacture at last brought better employment opportunities to the town and ushered in a more tranquil era.

In the years between the Restoration and the early nineteenth century, life in Leicester changed in many ways. In 1660 Leicester was a shabby, run-down place, but by the first decades of the eighteenth century the developing hosiery industry was bringing new wealth to the town and helping to change its fortunes. Leicester shared in the commercial success that swept Britain in the eighteenth century, and the repair and reconstruction of the road network connected the town satisfactorily with the rest of the country, radically improving communications. After the mid-century, when the market for hosiery proved volatile, the town still benefited from having a staple industry, even though the lot of the framework knitter was often extremely hard. The local economy was boosted when Leicester was linked to the canal system in the 1790s, and even more so when the railway arrived fifty years later. Building in brick changed the face of the town, and did much to give it a more modern appearance. However, the population had increased significantly, and by 1800 this growth gathered momentum – creating problems in a town that lacked a proper water supply, let alone a sewage system. The early nineteenth-century town was also still bitterly divided by politics and religion, as well as by social class. The takeover of the corporation by the Liberal reform party broke a political stranglehold, but bridges needed to be built between the different groups of residents. In the mid-nineteenth century there were at last some breakthroughs in the economy, and Leicester passed into a period of renewal.

*five*

# RENAISSANCE IN
# MID-VICTORIAN LEICESTER

New Industry, Improved Public Health and the Rebuilding of the Town

On the Whitsun bank holiday of 1882 the Prince and Princess of Wales visited Leicester to open Abbey Park and to admire the improvements that had been made to the town. As they were driven through Leicester, cheered on by the crowds, they passed under a decorative arch fashioned in Renaissance style that had been erected to celebrate the occasion. It was suitably symbolic of the renaissance that Leicester had gone through since the mid-century. Change in the town had many aspects, but three of the most important were improvements in the local economy that provided a more secure outlook for Leicester people, a focus on public health, in particular sanitation and water supply, and finally the rebuilding of the city centre and growth of suburbia.

Leicester was run by its middle classes, and local employers had put energy into town improvement, serving on the town council and donating their time and money to charitable and civic causes. The class divisions in local society were of course marked, and the majority of working people led hard lives and still had little or no input into the management of town affairs. However, in many ways things were better. Leicester was no longer the drab poverty stricken place it had been in the 1840s; it had economic prospects and had taken on the appearance of a modern provincial town. When the mayor and corporation welcomed the royal couple to Leicester in 1882 they naturally wished to create an impression of civic unity and pride, and this they succeeded in doing, for despite the difficulties of everyday life thousands of townspeople obligingly turned out to cheer and take part in the celebrations.

# Hosiery

One tragic aspect of Leicester during the 1830s and 1840s was the decline of the hosiery industry on which the local economy was built.[1] This stagnation blighted the town, as many framework knitters, or stockingers as they were known, found themselves reduced to grinding poverty. Framework knitting was characterised by low wages, long hours and irregular employment, and the image of the poor stockinger, pale and thin and often forced to seek poor relief, became a symbol of the industry. The systems by which the industry ran were ineffective and rife with abuse, and the technology used for production was antiquated. These difficulties affected the ability of the industry to compete on the international market, where the American hosiery industry had already overtaken the British, and the German industry was emerging as a powerful rival.

In the mid-century, framework knitters in Leicester still mostly worked in small workshops, while in the county they worked in their own cottages. The old system of frame renting continued, and the cost of the frame rent and additional charges greatly detracted from the workers' incomes, helping to keep them in poverty. In the town workshops, where as many as eighty frames were sometimes concentrated, the stockingers still had to pay frame rent, and often exploitative additional charges. Frames were rented by the manufacturers or sublet by middlemen, and the profits they made from rentals and the additional charges detracted from their incentive to change working practices and develop a factory based industry. It was not only the masters who resisted change, however. The framework knitters, although poor, prized their independence. Despite the drawbacks of the system, and although they worked very long hours, they could still enjoy some irregularity in the way those hours were worked. Change from this to the discipline of the factory held little appeal. The industry in which they worked brought them few benefits, and in view of this they were reluctant to sacrifice the one small advantage it did offer.

Up until the mid-century little technological advance was made in the industry, and the equipment that the framework knitters employed was very similar to that used by their forebears in the sixteenth century. Power-driven machinery was seldom used, as there was difficulty in designing a machine that could shape socks and stockings in the way customers required. This kind of fashioning could only be done successfully on a hand frame. From the 1840s, however, there were at last some advances in developing and improving knitting machinery. In 1844, Paget's of Loughborough introduced improved power-run frames, and in 1847 Matthew Townsend, a Leicester man, invented the latch needle, which also improved efficiency. By 1854 the Nottingham firm of Hine and Mundella was running machines that could produce batches of fully fashioned hose, and in 1864 William Cotton from Loughborough built on these achievements with his Cotton Patent machine, which was soon used extensively. The new technology brought better prospects for the hosiery industry, and hopes for a brighter future were also raised when hosiery benefited from a general improvement in economic conditions in the 1850s.

On 13 July 1865 the opening of the Corah hosiery factory and warehouse in Leicester, with its steam-powered machinery, signalled a new era in the local industry. The Corah buildings, known as the St Margaret's Works, formed a large complex in the north of Leicester, near St Margaret's church, and the brick and stone warehouse, designed in grand Italian style by local architect W. Jackson, was an impressive spectacle. A further notable sight was the boiler and engine house adjoining the factory; its chimney, 140ft high, towered above the complex.[2] It was not only the appearance of the complex and the steam-powered machinery that were impressive. Factory based work offered substantially improved wages for hosiery workers, with Corah's claiming a rise of 25 per cent in wages. Working in a factory, although it demanded more discipline, also meant shorter hours than working in domestic surroundings. Despite these advantages, though, full transfer to a factory system remained slow, as manufacturers continued to profit from frame renting and workers clung to their old traditions.

From the 1870s change became more rapid. One factor that spurred this on was the drive to provide universal primary schooling for children. Educational reform presented a real problem for domestic framework knitters, as children made an important contribution to the work. Under the Factory Acts it was illegal for children under 10 to work in factories, but many were put to work in small domestic workshops and given tasks such as winding, stitching and seaming. Even children as young as 4 undertook these tasks, and were kept up late so that the orders could be completed. This contrasted with the factories, where these jobs could be done by machine. Reliance on children's work no doubt encouraged some of the intense opposition among Leicestershire working men to educational reform. When a public meeting was called in

The 'finishing' room – Leicester Co-operative Hosiery Manufacturing Society in the 1890s. Image taken from T. Blandford and G. Newell, *History of the Leicester Cooperative Manufacturing Society* (Leicester, 1898).

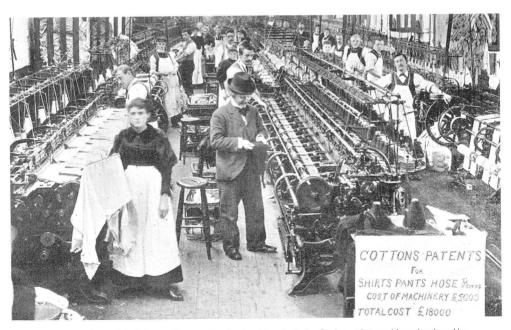

Hosiery workers of the Leicester Co-operative Hosiery Manufacturing Society using machines developed by William Cotton of Loughborough in the 1890s. Image taken from T. Blandford and G. Newell, *History of the Leicester Cooperative Manufacturing Society* (Leicester, 1898).

Hinckley in 1871 to discuss the formation of a school board in the town, it was reported that the hall was filled with a large crowd of working men, the majority of whom showed 'noisy and vociferous opposition' to the expansion of schooling, and were angry enough to break windows in the hall.[3] It was noted that when the authorities in Hinckley permitted girls to bring seaming work to school for the afternoon hours, school attendance radically improved.[4] Despite opposition, however, the wheels of reform were already in motion, and the outcome was inevitable. Five years later the 1876 Education Act brought in universal and compulsory schooling for children between the ages of 5 to 14.

A further death knell for the domestic system was the passing of legislation in 1875 that abolished frame rents. From the manufacturers' point of view, this meant the removal of a major source of profit from the domestic industry. It was clear that the long-term future of production lay with the factories, when this factor was taken together with the advances in technology and educational reform, although the domestic system struggled on for a while.

The leading Leicester factory was doing well. For Corah's of Leicester the 1870s were a time of success, as the factory extended its range of products beyond hosiery and plain underwear, and the St Margaret trademark became well known. The new garments included cardigan jackets and top-selling football jerseys, and the firm later ventured into stylish knitwear for women and girls. In 1878, Princess Alexandra and her children were photographed on board the royal yacht wearing St Margaret jerseys.[5] This underlined the widespread and enviable reputation that the firm had gained.

In the second half of the century the numbers of women employed in the hosiery industry began to increase. During the earlier years of the nineteenth century the heavy hand frames had been easier for men to work, and women had mostly taken responsibility for sewing tasks. However, with the development of power machinery and factory work this changed, and from the 1870s women workers began to outnumber the men; this remained a characteristic of the industry. It meant that Leicester offered good employment chances for women, although it was often claimed that because of the large number of women in the workforce wages could be kept low.

More positive economic conditions in the 1850s and 1860s and the improved fortunes of hosiery resulted in a more prosperous Leicester. In the last quarter of the century, however, international trade conditions were not so favourable:

serious competition from German manufacturers began to put some smaller Leicester firms out of business. Despite this setback, the advances that had been made over the previous decades meant that the town was far better placed to survive these difficulties than it had been earlier in the century. Moreover, another industry had been fast-developing locally, giving Leicester another string to its bow.

## Boots and Shoes

From the 1850s Leicester became an important boot and shoe town, and this meant that local people were no longer so dependent on hosiery.[6] Moreover, although both men and women were employed in the making of boots and shoes, this was a male-dominated workforce, creating a lucky counterbalance to hosiery manufacture, with its increasing number of women employees. This new local industry brought Leicester the opportunity for solid and long-term economic security.

Neighbouring Northampton had long been a town famed for boot and shoemaking, with a specialisation in heavy army boots. Although there was some history of shoemaking in Leicester before the 1850s, shoemakers had mainly supplied the needs of local people, or at least those who could afford shoes. For many people clogs were a cheaper alternative, and the poorest could not even afford those. In the early nineteenth century shoes were still handmade, and customers generally received a bespoke service, although some shoemakers kept a limited stock. By the 1830s there was some expansion when Leicester shoemakers developed a popular line of children's footwear. These ankle strap slippers and boots made from coloured morocco or black roan leather were commonly known as known as 'cacks', and were supplied for general trade.[7]

Real change came, however, thanks to the ingenuity of a shoemaker and wholesaler called Thomas Crick, who ran a workshop with about a dozen employees in Highcross Street, Leicester. Crick made a breakthrough when he tried riveting soles to shoes rather than stitching them. He then started to develop machinery to do this job, and patented his first machine in 1853. A few years later he was using steam power to run his workshop, paving the way for factory-based production.

A further breakthrough came in 1858 at the firm of Stead and Simpson, a firm that had previously been involved in the leather trade in Leeds but had recently relocated to Leicester. They were seeking to expand their shoemaking business, and pioneered the use of an American machine called the Blake sole sewing machine, which could stitch the insole and upper of the shoe to the outer sole. The shoes produced were of very good quality, and the machine radically increased productivity. There were both treadle- and steam-powered versions of the Blake sewer, and it was said that a workman using the steam-powered version could produce around 300 pairs of shoes a day. Here then was a way to mass-produce shoes that were genuinely attractive to the customer.

Boot and shoe manufacture and distribution expanded massively during the following decades, with large numbers of new firms opening up for business. Shoemaking was an enterprise that favoured the small businessman, as the machinery could be hired: very little capital was needed to get started. The new business owners came from a variety of backgrounds. Some were ex-hosiery manufacturers, who saw the opportunities offered by the new industry and decided to change direction, while others included genuine shoe craftsmen and men who had served an apprenticeship and wanted to branch out on their own. The pattern that emerged was largely composed of small family run businesses. Some maintained a mainly local reputation but others, such as Oliver Shoes, Stead and Simpson and Leavesley and North, later known as Freeman Hardy and Willis, were to become national names. Between 1861 and 1870 the number of wholesale manufacturers in Leicester increased from 23 to 117,[8] and the results of the 1871 census showed that in ten years the number of local people working in the industry had more than doubled from 2,315 to 5,087. The number of boot and shoe workers in Leicester now exceeded the number in Northampton. The growth continued, and by 1881 the census showed 13,055 boot and shoe operatives in Leicester; by 1891 this had almost doubled to 24,159.[9] The success of the boot and shoe industry also allowed certain related trades to achieve success. One of the most prominent examples of this was the local manufacture of elastic webbing, which gained particular momentum when elastic-sided boots became popular.

In the early decades of growth some boot and shoemaking took place in factories, but alongside this a system of outwork emerged that resembled the hosiery industry. Treadle machines were hired out to workers, who took baskets of work into their own homes to complete, and carts of material were sent to outlying villages in the county in order to use the cheaper labour available there. Some framework knitters who found that they could not make an adequate living from hosiery switched to making boots and shoes in their cottage workshops.

The American shoe industry led the way in machinery development, and their methods of production had a dynamic effect on British manufacture. Not only were the latest American machines imported, but British manufacturers also visited America to observe and learn. The American Civil War in the 1860s and the consequent demand for good army boots, served to stimulate creative development, and more and more machines of different types were produced in an effort to break down the different aspects of shoemaking into simple tasks that relatively unskilled operatives could perform. By the mid-1870s centralised factory production was strongly favoured in America, with many tasks performed by teams on assembly lines. In Britain, meanwhile, the use of outworkers continued, although productivity was lost, partly because these workers were not using power machines. Despite this, some manufacturers preferred the outwork system, claiming that outworkers were generally of a higher quality and ability than the average factory hand. By using outworkers they also avoided the tougher regulations that had to be observed in a factory. By the late nineteenth century, work patterns in Leicester moved nearer to the American model. Advances in machinery now meant that factory work largely outweighed any advantages of outwork, and many more boot and shoe factories were built in Leicester in the 1890s as a major transfer to factory based work was made.

## Public Health: Disease, Sanitation and Water

As in all the growing towns and cities of Britain during the nineteenth century, the struggle to make a living was matched by the struggle to keep healthy. Newcomers poured into Leicester looking for work, and the number of townspeople trebled from 16,953 in 1801 to 60,642 in 1851.[10] The inevitable result was poor housing and a squalid, unhealthy town environment. In the network of narrow streets and courts, where working people lived in cramped conditions with inadequate sanitation and water supply, disease could easily take hold. Typhus and typhoid fever, cholera, smallpox and an illness known locally as summer diarrhoea were all visitors to the town. In 1846, at a time when the framework knitters were particularly deprived, a fever epidemic broke out in Leicester. Although there was a small fever house, which had been built in 1820 and added to the Leicester Infirmary, this was entirely unable to house the numbers who fell sick. In 1848 the house surgeon, Henry Harding, himself developed the fever and died.[11] In the mid-1850s, it was smallpox that became a greater and continuing threat, and summer diarrhoea, the exact cause of which could not be identified, also continued to be a particular scourge in Leicester, claiming many deaths each year.

To counteract smallpox, legislation was introduced in 1853 making vaccination of infants compulsory. However, a hostility to this emerged in Leicester, with widespread belief that not only was vaccination ineffective but that it was responsible for the spread of skin disease. The town remained a centre of anti-vaccination protest until late into the century.[12]

After municipal reform in 1836, the Liberals stormed to victory in the newly elected town council, and they continued to hold an overwhelming majority for the rest of the nineteenth century. These new leaders were middle-class property owners, many of them manufacturers, who had a vested interest in creating an orderly environment in the town. At this time, however, there was little clear vision about the exact role of the municipality; what was the responsibility of the corporation and what was the role of private initiative. The town council was answerable to local ratepayers, always keen to protect their interests, and legal powers to make any significant town improvement had to be acquired from Parliament, usually by means of a local Improvement Act.

By the end of the first half of the century the corporation had still not started to tackle two major public health problems in Leicester: poor sanitation and inadequate water supply. There was no proper sewerage system in the town, and in many poor streets there were no sewers or drains at all. Parish authorities were officially responsible for dealing with sewage, but where facilities were provided they were haphazard and inefficient, and often added to rather than solved the problem. There were large numbers of open cesspits, and much of the town's filth drained into the River Soar. To make matters worse the low-lying areas near the river were regularly flooded, and St Margaret's parish was particularly badly affected. It was common, for example, for Churchgate, Sanvey Gate, Belgrave Gate and the surrounding areas to be 2–3ft deep in heavily polluted water, and then for the streets to be clogged with poisonous

1 The Jewry Wall and St Nicholas church. This photograph is from the author's own collection.

2 The burial of a Saxon lady, known as the Glen Parva Lady, c. AD 500. The illustration is by Mike Codd. This image is reproduced courtesy of Leicester Arts and Museum Service.

*Left* 3 Ethelfloeda, 'The Lady of the Mercians', whose forces regained Leicester from the Danes. This photograph was taken by the author and permission to use the photograph is credited to Leicester City Council.

*Below* 4 View of St Mary de Castro and Castle Gardens. This photograph was taken by the author.

*Right* 5  An Edwardian postcard of St Martin's church. This postcard is from the author's own collection.

St. Martin's, Leicester.

*Below* 6  The Magazine Gateway, and buildings of De Montfort University, 2012. This photograph was taken by the author.

*Left* 7 An Edwardian postcard of St Margaret's church. This postcard is from the author's own collection.

*Below* 8 A stone carving on West Bridge. This photograph was taken by the author.

9 Statue of Richard III in Castle Gardens. This photograph was taken by the author.

10 The statue of Cardinal Wolsey in Abbey Park. This photograph was taken by the author.

11 The remains of Cavendish House in Abbey Park. The house was built on the Leicester Abbey site in about 1600, and in 1613 came into the possession of Thomas Cavendish, the first Earl of Devonshire. It was burned down by Royalist forces in 1645 after the siege of Leicester. This photograph was taken by the author.

12 The Guildhall. This photograph was taken by the author.

13 The Guildhall courtyard. This photograph was taken by the author. Permission to use the photograph is credited to Leicester City Council.

14 The Old Grammar School building refurbished as a restaurant. The name of the restaurant, 1573, recalls the year the Grammar School was opened. This photograph was taken by the author.

*Above* 15  An Edwardian postcard of St Mary de Castro and the chantry house built by William Wyggeston in about 1513. This postcard is from the author's own collection.

*Right* 16  Statue of Robert Hall (1764–1831) who succeeded William Carey as minister at Harvey Lane Baptist Chapel. Hall was renowned for his talents as a preacher. This photograph was taken by the author.

17 Town Hall Square. This photograph was taken by the author.

18 New Walk was first developed as Queens Walk in 1785 and was originally planned as a promenade out of the town through open fields, leading to the racecourse. It is seen here on an Edwardian postcard. This postcard is taken from the author's own collection.

19 The Crescent, King's Street, built in 1826. This photograph was taken by the author.

20 An Edwardian postcard of West Walk. This postcard is from the author's own collection.

21  Suburban expansion: the Melton turn. This Edwardian postcard is from the author's own collection.

22  An Edwardian postcard of Gallowtree Gate. This postcard is from the author's own collection.

23  An Edwardian postcard of Granby Street. This postcard is from the author's own collection.

24  An Edwardian postcard of the market place. This postcard is from the author's own collection.

25 The top of London Road. This Edwardian postcard is from the author's own collection.

*Humberstone Gate, Leicester*

26 Humberstone Gate. This postcard is from the author's own collection.

*Right* 27 The war memorial at Victoria Park. This photograph was taken by the author.

*Below* 28 University of Leicester buildings. This photograph was taken by the author.

29  New Walk, 2013. This photograph was taken by the author.

30  Leicester Caribbean Carnival, 2012. This photograph was taken by the author.

mud after the water had receded. The health of the townspeople suffered, and although all industrial towns of the period faced environmental problems, Leicester had above-average mortality rates. The lack of a piped water supply further aggravated the situation. Leicester residents obtained their water from a variety of sources. One was an old conduit set up in the eighteenth century, which carried water into the marketplace from a local spring. In addition to this there were rainwater cisterns, the polluted river and wells, though frequently these were polluted too, often by proximity to cesspits and privies.[13]

National legislation eventually helped to stimulate change. In 1842 the social reformer Edwin Chadwick published his *Report on the Sanitary Conditions of the Working Classes*. The report, based on painstaking research in the expanding towns and cities of England and Wales, highlighted the squalor in which so many working people were forced to live, and linked living conditions to ill health. Public health came to the forefront of national debate, and led to the Public Health Act of 1848. Shortly afterwards, in 1849, Leicester town council assumed an additional new role as a local health board, with definitive responsibility for sanitation and water supply. In the same year, the first efforts were made to provide Leicester with a properly functioning sewerage system.[14]

A civil engineer by the name of Thomas Wicksteed was commissioned by the town council to construct the system, an additional plan being that the sewage should be treated and sold as manure, so that the new system made a profit as well as providing a public service. Work started on the scheme in 1851, and the system was in operation four years later. Although this clearly improved the sanitation of Leicester, the project was not entirely successful. There was a fault in the construction of the pipes, and the system discharged liquid sewage into the Soar, polluting the water further and causing an offensive smell. It was also a disappointment when the expected profits from the sale of manure did not materialise. Eventually this idea was given up, and the town council had to finance the system at a cost of £2,000 a year, an amount that was considered by some to be over-expensive. There were various attempts to improve the efficiency of the system over the following decades, but the problems were too difficult to solve. Because the scheme had cost about £40,000 to set up, there was a reluctance to admit that a entirely new system was needed. Finally, in 1880 a new and gifted borough surveyor called Joseph Gordon was appointed. Under his direction a new sewerage system was conceived and constructed, and by 1886 it was in operation: Leicester at last had efficient sanitation.

From the mid-century onwards there were also efforts to provide an adequate water supply, though this too took many years to sort out satisfactorily. In 1846 a private waterworks company was established, with the intention to build a reservoir at nearby Thornton from which water would be piped into Leicester. This scheme stalled when the required funds could not be raised, but in 1850 the town council obtained legal authority to finance the scheme from public money. The reservoir was constructed, and by 1853 water was being pumped into the town. The supply was still very limited, though, and there continued to be many homes without water. This was alleviated when further reservoirs were built at Cropston in 1866, at Oadby in 1886 and at Swithland in 1896.

The Public Health Act heralded a new era in which provincial town councils throughout Britain took on a widening number of projects. One further aspect of this was that by the 1860s and 1870s it became commonplace for town councils to take local gas and water supply into public ownership, usually by buying out private companies. In Joseph Chamberlain's Birmingham, the implementation of this policy was the inspiration for the phrase 'gas and water socialism', which came to describe the new municipal control of town environments. Leicester followed the trend and in 1878, with the agreement of the relevant companies and authorisation from Parliament, the town council took total control of both gas and water.

## Suburbanisation

From the mid-nineteenth century the suburbs of Leicester grew rapidly, building on roads out of the town increased and outlying villages were swallowed up by suburban sprawl. Most of the suburbs were unpretentious, consisting of red-brick terrace housing with the addition of a few grander houses. One outstanding exception to this was the select suburb of Stoneygate, and to some extent neighbouring Knighton, where many of the wealthiest manufacturers migrated. This area was characterised by its fine suburban villas, the construction of which gave a number of outstanding local architects such as Isaac Barradale and Joseph Goddard an opportunity to showcase their talents.[15]

One obvious reason for suburbanisation was the need to house a rapidly rising town population. As industrialisation gained momentum so did population growth, as people migrated into the town from the surrounding counties or from further afield, looking for work opportunities and a better life. Census returns show that from 1861 to 1891 the number of Leicester residents shot up dramatically, almost trebling from 68,056 to 174,624.[16] Spreading outwards was one way of accommodating everyone, and ameliorating squalid overcrowding in the heart of the town. There was also public awareness that housing built close to the river provided an especially unhealthy environment, and those who could moved away from that area. In addition to this, many townspeople were displaced from their homes when a large number of houses in the city centre were demolished in an attempt to encourage economic growth, by opening up space in the town for commercial and industrial premises.

On the north side of Leicester, housing development on and around the Belgrave Road was well underway in the 1850s, an early development that occurred because of the close involvement of Belgrave with the textile industry. This expansion increased in the 1860s, and soon the new housing crept up on the village of Belgrave. On the south side of Leicester, Stoneygate, Knighton and Clarendon Park all underwent significant development between 1860 and 1890. There were already a few grand houses in Stoneygate by the late 1840s, but when further land became available for building in 1858 the neighbourhood rapidly expanded, and continued to do so over the following decades. Nearby, the new suburb of South Knighton was also growing, and a little further out lay the rural village of Knighton, which gradually lost its separate identity and became swallowed up by suburban sprawl. In 1875 the private land comprising the Clarendon Park estate was sold, and this area was rapidly built up too. Land was also sold in Highfields in 1868, and many red-brick terraces were constructed in the years that followed. Other suburbs that underwent notable development in the 1870s and 1880s included Aylestone, Humberstone and, on the west side of the river, Westcotes and Dannetts Hill, while in North Evington, in 1885, Leicester architect Arthur Wakerley embarked on a long and innovative project to create an industrial suburb, a community combining housing, factories and services for local residents.[17]

The introduction of horse-drawn trams along the routes in and out of town both helped and consolidated this spread of suburbia. The first tramway was introduced in 1874 to carry passengers back and forth along the Belgrave Road, and it was not long before all the main suburban routes were catered

Suburban expansion: St Stephen's Road. This Edwardian postcard is taken from the author's own collection.

Suburban expansion: Narborough Road. This Edwardian postcard is taken from the author's own collection.

Leicester's first tram car. This Edwardian postcard is taken from the author's own collection.

for. Leicester resident Robert Read wrote with enthusiasm about the trams in 1882. He commented on the 'superior horses', the 'commodious' carriages and the regularity of the trams, which arrived every ten to fifteen minutes. However, he also suggested some improvements. These included lowering the fares and making the time of the last tram later on some of the routes. Apparently the last trams to Belgrave and Stoneygate left half an hour later than those going to other suburbs, and this was the cause of some envy and resentment in the town. He also helpfully suggested that the tram companies should employ more drivers and conductors, so that they could enjoy proper breaks and not have to eat their meals on the job.[18]

The suburbanisation of the mid- to late twentieth century created a greater level of class segregation than had existed previously. In the earlier part of the century, when employers had lived in the town, they had also lived close by their workers. In contrast to this, the suburb of Stoneygate created an exclusive social zone for the local elite.[19] In these prosperous surroundings, suburban living could be experienced not just as a pragmatic choice but as an ideal. This perception was influenced by a combination of contemporary thinking, including sanitary science, evangelicalism and romanticism.

# THOMAS COOK

Shortly after the death of Thomas Cook (1808–92) at his home in Stoneygate, *The Times* newspaper dubbed the Leicester businessman and his son John 'the Julius and Augustus Caesar of modern travel'. Cook's Tours had provided people with unprecedented opportunities for taking pleasant and more adventurous holidays, and as a result there had been a sharp increase in tourism. The newspaper observed that in the 1890s Cook's had a 'phenomenal list of Branch offices', including in Brussels, Brindisi, Chicago, Jerusalem, Sydney and Rangoon.

Thomas Cook was originally from Derbyshire, but as a young man came to Market Harborough to work for a bookseller with connections to the Baptist Association. Cook was himself a Baptist and a dedicated temperance advocate, and it was said that one day while he was walking from Market Harborough to Leicester to attend a temperance meeting he had an idea of how the railways could be used to help the temperance movement. Shortly afterwards he arranged with the Midland Counties Railway Company for a special train to take passengers on a one day trip to Loughborough to attend a temperance rally planned for 5 July 1841.

This excursion was advertised and proved to be a great success. The party, which was accompanied by a musical band, consisted of around 485 people all travelling on 1s tickets. A great crowd gathered to see the travellers off at the station in Leicester, people crowded on to bridges all along the line to view the train, and when it arrived in Loughborough a further crowd was waiting to meet it.

Shortly after this first trip, Cook moved with his family to Leicester. There he established a bookselling and printing business as well as developing an excursion and travel programme to a wide range of destinations – firstly in the Midlands and then further afield in the British Isles, including Scotland and Ireland. In 1851, Cook's excursions played a major role in transporting people from outside London to and from the Great Exhibition, and as the reputation of the company grew it expanded into continental and more ambitious overseas travel. Thomas Cook himself retired in 1878 and handed over the business to his son.

## *Sources*

P. Brendon, 'Cook, Thomas (1808–1892)' in *Oxford Dictionary of National Biography* (Oxford, 2004), www.oxford dnb.com/view/article/6152, accessed 20 October 2012; R. Ingle, *Thomas Cook of Leicester* (Bangor, 1981); D. Seaton, *The Local Legacy of Thomas Cook* (Botcheston, 1996); J. Simmons, 'Thomas Cook of Leicester', *Transactions of the Leicester Archaeological Society*, vol.49 (1973–4), pp.18–32.; *The Times*, 20 July 1892.

Public health concerns were an issue, and there was a clear intention to move to a safer, cleaner environment. There were also moral overtones, and the suggestion that suburbanites were avoiding the vice and corruption of the town by keeping their distance. Great emphasis was also placed on the peace and seclusion of the home, and the ample gardens that brought the beauty of the countryside to the town, a romantic refuge to return to after the working day.[20]

The red-brick terraced housing that composed so much of the less pretentious suburbs obviously created a very different living environment to that enjoyed in Stoneygate. The new housing, much of which still survives today, was solid, spacious and considerably better in quality than the back-to-back housing constructed in the earlier part of the century. These improvements were supported by new local building regulations that were enacted in 1859, and Leicester housing generally compared well with that of other industrial towns.

## Civic Participation and Civic Pride

Leicester, like the other rapidly growing industrial towns in Britain, needed capable leadership to manage the town, and it was generally thought that the ideal counsellor should have proven business skills. Joseph Chamberlain, that most famous of Victorian provincial mayors, demonstrated in Birmingham during the 1870s what could achieved in a short time; and outstanding among Chamberlain's talents were his business and financial acumen. This was developed by his early career working in the local family firm, which specialised in the manufacture of screws.[21] It was an illustration of how brilliance could emerge from very prosaic circumstances.

The job of town councillor was unpaid and time consuming, and there needed to be a good reason to participate. One reason could have been the attraction of gaining power and influence in the limited local arena. Another incentive might have been social prestige. In Leicester, as in other provincial towns, councillors were part of a wider middle-class circle who took part in chapel and church activities, supported local charities and charitable institutions, and participated in other voluntary associations, including business groups, the local Literary and Philosophical Society and the Freemasons. To become a town councillor meant gaining the respect of this group, and to do this the candidate normally had to be a person of financial substance who had social standing, gained through taking part in local affairs.[22]

A further motivation was religious in origin. In the 1840s a Birmingham Baptist minister called George Dawson started to cause a stir by preaching, to great effect, a creed that became known as the civic gospel. This acquired a great following not only among Baptists but more generally in Nonconformist congregations and beyond.[23] Dawson not only preached that involvement in local affairs was a Christian duty, but he helped to promote a vision of the provincial town that was heroic in quality. He told his listeners that 'a great town exists to discharge towards the people of that the town the duties that a great nation exists to discharge towards the people of that nation'.[24] This type of rhetoric gave a sense of mission to the process of town improvement, as well as encouraging a sense of duty and civic pride at the results achieved. The Birmingham civic gospel was an important part of Chamberlain's background, and Birmingham and its achievements helped lead a new public perception of civic participation.

While this new perception enhanced the dignity of candidates for local election, other social trends could discourage civic involvement. In some towns, including Birmingham, Leeds and Manchester, as the leading businessmen moved to leafy suburbs there was a growing tendency for some to become more detached from civic affairs and to leave this responsibility to smaller businessmen and shopkeepers, a tendency that gathered momentum towards the end of the century. This was not, however, a noticeable trend in Leicester. Although many Leicester manufacturers moved to suburbs such as Stoneygate and Knighton, an unusual number of the leading employers stayed involved in local politics and the management of town affairs. The relatively compact size of Leicester may have helped encourage this. While Stoneygate, for instance, featured many quiet and secluded residences, it was still only a very short ride from the town centre.

Leicester town centre was also compact, with the Town Hall, workplaces and the premises of leading societies and institutions within easy reach of each other, making it relatively simple to participate in town affairs. For a businessman working in Leicester in the 1870s there were a number of obvious choices. Many were active in the Chamber of Commerce, which was situated in Friar Lane, the Leicester Freehold Society and the Leicester Permanent Building Society, while a few doors away and around the corner in Horsefair

Street was the Leicester Trade Protection Society. All of these groups were run voluntarily by local businessmen. To demonstrate his public spiritedness, a businessman might seek election to the board of the Leicester Infirmary, and the short walk to the hospital would probably not be a great inconvenience. If he was kept late at his workplace it would not be too difficult to go on afterwards to a masonic lodge meeting at Freemasons Hall in Halford Street or to attend a lecture meeting at the Leicester Literary and Philosophical Society in New Walk. In this way a man could build up a following, and with relative ease become a well-known face about town. For those who then went on to serve as town councillors the geography of the town centre meant that the majority of workplaces were not far from the Town Hall, making acceptably regular attendance at town council meetings possible.[25]

Those who preached and followed the civic gospel believed that there was more to local development than good sanitation and public ownership of the gas and water supply. Town improvement was seen as a civilising mission that entailed providing townspeople with educational and leisure facilities, such as museums, libraries and public parks, and in the mid- to late nineteenth century it was expected that town leaders would provide these refinements to urban life. The earliest project of this type in Leicester was the town museum in New Walk, which was opened in 1849. The initiative for this came from the Leicester Literary and Philosophical Society, or the Lit and Phil as it was commonly known.[26] This society, established in 1836, was a middle-class body that held fortnightly lectures on a variety of literary, historical and scientific topics. Additionally, members collected a variety of 'interesting' objects, with the intention that this should be the basis of a Leicester museum. The rather homely collection included fossils, plants, shells, stuffed birds and scientific books, and was at first housed in a cupboard.[27] However, in 1845, after Parliament passed an Act that enabled large towns to establish museums, the Lit and Phil prevailed on Leicester Town Council to rehouse their growing collection and present it as the town museum. Their campaign was successful, and in 1849 the museum was opened in the vacant buildings of the old Proprietary School in New Walk. The opening was performed with civic ceremony by the president of the society and the Mayor of Leicester in the presence of distinguished guests from the town, county and '500 ladies and gentlemen seated in the large room'.[28]

The opening of the museum illustrates a number of important and developing aspects of Leicester life at this time. The men and women who assembled

The crossroads at Bridge Street, Castle Street and Bath Lane, and in the background the Mitre and Keys Inn: a late nineteenth-century view. This image is reproduced courtesy of the Record Office for Leicestershire, Leicester and Rutland.

at the museum to watch the opening were a sample of the professional and employing classes in the town, and among the men were voters whom the town council represented and ratepayers to whom they were accountable. Their attendance shows their interest in the development of their town. Moreover, the partnership between the Lit and Phil and the town council in creating the museum illustrates how town life was managed by a combination of the official authorities and private individuals and groups. Although the role of the corporation greatly increased in the mid- to late Victorian decades, the contribution of private residents and voluntary associations to town improvement remained vitally important.

It was not until twenty years after the town museum opened that Leicester acquired a free public library, another symbol of a modern provincial town. A subscription library known as the Leicester Permanent Library had been established since 1791, since the mid-nineteenth century in Granby Street, but the subscription rate was well beyond the pockets of most local residents. As the drive to make elementary schooling compulsory for everyone gained momentum, however, a town without a free library seemed backward. To remedy this, in 1871 the town council opened a free library and reading room in Belvoir Street, paid for by the rates. However, this still benefited considerably from private generosity, as individuals gave financial donations and provided books and periodicals to boost the stock. A decade later, in 1883, the first branch library opened at Garendon Street in Highfields. A small amount of public money was provided annually to maintain the branch, but the building itself and the initial stock of books were a gift from Councillor Israel Hart, a leading member of the local Jewish community and a future Mayor of Leicester.[29]

Around mid-century, the growing provincial towns of Britain not only developed better facilities but they also started to look more impressive. Civic pride was expressed by statues, Town Halls, monuments, attractive city centre streets and imposing public spaces.[30] Leicester followed suit, though development was more gradual than in the larger, leading industrial cities such as Manchester and Leeds. In the 1850s Leicester was emerging from crippling economic insecurity and was only just beginning to deal with very basic problems of infrastructure. Despite this, some attention was paid to smartening up the marketplace, with a new market hall and a stylish new corn exchange, and some impressive private buildings were constructed in the town centre. During the 1860s to 1880s there seemed more grounds for civic pride. The hosiery industry had emerged from depression, and the local manufacture

Hotel Street, showing the Saracen's Head Inn with advertisements for a show at the Royal Opera House. This image is reproduced courtesy of the Record Office for Leicestershire, Leicester and Rutland.

Drawing of the Royal Opera House in Silver Street, opened in 1877. This image is taken from R. Read, *Modern Leicester* (London, 1881).

A view of Granby Street, showing the distinctive columns of the General Newsroom and Library. The building was constructed in 1838 and demolished in 1901. This image is reproduced courtesy of the Record Office for Leicestershire, Leicester and Rutland.

of boots and shoes was developing fast. Although the problems of sanitation and water supply had not been entirely resolved, at least reasonable attempts were being made to tackle these issues, and by the 1870s plans to deepen, widen and alter the course of the Soar were at last being implemented in a serious and ultimately successful effort to deal with the river floods that had dogged the town for so long. It was during these decades that much of Leicester town centre was redesigned and rebuilt. Although some of those buildings have now gone, this mid-Victorian town centre was the basis of the Leicester we know today.

One monument, built in 1868, has become an icon of Leicester: the Clock Tower that stands in the city centre. This had a very humdrum, practical function, and was built after the town council and interested individuals had put work into reducing traffic congestion. The site on which the tower stands had long been an important and busy junction, where five major thoroughfares converged. This spot was known by a number of local names, one of which was Coal Hill (it was where coal brought from the local collieries was unloaded). It was also called Haymarket, after a regular market that was held there until it was moved to Humberstone Gate in 1866. A further and ancient name for the place,

Wyggeston Boys School in 1893. This image is taken from G. Cowie, *The History of Wyggeston's Hospital, the Hospital Schools and the Old Free Grammar School* (Leicester and London, 1898).

dating back to the Danish occupation of the ninth century, was East Gates. Assembly rooms had been built at this spot in 1750, but by the mid-nineteenth century the building was just an awkward obstruction to town traffic. When it was pulled down in 1862 there was more space, but a further problem arose: traffic converged on the spot from all directions, and without a central point to circulate around the flow became haphazard and dangerous. From this problem the idea of the Clock Tower emerged. When built, it reduced the traffic problem – and also became one of the most distinctive sights in the town.

Despite the practical function of the clock tower, it was intended that it should be a monument to civic pride. A competition was held to find an appropriate design, and this was won by local architect Joseph Goddard. The tower is adorned with four statues, depicting Simon de Montfort, William Wyggeston, Thomas White and Alderman Gabriel Newton, characterised as benefactors of Leicester. By decorating it in this way Goddard added symbolic meaning: not only did the monument represent the achievements of modern Leicester, but the statues made reference to the historic traditions of the town, seeming to draw a line of continuity between past and present.

East Gates with the Clock Tower which was built in 1868. This image is reproduced courtesy of the Record Office for Leicestershire, Leicester and Rutland.

The contribution made to Leicester by Montfort was dubious and Thomas White's connection with the town was tentative, but the representation of Leicester as a historic town of significance created an appropriate gravitas. The cost of building the Clock Tower was supported by a grant from the town council, but again, the input and interest of local townspeople was just as important. The idea originally came from a group of private citizens and private subscriptions carried the majority of the cost, demonstrating that civic involvement and pride in the town were held dear not only by local politicians but also by members of the more general public.[31]

*Spencers' New Guide to Leicester*, published in 1888, described some of the improvements that had been made to the appearance of central Leicester during the mid-Victorian decades.[32] New roads and public spaces had been laid out and planted with trees, while the old major thoroughfares had been widened. The newly widened Granby Street was particularly admired, and the profusion of public and private modern buildings that had sprung up in the heart of the town, including 'clubs, public offices, banks, baths, restaurants, warehouses, factories and other business establishments', was commented on.[33]

Among the buildings that the writer chose to describe more specifically were the modern Town Hall, the Freemasons' hall, the Temperance Hall and the Victoria Coffee and Cocoa House.

The new Town Hall, still in use today, was an imposing red-brick building that had been opened with full civic ceremony in 1876. It was situated between Horsefair Street and Bishop Street and was designed in Queen Anne style by London architect Francis Hames. The borough arms were emblazoned on the front of the hall, and it boasted a 145ft-high tower surmounted by a cupola and four clock dials. Rising proudly above the centre, this was a proclamation that Leicester was flourishing and could

The Magazine, also known as the Newarke Gateway. This image is reproduced courtesy of the Record Office for Leicestershire, Leicester and Rutland.

A crowded carriage outside the Three Crowns Hotel on the corner of Horsefair Street and Gallowtree Gate. This is thought to be a picture of the last stagecoach to leave Leicester in 1866. The Three Crowns was demolished in 1870. This image is reproduced courtesy of the Record Office for Leicestershire, Leicester and Rutland.

Hallam's shop, 'The Family Fry Pan', on the corner of High Street and Highcross Street. This shop was demolished in 1902. The image is reproduced courtesy of the Record Office for Leicestershire, Leicester and Rutland.

The Town Hall, built between 1874 and 1876. This image is taken from R. Read, *Modern Leicester* (London, 1881).

compete with other towns. The construction of the Town Hall was, like the Clock Tower, important for both practical reasons and reasons of civic pride. The public business of the town had been run from the Guildhall since the fifteenth century, but the accommodation that the medieval building offered had become hopelessly inadequate for the purpose, especially as the municipal buildings were also the site of the town courts. The new building by comparison was extremely spacious and well appointed. As well as a range of different offices, there was also a handsome mayor's parlour, two courtrooms and retiring rooms for judges, lawyers and jury, while in the basement there were cells for the prisoners. The decoration of the Town Hall followed the Clock Tower in its recollection of Leicester's past, reinforcing the impression of a town steeped in history. There were painted-glass windows overlooking Bowling Green Street that depicted images including Simon de Montfort, John of Gaunt, Hugh Latimer, William Wyggeston, Alderman Newton and Thomas White; while in the council chamber a portrait of Thomas Paget, first mayor of the reformed corporation, was displayed over the fireplace, making the connection between Leicester's distant and more recent past.[34]

*Spencers' Guide* also picked out a number of other mid- to late Victorian buildings and developments for special comment. One of these was the Royal Opera House in Silver Street. Another striking red-brick building, this was designed in Queen Anne style. Built in 1876–77, it stood three storeys high and held 2,550 people. The writer remarked with some amazement that 'notwithstanding the immense and rapid growth of Leicester, few persons could have anticipated the erection of such a noble building for the purposes of drama'.[35] Further plaudits were reserved for the Temperance Hall in Granby Street, with its 'commanding' front decorated by Corinthian pillars,[36] and the elegant Freemasons' Hall in Halford Street, built in Italian style.[37] The guide writer was also very taken with Leicester's seven coffee and cocoa houses, designed to keep residents away from the demon drink by providing food and non-alcoholic beverages at affordable prices. A particularly enthusiastic review was reserved for the new Victoria branch, a five-storey turreted building opposite the post office in Granby Street, where one imagines the writer may have stopped for coffee after walking round the town. After commending the attractive and capacious interior, thought to 'far exceed' the other branches, the guide finally declares that the establishment is 'considered one of the best in the kingdom'.[38]

## The Opening of Abbey Park

In the 1880s, Abbey Park, Victoria Park and Spinney Hill Park were laid out and opened to the public, and particular celebration accompanied the opening of Abbey Park in 1882, which was performed by the Prince and Princess of Wales.

Public parks were a further symbol of a successful modern town, and reformers had long argued that they provided townspeople with fresh air and a healing contact with nature that gave much-needed relief from urban surroundings. More moralistic voices also gave their support to the provision of public parks. Libraries, museums and parks were all considered to be places of 'rational recreation', or in other words 'respectable' leisure pursuits, as opposed to pubs and beershops. Organised sport was particularly favoured, and the new town parks were generally supplied with sporting facilities. Birkenhead was the first provincial town to boast a public park, and by the 1840s Manchester had three; by the 1880s the Leicester parks were perhaps somewhat overdue.[39] Nevertheless, when they were established they were a source of great civic pride, especially Abbey Park, which the colour and theatre of the royal visit dramatically expressed.

The plans for Abbey Park emerged from the flood prevention measures undertaken in Leicester in the 1870s. Abbey Meadows and St Margaret's Pasture were scheduled for flood-works, and it was decided that 66 acres of the meadows would be set aside for a park and approach road, while 10 acres of the pasture would be reserved for a new cricket ground.[40] By January 1882 the work was progressing well, and the town council decided to ask Albert Edward, the Prince of Wales, to open the park in the following May. The prince was due to pass through Leicester on 9 January 1882, on his way to stay with the Earl of Stamford, and it was arranged with Buckingham Palace that this would be a suitable time for the town leaders to meet the prince, present him with an address of loyalty and a formal invitation. This was done, and all was set for the big day.[41]

The opening of the park took place on 29 May 1882, the Whitsun bank holiday.[42] Prince Albert Edward, Princess Alexandra and their party, including the Duke of Rutland, Countess Suffield and royal attendants, took a specially scheduled train from St Pancras at 10.50 a.m. and arrived at the Midland station in London Road just before 1 p.m. As the train steamed into the station

The Prince of Wales visits Leicester, 1882: a preliminary visit before the opening of Abbey Park later that year. This image is taken from W. Kelly, *Royal Progresses and Visits to Leicester* (Leicester, 1884), courtesy of the University of Leicester Special Collections.

the Royal Standard was raised on a flagpost just outside the building, cheered on by crowds of spectators. The platform at which the party alighted had been elaborately decorated under the supervision of Mr Mitchie, the stationmaster, and Mr Loveday, the chief traffic inspector; there was bunting as well as a profusion of red, white and blue streamers, and the station walls were covered with a multitude of wreaths, shields and trophies. Above the entrance to the equally decorated booking hall the word 'Welcome' had been placed.

The royal couple were greeted on the platform by the band of the Leicester Volunteers, and were met by a civic reception committee led by the mayor and mayoress and composed of aldermen, councillors and various members of the Leicestershire Regiment. The princess was presented with a bouquet of flowers, following which the group went out into the station yard where, cheered by the onlookers, they embarked in waiting carriages.

The procession set out along Granby Street led by mounted police and the fire brigade, followed on foot by 900 members of Leicester's Friendly societies and behind these twenty-eight carriages arranged in order of hierarchy, with the royal couple at the rear. The first carriage carried borough officials and then came leading citizens, councillors, aldermen, justices of the peace, mayors of neighbouring towns, ex-mayors, queen's counsel recorder, the High Bailiff of Leicestershire, the Mayor of Leicester for 1881 and the current Mayor and Mayoress of Leicester. Finally, along with a yeomanry escort, came the royal carriage driven by four bay horses, trailed at the back by a carriage carrying members of the Leicester, London and Manchester press. The procession made its way to the marketplace, with dense crowds watching and cheering from the pavements, while the windows of every shop and house were packed with spectators trying to get a good view.

The procession was clearly intended to send a message of unity and loyalty to all onlookers. The civic authorities and other town leaders were showcased with the royal couple, suggesting that Leicester was proud of its own identity but loyal to the nation. In addition, the presence of representatives from the county and other mayors conveyed the impression that the town of Leicester maintained a cordial relationship with its hinterland as well as with other towns, while the attendance at the parade of so many Friendly society members also seemed to suggest that there were harmonious class relations in the town.

By taking the parade through the centre of Leicester, town leaders were able to show off the new buildings and developments; the whole town was elaborately decorated and shown to good advantage. Private shops and firms had festively decked out their own buildings, and £3,000 had been collected to pay for the decoration of public buildings and spaces. Particularly memorable were a series of decorative triumphal arches that had been erected along the processional route, one of which was the Renaissance arch (referred to at the beginning of the chapter), most likely intended to symbolise the rebirth of the town. The decorations conveyed the same messages as the procession: self confidence, unity and loyalty. Buildings and triumphal arches were adorned with heraldic symbols of the Prince of Wales, with messages of welcome and loyalty, while the cheers of the spectators consolidated the message to good effect.

At the marketplace the royal party was received by a great mass of over 6,000 local schoolchildren, who had passed the time in waiting by singing 'Rule Britannia', 'Men of Harlech' and 'God Bless the Prince of Wales'. There then followed a short Masonic ceremony: the prince was the Grand Master of Freemasons in the United Kingdom, and indeed one Leicester lodge was called the Albert Edward Lodge in honour of him. On this occasion all eight lodges from Leicester and the county were in attendance, wearing full regalia and carrying lodge banners. Many local manufacturers and professionals were Freemasons, and their participation demonstrated their interest not only in the Masonic connection with Albert Edward but also in civic affairs.

After this interlude the royal visitors and procession continued on their way to Abbey Park, where all was prepared for the opening ceremony. On arrival, the royal couple were taken along the various drives in the park, with Friendly society members lining the route. Following this they were seated on a platform among 'a distinguished company of ladies and gentlemen'.

On the ice in Abbey Park. This image is reproduced courtesy of the Record Office for Leicestershire, Leicester and Rutland. Thanks also are due to Malcolm Noble for help in reproducing this.

The opening ceremony began with a speech from the mayor, which included a history of the planning of the park. He emphasised that 'this is truly a people's park', and that the land had been purchased and laid out at public expense. He expressed the hope that 'this park will afford means for rational recreation and healthy exercise to future generations and be to them a source of strength and gladness'. Handing a golden key to the prince, he declared, 'In the name of the corporation of this ancient borough I have now the honour to ask your royal highness to accept this key as a memento of the proceedings of this day'. Taking the key, the prince said, 'I declare this people's park open.' The royals then left the platform and walked to a nearby site where the princess planted an English oak, following which the Mayoress, on behalf of 'the ladies of Leicester', presented her with a silver spade. As ever, the ceremony, with its references to the 'ancient borough', and the park setting that recalled Leicester's medieval abbey, made much of the town's historic tradition, and linked it to the present, underlining a further reason for civic pride.

The opening ceremony was followed by a luxurious luncheon served under a marquee on the green, and in the afternoon there was a lengthy programme of speeches. At five o'clock the prince and princess departed for the station. The Leicester Volunteers were at the station platform to give them a send-off, and after the band had played 'God Save the Queen' the royal party left for London. Meanwhile in the town, celebrations continued into the evening, with elaborate firework displays at Abbey Meadows and Victoria Park, during which dramatic fire portraits of the royal couple were created for the entertainment of the crowds.

This celebration was a considerable achievement for the leaders of the town. The visit had been a chance to present Leicester as an up-and-coming modern town, where public health was under control, with productive industries, attractive facilities and an impressive town centre. In addition to this, they had succeeded in creating the impression of a flourishing city community. Leicester, like all the growing industrial towns, was a mass of different interest groups and the townspeople were divided in many ways, including by class, sex, religion and party affiliation. The challenge had been to create an image of unity, all groups united under a single civic identity celebrating a shared civic pride, and this was successfully expressed.

*six*

# LATE VICTORIAN AND EDWARDIAN LEICESTER

## The Yearly Calendar

As part of the New Year celebrations in January 1875 a local newspaper, the *Leicester Chronicle and Leicestershire Mercury*, published a retrospective diary of the year that had passed. This was a strictly local diary, mainly concerning events in Leicester, with some additional information on the county. The diary proved a great success with the readership, so much so that it was introduced as a regular feature every New Year. The rapidly growing population of Victorian Leicester and the new suburban sprawl made it increasingly difficult for townspeople to experience Leicester as a unified whole. This division of the population by location added to other obvious divisions, such as the hierarchy of social class and differences in religious belief. Against this backdrop the local newspapers helped to maintain a sense of collective Leicester identity, a perception that the town was a coherent society and not just a formless mass of people. While it was not possible for Leicester residents to have direct knowledge of everything going on in the town outside their own social circle, they could at least read about a variety of local activities in the newspaper and imagine themselves as part of a wider Leicester community. Features such as the New Year diary helped create this sense of belonging.

The events recorded in the diary for the most part fell into two categories. First there were meetings and occasions organised by the town council and other authorities such as the school board, which managed the new schools created by the 1870 Education Act, and the Poor Law guardians, who managed the affairs of the workhouse. Second, there were the meetings and events of local, voluntarily run institutions and associations, including commercial and trade organisations, medical and benevolent institutions, educational, musical

*Left* St Martin's Church, late nineteenth century. This image is taken from Mrs T. Fielding Johnson's *Glimpses of Ancient Leicester* (Leicester, 1891) courtesy of the University of Leicester Special Collections.

*Below* Children near the town museum. This Edwardian postcard is taken from the author's own collection.

and literary societies, Friendly societies, temperance societies, religious groups, floral and horticultural societies and social clubs. Although these groups differed in interest and focus, what they shared was that they were run by unpaid volunteers, independent of local government. They helped manage the life of the town, brought people together and provided an organised Leicester social life.[1]

The annual diary published in the *Leicester Chronicle and Leicestershire Mercury* was really just a summary of the local events the paper had already reported on during the year. Although each year the diary differed in detail, at the heart of it was a repetitive cycle of events that took place annually: as well as being a record of the year that had passed, the diary was also a calendar of the year to come. The cycle of meetings, celebrations, concerts and other functions was an ongoing schedule with its own patterns and rhythms. It was, in fact, a local way of life.

By the mid-1870s a range of local newspapers were published in Leicester. There were two leading weekly papers: the Liberal *Leicester Chronicle and Leicestershire Mercury* and the Conservative *Leicester Journal*. The energy and activity surrounding the rebuilding of the town during the mid- to late century also produced two new daily newspapers, the *Leicester Daily Post*, first published in 1872, and the *Leicester Daily Mercury*, launched in 1874.[2] Both these new papers were Liberal, reflecting the dominance of the Liberals in the town, which had persisted since the old corporation was disbanded in 1835. All these Leicester papers gave full reports of national news and local government affairs, and all of them reported in detail on the associational life of the town.

## The Leicester Calendar in the 1870s and 1880s

The shape of the Leicester year was moulded by a number of influences, including the four seasons, the municipal calendar, the programmes of societies and clubs and the Church calendar, with its major holidays and festivals such as Christmas, Easter and Whitsun. These different calendars overlapped and intertwined to form an overarching town calendar.

As far as many people were concerned, the Leicester annual calendar did not really start in January; it started in autumn after the summer holidays were over. One important occasion that opened the year in September was the annual meeting of the Leicester School of Art, held a few weeks before the term started in October. This school, the origin of De Montfort University, was a private initiative founded in 1870 by a group of local businessmen to train students in commercial art and design, for the benefit of Leicester trade and industry. It was first set up in Pocklington's Walk before moving to a site adjoining the town museum in 1877. Both the daytime and evening classes were held at the school, and artisans who wished to attend were offered evening classes at a special low fee. Although the town council at this time was not legally allowed to subsidise higher education, there was widespread support for the School of Art among the wider middle classes, and the governing committee was composed of prominent clergymen and businessmen from the Chamber of Commerce and Trade Protection Society, many of whom doubled as councillors and aldermen. The meeting in September no doubt provided an excellent networking opportunity for all after the summer break.[3]

Two important outdoor social events took place in October: the Leicester races and the October pleasure fair. The race week was at the beginning of the month, and on the Thursday and Friday there was a holiday, which allowed large numbers of people to attend. The racecourse was still on the South Field of Leicester adjoining London Road, and the races were run by an independent committee on a non-profit-making basis. People of all social classes attended each year, although by the 1870s the occasion had become less popular with the county gentry and more popular with the working classes of the town. Entry was free, and for those who were not so interested in racing there were refreshment booths and fairground attractions. This annual tradition came to an end in 1883, when the last race was run at South Field and the yearly holiday was abolished. The green then became known as Victoria Park, and a new racecourse was opened at Oadby. This was run on a more commercial basis, with races taking place every three months and an entry fee charged at the gate.[4]

The October pleasure fair was held in mid-October in Humberstone Gate, and was the direct successor of the Michelmas fair that had been held in Leicester for centuries. After the Gregorian calendar was adopted in Britain in 1752 the date was moved from September to October.[5] The fair always had a variety of attractions: 1871 was typical, with amusements including several menageries, waxworks, a theatre, a German band, nut and gingerbread stalls and various curiosities, including 'Sampson, the largest horse in the world' and

The Grand Hotel. This Edwardian postcard is taken from the author's own collection.

The Clock Tower and trams. This Edwardian postcard is taken from the author's own collection.

The workhouse inmates. This image is reproduced courtesy of the Record Office for Leicestershire, Leicester and Rutland. Thanks are also due to Malcolm Noble for help in reproducing this.

performing dogs and monkeys.[6] This fair and the traditional May fair, which had also survived, were finally discontinued in the early 1900s, when they were held to be incompatible with the new electric tramways.[7]

The build up to the annual town council elections also began in the autumn. October was the time for nominations, and meetings took place in the electoral wards throughout the month. In November, after the elections were over and the new mayor installed, the municipal year began, and the regular beat of town council meetings punctuated the calendar. These were recorded very fully in the press during the 1870s and 1880s, often with four or five columns of small print spread over a broadsheet newspaper page, giving a level of detail that was almost a substitute for attending the meeting.

Autumn also marked the beginning of a new cultural and social season. One strand was contributed by the Leicester Musical Society, which organised a series of high-quality classical music concerts between November and March each year. In 1884, a not untypical season, the Hallé Orchestra visited Leicester and played the first concert of the series.[8] Other music societies were

A charity tea for elderly people, around 1900. This image is reproduced courtesy of the Record Office for Leicestershire, Leicester and Rutland.

also establishing themselves at this time, and in the same month the Leicester Amateur Harmonic Society also gave their first performance of the season, a vocal and instrumental concert at the Temperance Hall.[9] In 1886 the Leicester Philharmonic Society joined the local musical scene: this was a choir with around 250 members founded by Herbert Marshall, a local piano dealer and future mayor of the town.[10]

The social gatherings that dominated the autumn and winter months more than any other, however, were the lecture meetings. The leader in this was the Leicester Literary and Philosophical Society, or Lit and Phil, which held its 'members only' lectures fortnightly on Tuesday evening at the town museum. The lectures dealt with a range of scientific, historical, musical and literary topics, and were delivered by a mixture of visiting and local speakers. The 1875 to 1876 season included such items as 'The Personality of a Poet', a lecture given by R. Laird Collier of Chicago, 'Richard Wagner and the Music of the Future', delivered by local man Thomas Carter, and 'The Arthurian Legends', presented by the Revd A. MacKennal, a well-known Leicester clergyman.[11]

The content of these lectures, like that of the town council meetings, was reported in minute detail by the press, reflecting the local prestige of the society.

The town council also put on a fortnightly series of Saturday evening lectures at the museum. These were free of charge and were intended to cater for a wider audience than the middle-class elite who attended the Lit and Phil meetings. There were no visiting lecturers, and many of the talks were delivered by Lit and Phil members who ran the museum in collaboration with the town council. The lectures were generally less highbrow than those at the Lit and Phil and tended to veer away from literary topics, favouring more practical and scientific subjects such as 'magnetism' and 'the weather instruments at the museum'.[12]

Generally speaking, the subjects chosen for both the Lit and Phil and the town council lectures were uncontroversial. The Lit and Phil maintained its ban on religious and political topics, which had been imposed to play down divisions among the members, and this was also the practice at the town council lectures. Sometimes, however, there was something a little more contentious. In 1871, Dr W. Romanis, the first visiting lecturer to speak at the Lit and Phil, opened the season with a lecture on Darwinism,[13] and in 1875 a lecture entitled 'Evolution or the Origin of the Species' was one of the talks in the Saturday night season at the museum, showing that while it was not acceptable to pit one religion against another in debate, it was possible to discuss scientific challenges to religious belief.[14]

Christmas and New Year heralded a season of charity parties, entertainments and chapel tea meetings. January 1871 was typical, with events including a 'customary treat' at All Saints' open mission room, where sixty old men sat down to roast beef and plum pudding,[15] an annual dinner at Carley Street Ragged School for 200 poor children, and an invitation by the lessee of the Theatre Royal to the workhouse children to see the pantomime free of charge, along with free buns and milk.[16]

The Christmas and New Year break was a dividing line between two phases of the cultural and social season. The programme of lectures and concerts continued between January and Easter, but there was an increase in other types of social gatherings as well. January and February were months in which prestigious balls took place; some of the organisations that held these during the 1870s and 1880s were the Leicester Infirmary, the Freemasons, the Licensed Victuallers Association and Leicester Conservative Club.

Drawing of the Bell Hotel, nineteenth century. This image is taken from R. Read, *Modern Leicester* (London, 1881).

The Leicester Infirmary ball of February 1871, at which the centenary of the hospital was celebrated, took place on a Tuesday evening at the assembly rooms in Leicester. This was a glittering occasion attended by the Mayor of Leicester and representatives of the county gentry, and the *Leicester Chronicle and Leicestershire Mercury* reported that 'Nicholson's band was in attendance and dancing was kept up with unflagging activity until four o'clock on Wednesday morning'.[17]

January was also the start of a season of annual dinners, which ran through from the beginning of the year to summer. Many organisations, from philanthropic associations to business groups, held an annual dinner, and these generally followed a standard format. The ritual was a shared meal followed by a series of toasts and speeches, then sometimes music provided by a local glee club or band. In March 1871 members of the Leicestershire Trade Protection Society gathered together for just such a dinner at the Bell Hotel. The mayor, various councillors and many leading local businessmen attended, and according to the local press they greatly enjoyed the excellent catering provided by Mr Thompson of The Bell. After dinner, patriotic toasts were drunk to queen and country, and to the mayor, magistrates and corporation. The evening then continued with further talking, toasting and camaraderie.[18]

Reports of Friendly society dinners showed that with some variation they followed the same format, although the dinners were less grand and the guests were working people rather than well-heeled businessmen. On one such occasion, in July 1871, the St Andrew's Lodge of Oddfellows met for dinner at St Andrew's schoolroom. The guests first enjoyed a meal, supplied this time by Mr Faulkes of the Blue Boar Inn, after which there followed patriotic toasts and toasts to the future and prosperity of the society. Finally, at midnight, the company marched in procession with their band to the marketplace, where they cheered and sang the national anthem before bringing their evening to an end.[19]

Annual business meetings could occur at any time between September and the summer, but the greatest number occurred in the months between January and June. These often took place in clusters, with organisations of a similar type holding their meetings round about the same time. One example of this was a cluster of meetings held by local banks and building societies in January, and another was a knot of meetings held by philanthropic bodies in the spring. Like the annual dinners, these annual business meetings followed a set format: a report was presented with accounts and officials for the next year were elected, all intertwined with votes of thanks and good wishes expressed for the future of the organisation. Here again working-class organisations, such as Friendly societies, adopted the same procedures as middle-class bodies, and all were duly reported in the press, although the leading middle-class groups and institutions were given far more column space, reflecting the hierarchical nature of local society.

Easter, like Christmas, marked a break in the rhythm of the calendar. There were special church services and often church bazaars, and the Easter bank holiday gave an opportunity for an excursion or for a day spent relaxing in Leicester. With Easter over, a new season of outdoor events began. This was the opening of the cricket season, and from April until August a Leicestershire cricket side played matches against visiting teams. In 1874 the Leicestershire Cricket Association acquired a new ground at Aylestone, and this helped increase the popularity of the game locally.[20] By the early 1880s there was a proliferation of amateur cricket clubs in Leicester, and new cricket facilities provided at Abbey and Victoria Park helped to encourage the game. One of the earliest groups boldly called itself the Leicester Cricket Club, but there were other clubs named after streets, workplaces and churches, in which friends, neighbours and workmates came together to form teams.[21] There was, of course, the inevitable hierarchy among the clubs in terms of social status. One of the more exclusive options was the Banks' Cricket Club. The president of this club was Thomas Paget of Paget's Bank, one of the leading banks in Leicester, and his five vice-presidents were the five other local bank managers. Prospective members of this club, if they were allowed to join, paid a substantial 10s 6d a year for the privilege. This top-priced subscription contrasted with cheaper options such as the Half-Holiday Club, the contact details of which were a modest terrace house in Highfields and which charged its members 5s a year. Many different types of people played cricket in Leicester, and it became part of the local way of life. In the late 1870s and early 1880s, however, 5s subscriptions were not cheap in relation to some workers' wages, and would have excluded those on a very low income. According to official statistics the highest paid boot and shoe workers in 1879 received 28s a week, while some of the lower paid only received £1: in 1884 the *Leicester Daily Mercury* printed a letter from a reader with a wife and two children who earned this salary. A breakdown of weekly household expenses showed that after buying food, and other expenses, he was left with 3½d. The typical sports subscription of 5s a week was the same amount he paid for his weekly rent.[22]

As well as cricket, gardening was an increasingly popular pastime, and a season of floral and horticultural shows from July until the end of August was also an important feature of the summer. In the early 1880s, the North, South, East and West Leicester Floral and Horticultural Societies represented different parts of the town, and each held an annual show. The North Leicester Society show of June 1882 was held in Central Northgate Street and, according to the *Leicester Daily Mercury*, not only members but 'throngs of visitors' came to look at the exhibits. The yearly subscription fee for the society was a relatively modest 2s 6d, and people were encouraged to participate by the fact that entries to the show did not have to be too ambitious. Many competitors entered plants they had grown in a windowbox, and children were allowed to enter bunches of wild flowers.[23]

In 1886 the town council drew on this enthusiasm for gardening to launch a regular August bank holiday event – the Abbey Park Flower Show. From initial low-key success the flower show mushroomed by the 1890s into an elaborate civic occasion with a grand opening ceremony, an official luncheon with speeches and toasts, musical entertainment and a water sports gala and fireworks. The Town Council Parks Department was responsible for the event, but it was managed in partnership with a range of voluntary associations. The Leicester rowing and swimming clubs organised the aquatic sports, local brass bands provided the music, the Leicester and Leicestershire Beekeepers Association organised a bees and honey exhibition, and the Leicester St John's Ambulance volunteers were present to deal with any medical emergency.[24]

The summer months were also a time when clubs, societies, evening classes and sometimes workplaces organised an annual group excursion. The grandeur of these events depended on the group concerned. Every June, members of the Leicester Lit and Phil embarked on an excursion to a local beauty spot. Swithland was the destination in 1881, and the outing followed a well-worn routine. Members left Leicester on a Saturday morning in a procession of carriages, and on arrival at their destination admired their natural surroundings. On this particular occasion the *Leicester Chronicle and Leicestershire Mercury* reported that they 'sat on the summit of the lofty crag enjoying the beauty of the scene and a little poetic and philosophical chat', after which they listened to a talk on an aspect of local botany. The day was rounded off by tea in an inn at Newton Linford, before returning to Leicester in the early evening.[25] This was certainly a more showy event than humbler equivalents, such as the 'All Saints Discussion Group annual walk to Swithland', although in both cases the outline of the day was very similar, with both parties going to the same venue, listening to a lecture on their surroundings, enjoying refreshments together and coming home.[26] The tone and social status were different, but the two occasions belonged to the same way of life.

Further summer attractions were public military reviews conducted by the various sections of the Leicestershire Regiment. A regular annual event in August that drew large crowds was the yearly review of the local Rifle Volunteers, held at the old racecourse, which had since become Victoria Park. The Rifle Volunteers were amateur soldiers, precursors of the Territorial Army, originally formed in 1859 to supplement home defence at a time when there was renewed and widespread anxiety about the military intentions of the French. There were town and county companies of volunteers, each company being a small club where members drilled together, enjoyed annual dinners and competed in shooting competitions against other local companies. Recruits were drawn from both the middle and working classes, and individual companies sometimes developed a particular class character. From 1879 onwards the town and county volunteers camped together each year at various sites in Leicestershire, an occasion that was open to spectators and attracted large crowds.[27]

As August drew to a close the annual cycle had passed through a whole year, and with the autumn coming on it was time for the new one to begin. The sequence of events that has been described here has picked out only some of the more prominent aspects of the Leicester calendar reported in the press during the 1870s and 1880s, but it shows the basic shape of the year at this time.

## Social Networks

The Leicester newspapers of the period conveyed the impression of a vibrant local community, and there was in fact some reality to this. The clubs, societies and other associations in the town genuinely did bring people together, added to which there were often connections between the separate groups – making them part of a larger social network.

A closer look at some of the educational organisations in the town illustrates this. The Leicester Lit and Phil, the Leicester Working Men's College and Institute, the All Saints' Discussion Group, the Leicester Secular Society and the Leicester Ladies' Reading Society all met regularly and all had links to other groups. The Lit and Phil and the Working Men's College were two of the largest and most high-profile educational organisations in Leicester in the 1870s and 1880s. The contrast in social class between the members of the first and the students of the second was marked, for while the Lit and Phil provided for 'leisure time cultivation of scientific interest by the professional and employing classes', the Working Men's College supplied 'institutional instruction for artisans' who had received little or no formal education.[28] Despite this, the two organisations shared some things. They both ran a yearly programme that started in the autumn, were managed by unpaid volunteers and received coverage in the local press. Both also deliberately set out to bring people together and create unity.

In the case of the Lit and Phil, measures intended to keep people together, including the ban on political and religious discussion, proved successful. In the 1880s, fifty years after the society was founded, there was a solid membership of around 300, lectures were well attended and members were a mix of Liberals, Conservatives, Anglicans and Nonconformists.[29] The approach at the Leicester Working Men's College, on the other hand, was to promote unity through Christian Socialist principles. The college was established in 1862 and was the origin of modern Vaughan College, which finally closed in 2013. The college started out in Friar Lane, where a few small rooms were used to provide a reading room, and the founder was the Revd David Vaughan, the vicar of St Martin's church, who modelled his college on the London Working Men's College, which had been established by F.D. Maurice, a well-known Christian Socialist and educationalist. Vaughan conceived the Leicester college as a community where students would bond through Christian conviction, fraternal cooperation and their desire for self-improvement. Edward Atkins, a teacher who was associated with the college from its first meeting and became the director in 1912 after Vaughan's death, wrote that Vaughan's approach was summed up in the motto 'Sirs ye are all brethren', which was emblazoned over the college door. People of all religions were invited to enrol, and every November a non-denominational service was held in St Martin's church, to which the students walked in procession through the town. Tea parties open to both students and their families were another feature of college life, and there was an annual summer outing. Vaughan also invited students to participate in the college management committee. The student numbers grew impressively, the college was rehoused in Blackfriars Street, and in 1892 a women's section was opened.[30] Vaughan's personality seems to have created an atmosphere of goodwill, and his efforts at building a community were successful enough to persuade former students to return as teachers, organisers and administrators.

Personal connections between the Lit and Phil and the Working Men's College were maintained by a small but influential group of middle-class individuals who held official positions in both organisations. One of these was David Vaughan himself and another was Thomas Cotchett Lee, a local manufacturer who served as college treasurer during the 1870s. Vaughan and Lee were re-elected year after year to the Lit and Phil council, the committee that organised the society. The length of their involvement promoted personal continuity and a stable though informal link between the two groups for more than forty years.[31]

The ideal of active citizenship was also a part of the ethos of both the Lit and Phil and the Working Men's College. The Lit and Phil members provided

Vaughan College, Great Central Street. The college moved to this building in 1908, where it stayed until 1962. This image is reproduced courtesy of the Record Office for Leicestershire, Leicester and Rutland.

Leicester with a museum, took an interest in preserving historical features of the town and encouraged local educational projects. Already in the 1880s there was talk of creating a local university, though at this point that remained just talk. At the Working Men's College, Vaughan tried to promote citizenship through education and open discussion. One strand of Christian Socialist belief held that working men could not take on the role of citizens or feel part of a community if they could not discuss the subjects of most interest to them.[32] A Friday evening discussion class was established and, unlike the Lit and Phil, there was no attempt to avoid controversy by imposing a bar on religious and political discussion. In January 1871 the *Leicester Chronicle and Leicestershire Mercury*

# ERNEST GIMSON

Ernest Gimson (1864–1919) was an architect, craftsman and a leading furniture designer associated with the Arts and Crafts movement. Born in Leicester, he was the fourth son of Josiah Gimson, a freethinker and local entrepreneur who had established the Vulcan engineering works near Humberstone Road and in the early 1880s provided financial backing to build the Secular Hall in Humberstone Gate.

As a young man Ernest Gimson was articled to the well-known Leicester architect Isaac Barradale, and also attended the Leicester School of Art. A turning point in his life came in 1884 when he heard William Morris speak on art and socialism at the Leicester Secular Hall. After the meeting Morris returned to the Gimson home for dinner, allowing Ernest to make his further acquaintance.

The following year, with Morris's help, Gimson obtained a position at the offices of the architect John Dando Sedding, which were situated next to Morris and Co. in Oxford Street. While in London he became part of a social circle of young architects influenced by Morris, and he participated in the Art Workers Guild and the Society for the Protection of Ancient Buildings, associations linked with this milieu. Also part of the circle were Ernest and Sydney Barnsley, the sons of a Birmingham builder, with whom Gimson became close friends.

In the early 1890s, Gimson and the Barnsleys moved to rural Gloucestershire together and settled in the Cirencester area – first at Pinbury and then at Sapperton – where they set up workshops. Gimson took a practical approach to design, and acquired and developed skills in chair-making and plasterwork. He was deeply interested in the history and techniques of traditional craftsmen, and this attracted him to rural life and surroundings. He and his wife Emily, whom he married in 1900, also shared an interest in traditional music and dancing.

Gimson's architectural work included two houses in Leicester, the White House in North Avenue and Inglewood in Ratcliffe Road. His furniture designs, produced by a team of skilled craftsmen, were prized pieces that attracted a range of wealthy buyers. These won him particular prestige as well as a lasting legacy.

## Sources

M. Comino, *Gimson and the Barnsleys: Wonderful Furniture of a Commonplace Kind* (London, 1980); F. MacCarthy, 'Gimson, Ernest William (1864–1914)' in *Oxford Dictionary of National Biography* (Oxford, 2004), www.oxforddnb.com/view/article/37458, accessed 27 October 2012; W.H. Lethaby, A.H. Powell and F.L.Griggs, *Ernest Gimson His Life and Work* (Stratford on Avon, 1924).

reported that at the weekly discussion class there had been a 'long and animated' discussion about the school board, during which 'the parsons' came in 'for a large share of hard knocks'.[33] This seemed to show a genuine tolerance of free discussion, especially as David Vaughan sat on the school board himself.

Middle-class initiatives for the working classes in the first half of the nineteenth century were often unsuccessful, because the founders and organisers were too busy trying to mould the students to their way of thinking. The education provided was too obviously directed at strengthening the social fabric rather than educating the individual, and this was one of the reasons why the earlier Leicester Mechanics' Institute eventually failed.[34] By the mid-nineteenth century the working classes expected better than this: for a college or a class to work there needed to be a compromise between middle-class and working-class expectations, a balance that was more successfully achieved by the Leicester Working Men's College.

The same tolerant approach to free debate was also taken by another high-profile group in the town, the All Saints' Open Discussion Class, which was founded in 1850 for a group of working men by Joseph Dare at the Unitarian Domestic Mission.[35] In 1870 the discussion class was one of a range of activities for both men and women run by the Domestic Mission, including a Sunday School, sewing classes, tea gatherings and window box competitions.[36] At a meeting of the class reported in the press in 1871, the speakers agreed that it was the free exchange of ideas and the encouragement for all to participate that had allowed the students to bond. One student spoke of his satisfaction at the 'perfect freedom' members of the class enjoyed, where 'any subject might be introduced, whether political or religious, and discussed, without let or hindrance', while another stressed that 'all were desired to take part, composing a paper or speaking in turn'. Another speaker praised the longevity of the class, remarking that it had been so long in existence that it reminded him of Tennyson's brook: 'Men may come and men may go but I flow on forever.'[37] Enthusiasm for the class also encouraged members to write poetry themselves, and in 1873 a poem was published celebrating the twentieth summer outing of the group and the long friendships of those who took part.[38] This class, like the Working Men's College, was far from isolated. The president, secretary and treasurer at the Mission were all Lit and Phil members, as were many of the individuals who subscribed to the Mission and kept the All Saints' class afloat.

**SOCIALIST LEAGUE.**

THE FOLLOWING

**COURSE OF LECTURES**

WILL BE GIVEN IN

**THE CO-OPERATIVE HALL,**

HIGH STREET.

| | |
|---|---|
| TUESDAY, FEB 4. | **H. HALLIDAY SPARLING,** (OF LONDON). *Sub-Editor of "Commonweal." Author of "Irish Minstrelsy."* SUBJECT: "THE EVOLUTED CANNIBAL." |
| TUESDAY, FEB. II. | **ANNIE BESANT,** (LONDON SCHOOL BOARD), Subject: "The BASIS OF SOCIALISM." |
| TUESDAY, MARCH 4. | **STEPNIAK, (Nihilist),** *Author of "The Russian Storm Cloud," "Underground Russia," "The Career of a Nihilist," &c.* SUBJECT: 'RUSSIAN DEMOCRACY.' |
| TUESDAY, MARCH II. | **WILLIAM MORRIS,** *Author of "The Earthly Paradise," A Dream of John Ball," "Pilgrims of Hope." Editor of the the "Commonweal," &c.* SUBJECT: "THE CLASS STRUGGLE." |

*Doors open 7.30 p.m.     Commence 8 p.m.*

ADMISSION FREE.   Collection to defray Expenses.   Discussion Invited.

Notice for lectures at the Cooperative Hall, reflecting the increasing interest in socialism in the late nineteenth century. William Morris also lectured on art and socialism at the Secular Hall in 1884. This handbill is from the Gorrie Collection and reproduced courtesy of the University of Leicester Special Collections.

**Rutland Skating Rink.**

**VISIT OF**

**J. KEIR HARDIE, M.P.**

**TO LEICESTER.**

Under the auspices of the Labour Club, Belgrave Gte.

**A Public MEETING**

WILL BE HELD ON

**SUNDAY, MAY 27, 1894,**

When an Address will be given by Mr. KEIR HARDIE on

**"Social Democratic Government."**

**T. F. RICHARDS,**

(Of the Boot and Shoe Operatives Union) will preside

☞ Doors open at 7 p.m.; chair to be taken at 7.30.

On Tuesday & Wednesday, May 29 & 30

**Mr. FRED. BROCKLEHURST,**

Secretary of the Labour Church, Manchester, Candidate for Bolton, will address two MASS MEETINGS:

**Tuesday, HUMBERSTONE GATE;**
**Wednesday, MARKET PLACE.**

SUBJECTS—"Socialist Aims and Methods," and "The Ethics of Socialism."

**Meetings to commence each Evening at Eight o'clock.**
**Collections towards Expenses.**

*HAMMOND & SON, Printers, &c., 1, Newarke Street. Leicester.*

Notice for a lecture by Keir Hardie. This handbill is from the Gorrie Collection and reproduced courtesy of the University of Leicester Special Collections.

The All Saints' Open Discussion Group was a particularly long-standing class, but it was not the only one of its type in the town. There were others springing up, which became known as adult schools. Often they had a connection to a Nonconformist church, one well-known example being the Soar Lane Adult School set up by the Quakers. Other adult schools in Leicester included those held at Sanvey Gate, Dover Street, Paradise Mission, Belgrave and Clarendon Park. It seems likely that enthusiastic students of these schools and the Working Men's College would have also taken advantage of the free lectures at the museum, making these talks occasions that linked up the self-improvement groups.

The Leicester Secular Society was another organisation that offered opportunities for debate but in a very different context. The society was founded in the 1850s, and provided a haven and a forum for those who either questioned or rejected the value of religion. Lancaster's account of working-class politics in the late Victorian period draws a direct line of descent between the Secular Society and the radical artisan culture that flourished in Leicester in the first half of the century.[39] The membership was from a mix of social backgrounds: the group was not about the middle classes providing educational opportunities for working people but about free-thinking individuals meeting on an equal basis to listen to speakers and discuss related issues. In 1881 the society increased its profile significantly when the Secular Hall, a handsome, custom-built meeting place, was opened in central Humberstone Gate, a venue that was used not only for lectures but was also a thriving social club. Busts of Tom Paine, Voltaire, Robert Owen and, rather surprisingly, Jesus decorated the façade of the building: these figures were chosen because of the example they had set in questioning 'priestly pretensions'. A grand ceremony was held to celebrate the opening of the hall, and among the guests was Charles Bradlaugh. He was the elected MP for Northampton and a prominent atheist, who at the time was fighting his exclusion from the House of Commons for refusing to swear an oath of loyalty on the Bible. The society's lecture programme in the following years lived up to the grandeur of the hall with an impressive array of visiting speakers, including George Bernard Shaw and William Morris.[40]

There were some local manufacturers involved in the Secular Society, most notably Josiah Gimson, proprietor of a local engineering firm, on whose initiative the Secular Hall had been acquired. Gimson had been involved in the society from the outset, and he represented a moderate strand of secularism that

Drawing of Gimson and Co. engineering works established by Josiah Gimson. Gimson's money was used to build the Secular Hall in 1881. Josiah's son Sydney Ansell Gimson was for many years president of the Secular Society, and another son, Ernest, was an architect and furniture designer associated with the Arts and Crafts movement. This image is taken from R. Read, *Modern Leicester* (1881).

promoted self-improvement and social reform through rational morality rather than exhibiting aggression towards Christians or preaching revolution. An exchange between London secularists and Gimson on the pages of a secularist periodical, *The Freethinker*, gives a flavour of this, as well as demonstrating the strong local identity that the Leicester group claimed. The London editors acidly offered the Leicester Secular Society 'a piece of advice', suggesting that a little respectability might be exchanged for a little free thought. To this Gimson replied that it was possible to discuss secularism 'without endlessly hammering away at God and the Bible ... or so we think in Leicester'.[41]

There were, however, more radical voices in the Secular Society. In the 1880s and 1890s the working-class membership grew, and many of these members were attracted by socialist ideas that were having an increasingly widespread impact in Britain. One prominent member was Tom Barclay, a hosiery worker of Irish parents, who worked at Corah's and was active in the Leicester Amalgamated Hosiery Union. Barclay had been a student at the Leicester Working Men's College, had spent a great deal of time in self-study and had gradually gravitated towards the Secular Society. He became a socialist after hearing William Morris speak at the society in 1895, and he formed a local branch of the Socialist League in Leicester. In the 1890s he also founded a local labour and socialist newspaper called the *Leicester Pioneer*. As well as reporting news and giving a socialist angle to current issues, this advertised meetings, talks and other events of interest to political sympathisers in Leicester.[42]

Unsurprisingly there was some local disapproval of the Secular Society. Religion was embedded in the social and cultural life of the town, and overt questioning or rejection of religious faith was clearly going to offend some devout churchgoers. David Vaughan, for example, was wary of the Secular Society, for despite his encouragement of free speech he regarded religion as a necessary ingredient of community, and thought irreligion a serious threat to class cooperation.[43] Despite the hostility from some quarters, the society was an accepted part of the local scene, as illustrated by the extensive and respectful coverage the press gave to the opening of the Secular Hall in 1881; and indeed is easy to see how the restrained style of secularism espoused by Josiah Gimson could fit into the social landscape without undue disruption. Gimson was also a member of the Lit and Phil as well as a town councillor, and in this way created

The Midland station was built in 1892 to replace the original Campbell Street station, erected in 1840. This Edwardian postcard is taken from the author's own collection.

a link between the Secular Society and other more mainstream institutions.

Women as well as men participated in educational groups in Leicester during this period, but for the most part male domination of local intellectual life in the mid- to late Victorian period remained unchallenged. By 1870, however, women's roles and rights were prominent in national public debate, and some headway had been made in improving opportunities for their secondary and higher education.[44] At the Lit and Phil women had attended lectures as visitors since the 1830s, but for many years were not allowed to become members. In 1870 a breakthrough was made when women were permitted for the first time to become associate members, but relatively few women took up this offer at first, suggesting perhaps that they did not find the option particularly appealing.

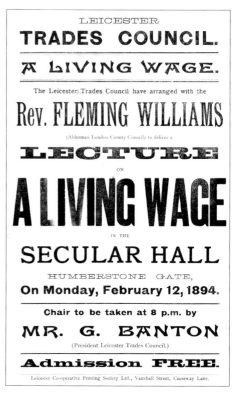

LEICESTER
# TRADES COUNCIL.
## A LIVING WAGE.

The Leicester Trades Council have arranged with the

### Rev. FLEMING WILLIAMS

(Alderman London County Council) to deliver a

## LECTURE

ON

# A LIVING WAGE

IN THE

# SECULAR HALL

HUMBERSTONE GATE,

**On Monday, February 12, 1894.**

**Chair to be taken at 8 p.m. by**

## MR. G. BANTON

(President Leicester Trades Council.)

**Admission FREE.**

Leicester Co-operative Printing Society Ltd., Vauxhall Street, Causeway Lane.

Notice for a lecture at the Secular Hall. This handbill is from the Gorrie Collection and is reproduced courtesy of the University of Leicester Special Collections.

Meanwhile, the Leicester Ladies Reading Society was established. The story of this society is told by long-standing member Gertrude Ellis, who wrote a history of the group in 1930 when it was finally wound up.[45] It was a private society, not publicised in the local newspapers, and it met in members' homes. The membership was entirely middle class and included women from some of Leicester's most well-known business and professional families: Corah, Gimson, Ellis, Paget and Clephan. An important bond within the group was the desire to undertake serious study, for the members committed themselves to producing regular papers on historical and literary topics. This was probably the reason why the women preferred their own society to the Lit and Phil, where they would have played a more passive role, with no chance of contributing a paper or sitting on the organising council. As members of the Leicester Ladies Reading Society they could be more genuinely involved, and this sustained the group. Ellis recalled how important the society was to members, and how close they became. She related how 'the meetings came round as regularly as the winters themselves and wove themselves into the fabric of life through youth and maturity, marriage and bereavement to old age'.[46] Although the Leicester Ladies Reading Society was in some ways rather inward-looking, Ellis perceived the group as 'a small local development in a countrywide, stirring of life in the education of women', implying that the founder members were consciously aware of their contribution to a national pattern. With regard to local society, the women expressed their identification with the town through their name, and the rather formal way the reading society was organised, with an appointed president and secretary and a regular annual meeting, suggested that despite the private nature of the society's activities there was an aspiration among the members to be considered part of local public life; though in the male-dominated society of the 1870s and 1880s this was difficult to achieve.

## New Influences, New Organisations and a Growing Social Calendar: 1890–1914

In the decades between the 1880s and the outbreak of the First World War the number of clubs, societies and other volunteer-run organisations in the town increased in number, and the memberships of some of the organisations that were already established also grew. The framework of the annual calendar remained much the same, but the growing level of organised social activity in the town meant that the Leicester newspapers had a far more complicated schedule to report.

A new social and cultural season still began each autumn, and the press continued to report on long-standing events such as the fortnightly lectures at the Leicester Lit and Phil. By the 1890s, however, reports of the lectures were less detailed as there was so much else to report. One feature of this fuller social calendar was that the middle ground between the activities of the town elite and the events organised by traditional working-class associations, such as the Friendly societies, began to fill out. Against a nationwide trend of increased incomes and better educational provision, a growing lower middle class of white collar workers was emerging, and a greater number of unpretentious middle of the road dinners, concerts and other events were reported in the press.

Groups such as the Leicester Philharmonic Society continued to provide 'serious' musical entertainment, but there were also many informal concert parties with less highbrow musical programmes. In Leicester in the 1890s there was a pool of local singers who were often called upon for these occasions, events such as the Leicester Football Club annual smoking concert of 1893, at which local singer James McRobie, who performed songs such as 'The Jovial Beggar' and 'Little Sue', helped provide the entertainment.[47]

By the 1890s working people generally had more leisure time, and the number of sports clubs in Leicester multiplied. Cycling, rowing and swimming all became popular, and there were very large numbers of cricket and football teams in the town. Club teams were organised into associations and leagues, which competed with each other, adding to the local social networks based around sport. Many churches in Leicester now had a church hall, and these were used for a range of social activities, such as mothers' meetings, clubs for adolescents, literary societies and often a football or cricket team, which gave people living on a low income a chance to play. Pubs were also sometimes the base for sports teams, such as the cycle club linked to the Marquis of Wellington on London Road.

Football was also becoming a very popular spectator sport throughout the north of England and the Midlands, and this was the case in Leicester. The Fosse Football Club, later to become Leicester Football Club, was the most successful club in town. It was based at its own Filbert Street ground, and in the early 1890s had a large and enthusiastic membership of well over a thousand. Both men and women went to see the matches, and a young couple could buy a cut-rate 'lady and gent' annual subscription for 7s 6d a year if they wanted to keep costs down. Going to rugby matches was another very popular outing at this time, and the Leicester Tigers rugby football club also had a membership of around a thousand.[48] This intense enthusiasm for sport, both participatory and as a spectator, continued to gather momentum throughout the 1890s. Sport as the number one pastime had come to stay.

A further strand of activity that shaped the yearly calendar and gave it a civic stamp was the mayor's annual schedule of visits to the municipal institutions and leading voluntary associations of Leicester. This symbolised the link between the town council and the organisations visited, stressing the importance of all those involved in the life of the town; this was further underlined by the press publicity. Towards the turn of the century Leicester benefited from a

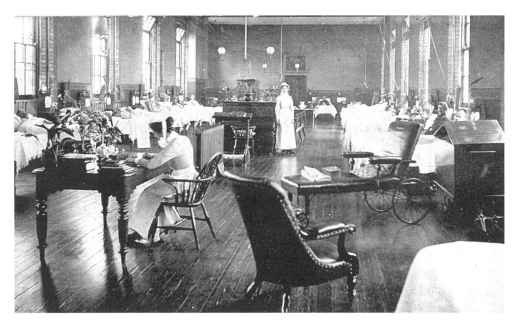

St Luke's Ward at the infirmary. This Edwardian postcard is from the author's own collection.

series of high-profile and active mayors, the most notable of whom were Israel Hart, Thomas Wright and Edward Wood. They all served more than once, and added new items to the mayoral schedule. The mayor's Christmas visit to the workhouse was just one event that always received extensive newspaper coverage. National attitudes to poverty and social welfare were at last becoming less punitive, and this visit gave the mayor a symbolic opportunity to express a communal responsibility for the town's poor, reflecting this change.

By the Edwardian and pre-war years the mayor's programme continued throughout the year. This was not just a public relations exercise imposed by the town council: a book of correspondence belonging to Charles Lakin, elected mayor in 1909, shows that he received a constant stream of eager invitations from all types of organisations including commercial, educational and sporting groups as well as churches and schools.[49] The range of invitations Lakin accepted shows that he encouraged contact with a wide variety of groups, recognising all sorts of social activity as a valuable part of urban life. Priority, however, was always given to philanthropic organisations. Thus an invitation to the Leicester Glee Club or the Rovers' Bicycle Club dinner could be turned down if necessary, but events organised by organisations such as the Leicester Wycliffe Society for Helping the Blind or the Leicester Guild of the Crippled were routinely accepted.

# Politics and Protest

By the end of the nineteenth century Britain was edging towards democracy. Electoral reform acts in 1867 and 1884 had extended the vote to approximately 60 per cent of adult males, and in the early 1880s the number of political clubs and associations in Leicester and its hinterland increased as both the Liberal and Conservative parties tried to influence voters. The Liberals had dominated the town since the 1830s, and it was the Liberal Party that for the most part attracted the new working-class vote.

Historically, relationships between the employing classes in Leicester and their workers had been better than in bigger northern industrial towns such as Manchester or Leeds. Leicester had been late to fully industrialise, and the small and intimate workplaces of the town where an employer had more direct relationship with his workforce tended to support harmonious inter-class relations rather than aggravate hostility. Even when the bigger factories were established, some employers, such as Corah's, tried to maintain good relationships by taking a paternalistic approach to their employees, and for much of the time they responded with deference. By the last decades of the century, however, attitudes were changing. Trade unions had held full legal recognition since 1871 and were an accepted part of society, but in the 1890s the nature of trade unionism changed. This was a time of increasing class consciousness among the working classes, and union membership increased and became politicised. Whereas previously the unions had sought merely to improve working conditions, now socialist ideas were more widespread and there were voices calling not just for reform but for radical change in society and the redistribution of wealth. During the 1890s many employers, alarmed by these changes, set out to undermine union power.

The Leicester town directory of 1894 listed nearly forty trade union groups affiliated to the Leicester Trades Council. The largest by far was the National Union of Boot and Shoe Operatives (NUBSO), which had 10,000 members in Leicester, around a quarter of the national membership. Second to this was the Leicester Amalgamated Hosiery Union, with approximately 3,000 members. The rest were much smaller, including branches of railway worker unions, engineers and groups representing particular areas of the footwear and hosiery industries. Small groups regularly held meetings at a string of town centre pubs. Typical were the engineers who met at the Red Cow in Belgrave Gate and the woolsorters who met at the Red Lion in Highcross Street.[50]

By 1895 a crisis had long been simmering in the boot and shoe industry. There was increasing competition from America, where footwear manufacturers had developed more advanced technology. British manufacturers argued that the industry needed to adopt new forms of mechanisation and updated practices in order to survive, but the workforce resisted this, fearing that it would result in the loss of jobs. Despite growing intransigence on both sides, national confrontation between the manufacturers and workers was headed off between 1892 and late 1894. The showdown finally came on 13 March 1895, when the employers launched a factory lock-out. This meant that shoe workers in many factories throughout the country, including Leicester, were

# The LOCK-OUT
IN THE
# BOOT AND SHOE TRADE.

TO THE

### Boot and Shoe Operatives, Male and Female, Unionists and Non-unionists.

Fellow Workers,—We have decided to hold a

# Monstre Demonstration

## ON THURSDAY AFTERNOON NEXT,
MARCH 21st. 1895.

And parade some of the principal streets of the town, and then walk to the

### Belgrave Road Grounds,

Where Addresses on the crisis will be delivered by the responsible officials of the Union.

Every man and woman whether Unionist or Non-Unionist are requested to be in the

## Market Place,

Promptly at **2 o'clock,** as the procession will start at **2-15** sharp, taking the following route :—

Leave the Market Place by way of Cheapside, and proceed down Humberstone Road, Colden Street, Willow Street, Wharf Street, Rutland Street, Granby Street, London Road, De Montfort Street, Princess Street, Regent Street, Carlton Street, Infirmary Square, Jarrom Street, Asylum Street, The Newarkes, Oxford Street, Southgate Street, High Street, Belgrave Road.

Marshalls will be appointed with full powers to act, and the Procession will be required to be **three deep.** The Females to head the Procession after the first banner.

By Order of the Executive,

No. 2 Branch.
E. BUSH, President.
W. H. LOWE, Secretary.

No. 1 Branch.
R. CORT, President.
T. F. RICHARDS, Vice-President.
H. H. WOOLLEY, Secretary.

Leicester Co-operative Printing Society Limited, Vauxhall Street, Causeway Lane.

Notice for the shoeworkers' demonstration in 1895, the year of the factory lock-out. This handbill is from the Gorrie Collection reproduced courtesy of the University of Leicester Special Collections.

barred from their factories until they complied with manufacturers' demands. The workers held out for six weeks, and there was a large demonstration in Leicester on 25 March that many townspeople turned out to watch. However, after six weeks the union strike fund had completely run out and the shoe workers were compelled to give in, with a settlement made to the advantage of the manufacturers.[51]

The impact of socialist ideals, combined with the need for better political representation of the working classes, led to the founding of the Labour Representation Committee in 1899. By 1906 this had become the Labour Party. With its broad church of socialist ideas and support from the trade unions, it set British labour politics firmly on the road to evolutionary change and reform rather than radical change. In 1900, Ramsay MacDonald became a Labour candidate for Leicester, but by splitting the Liberal vote he allowed a Conservative candidate to be returned. This was a notable change for a town that had been Liberal for so long, and in reaction to this the Liberals and Labour created a working relationship for their mutual political benefit.[52]

In the decade following the lock-out the decline in the boot and shoe industry worsened, and by the early years of the twentieth century poverty and unemployment were biting hard. By this time, Christian Socialists had established several Labour churches in Leicester, in an attempt to link the Labour movement with Christian ideals, and they held Sunday lectures at which working-class politics and social welfare issues were discussed in a Christian context. George White and Amos Sherriff, two local men who were involved in this circle, took the lead in organising a march of unemployed shoemakers to London in June 1905.[53] The support shown by the town was exceptional, apparently a genuine expression of community. The *Daily Mercury* reported that thousands of townspeople, men, women and children came out on the streets and crowded into the marketplace to witness the 500 unemployed men set out on their journey.[54] The men lined up in twos, stretching in a long line from one side of the marketplace to the other, with their leaders busy among them. Amos Sherriff was 'a veritable soul of energy, commanding here, cajoling there and making his presence felt everywhere'. George White issued instructions from the back of a vehicle in the centre of the marketplace 'with tact and unfailing good humour'. The men carried very little with them: some had water bottles and others a greatcoat or a blanket slung over their shoulder; they only took enough food for the first meal after their departure. The reporter commented on the seriousness and 'respectability' of the marchers, and noted that 'several men by their gait and stiff upright carriage showed at once that they had been in the army'; this was confirmed by 'the medals proudly displayed on their breasts'. As midday approached the crowd reached 'multitudinous proportions'. The reporter observed that 'all classes of the community' were there, and that 'they stood in a mass of sympathetic humanity extending from one side of the marketplace practically to the other'. At midday the vicar of St Mark's got up on the vehicle that was serving as a stage and addressed the crowd; he was the Revd F. Lewis Donaldson, known throughout Leicester as the 'vicar of the unemployed'. He gave a stirring sermon on the righteousness of the marchers' cause, and after he had given a blessing the march to

Leicester welcomes the unemployed shoeworkers back from their march to London in 1905. This postcard is from the author's own collection.

London began. A band played the hymn 'Lead Kindly Light' and the crowd and marchers sang together as the procession left the marketplace, making its way to Granby Street and up London Road. The reporter observed that 'the whole scene was remarkably impressive and never likely to be forgotten by those who witnessed it'. The route through the town was 'literally packed with spectators', and it was said that even when the Prince of Wales visited in 1882 to open Abbey Park the crowds were not so dense.

It is uncertain how much the march achieved, but it drew attention to the distress and poverty caused by unemployment. Lancaster observes that the attention given by local Labour activists to the problems of the unemployed attracted support to Labour, and, in the 1906 election Ramsay MacDonald was returned as a Labour MP for Leicester.[55].

The idea that there was a town community in late Victorian and Edwardian Leicester should not be exaggerated, for there were significant divisions between local people in terms of class, wealth, politics, religion and sex. Yet it is also true that thousands of people shared enough sense of a local identity to attend the opening of Abbey Park in 1882, to celebrate the improvements that had been made. In 1905 townspeople came out again in full force, this time to express a shared local sympathy for the Leicester boot and shoeworkers, who had been reduced to poverty by unemployment.

The calendar of associational events described each year in the local newspapers gives a clue to how this sense of local attachment and solidarity was created and sustained. Leicester people came together socially in many different groups according to their class, sex and interests, and these were genuinely small communities where they got together with friends. They were often linked to each other by overlapping memberships or personal contacts, and even when there were no links the groups, with their annual meetings, dinners and summer outings, shared a similar way of doing things that all could relate to. The newspapers underlined this with the extensive coverage they gave to these activities, representing Leicester as a place with a coherent local culture to which townspeople could feel they belonged.

seven

# THE GREAT WAR AND
# THE INTERWAR YEARS

On 28 June 1914 the assassination of Archduke Franz Joseph Ferdinand in Sarajevo heralded the outbreak of war in Europe. Bank holiday weekend began in Britain on 1 August and the people of Leicester, for the most part unaware of what was coming, enjoyed the break in the usual way. Some stayed at home to relax, perhaps taking time to visit the popular Abbey Park Flower Show,

while others left the town on excursion trains, often heading for the east coast seaside resorts. Then, on Tuesday 4 August, the first day back from the holiday, war with Germany was declared. International tensions had been building for many years, but when war came it was unexpected: national news had been more focused on industrial disruption led by the dockers, miners and railway workers, instability in Ireland and the suffragette campaign.

The struggle for women's suffrage had made an impact in Leicester, with both militant and non-militant groups campaigning for change. A Leicester branch of the Women's Social and Political Union, founded in 1907, was strong enough by 1910 to open a permanent shop in Bowling Green Street in the town centre. The women were active in rallies and demonstrations both locally and nationally,

Leicester suffragettes in the town centre. This image is reproduced courtesy of the Record Office for Leicestershire, Leicester and Rutland. Thanks are also due to Malcolm Noble for help in reproducing this.

and several were imprisoned. One outstanding local activist was shoe machinist Alice Hawkins who worked at Equity Shoes, invited the Pankhursts to Leicester, and was imprisoned no less than five times in support of the cause. During the militant campaign between 1912 and 1913 the suffragettes made various attacks on property in Leicester and the county, the most dramatic of which was the burning down of Blaby railway station in 1913.

In Leicester things had improved economically since the difficult days of the boot and shoemakers' march to London. A light engineering industry that had emerged in the 1890s had further developed and brought new employment opportunities, a welcome addition to the two staples of knitting and boot and shoe manufacture. Improvements to town facilities had also continued, including a new concert venue, the De Montfort Hall, designed by Leicester architects Stockdale Harrison and opened with civic ceremony in 1913. Unfortunately, however, these local preoccupations were now seriously disrupted.

## The First World War

With the declaration of war the mobilisation of the army and reservists began, and there was an immediate recruitment drive. The patriotic fervour with which men all over the country rushed to join up has been well recorded. In Leicester, however, despite an early burst of enthusiasm, recruitment was not as successful as in many other parts of the country. From the outset Ramsay MacDonald was forthright in his opposition to Britain's involvement in the war, and before long he resigned as chairman of the Labour Party. The extent to which his stance affected local attitudes is uncertain, but by the spring of 1915 the low level of recruitment in Leicester was well known outside the town, and an embarrassment to the corporation. Nevertheless, when the battalions of the Leicestershire Regiment departed for war they were seen off by cheering crowds. [1]

As soon as the war began so did the preparation for casualties, and the old county lunatic asylum next to Victoria Park was commandeered for this purpose; it was refurbished and renamed the Fifth Northern Military Hospital. The hospital, now the administrative building of the University of Leicester, was in a healthy position high up on Welford Road, with easy access to major roads and the Midland railway station. A string of auxiliary hospitals was prepared as back-up: these included the Leicester Royal Infirmary and the Poor Law

Wounded soldiers at the railway station during the First World War. This image is reproduced courtesy of the Record Office for Leicestershire, Leicester and Rutland.

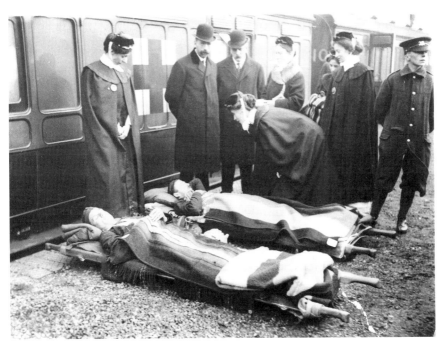

Wounded soldiers at the railway station during the First World War. This image is reproduced courtesy of the Record Office for Leicestershire, Leicester and Rutland.

Lord Kitchener inspects the Leicester Scouts. This image is reproduced courtesy of the Record Office for Leicestershire, Leicester and Rutland.

Infirmary in North Evington, as well as several large houses in the county which were converted for the purpose.

For the families of men who had gone to the Front this was often a time of severe hardship. Some men who had worked as public servants retained their pay while away fighting, but others were left dependent on inadequate separation allowances from the army or navy or, if they were lucky, help from special relief funds. Ben Beazley has vividly recounted how in August 1914, after the Leicestershire and Leicester Patriotic Fund had been established to help support the families of men who had joined up, women queued for hours in the hot sun outside the Magazine drill hall in order to register for assistance. Such was the heat that several women fainted during this ordeal, and many found after their long wait that if they were receiving any other allowance, no matter how paltry, they were not entitled to any further help.[2]

In the autumn of 1914 there was widespread belief that the war would be over quickly, and those suffering hardship held onto the hope that the men would be home by Christmas. This, of course, proved to be a vain hope, and it was not long before the news of mass casualties filtered through. As the years dragged on, with shortages of basic commodities, price rises and no end in sight, life became more difficult.

*Right* Soldiers outside the Fifth Northern General Hospital, now the Fielding Johnson building of the University of Leicester. This postcard is from the author's own collection.

*Below* Patients in the Fifth Northern General Hospital. This postcard is from the author's own collection.

Civilians wait in the breadline during the First World War. This image is reproduced courtesy of the Record Office for Leicestershire, Leicester and Rutland.

Everyone was expected to support the war effort, and civilians were constantly called upon to contribute to fundraising initiatives and projects to keep the men at the Front supplied with comforts such as woollen clothing and cigarettes. Many women and men also gave their time by putting themselves forward for the Voluntary Aid Detachment, an organisation that recruited volunteer nurses and auxiliary helpers such as cooks and clerks for work in British hospitals, as well as overseas in the field. The great majority of VADs, as they were known, were women. The war famously enabled women to take a more active role in society. In addition to VAD work, they took on paid jobs that had previously been done by men, including work in banks and offices, jobs that became available with the men away at the front. In Leicester the workforce of the boot and shoe industry was much depleted after a fifth of the operatives were mobilised. The war, however, resulted in increased demand for boots by armed forces, which meant that the boot manufacturing firms in Leicester had jobs to offer, vacancies that could be filled by women.

When the war came to an end in November 1918 the town celebrated with bonfires, torchlit processions and church services. Nearly 10,000 men from

Leicester and Leicestershire had been killed during the four years, and many more had been wounded and left disabled. As well as this, 1,600 civilian lives in the town were lost in the influenza epidemic of 1918–19. In May 1919 the first demobilised troops returned to Leicester, and the townspeople tried to resume their normal lives.

## The Interwar Years: Civic Pride, Economic Success and Social Activity

There is a perception that by the post-war decades civic pride had gone into decline in provincial towns. In the late nineteenth century, London had grown as a financial and social centre, shifting the focus away from provincial town life. Other factors, including the impact of the railways, telephone and the mass circulation of newspapers, had made society more heterogeneous, highlighting the national at the expense of the local.[3] In the large northern industrial towns of Manchester and Leeds it seemed that the appetite for civic celebration and ceremony was less intense, while in nearby Birmingham the grand civic funeral of Joseph Chamberlain in 1914 has been cited as a final, important ceremony that marked the end of an era.[4] This was not the case in Leicester, where the 1920s and 1930s were a highpoint of civic celebration.

One thing that Leicester had to celebrate was its promotion from town to city. Before the war, several unsuccessful applications had been made for city status, but after George V visited the town in 1919 the request was at last granted. In 1926 the city gained further prestige when a new Leicester diocese was created, and St Martin's church became a cathedral.

In the post-war years, long-held plans to create a university college in Leicester were also coming to fruition. The idea of a university college had been floated first in 1880 by the Leicester Literary and Philosophical Society, and in 1912 the new president of the society, Dr Astley Clarke, reintroduced the idea in his inaugural lecture. After the war, when the fifth Northern Military Hospital on Victoria Park closed, Thomas Fielding Johnson, a Leicester textile manufacturer and member of the Lit and Phil, bought the building to house the proposed college, presenting it as a gift to the city. The project was given an added boost by attracting the active support of the shoe manufacturer Sir Jonathan North, who had served as mayor throughout the war. When an inspired suggestion

An early student of the new Leicester University College was the novelist, scientist and public commentator Charles Percy Snow (1905–80). Snow was born into a lower-middle-class Leicester family, the second of four sons. His parents, William and Ada, lived at Richmond Road in Aylestone, and his father, who worked as a cashier for a shoe manufacturer, was the organist first at St James's, Aylestone Park, and then at St Mary de Castro.

Snow attended Alderman Newton's School, where he was an outstanding student, and in 1925 he went on to Leicester University College, where he took a first and higher degree in science. Subsequently he won a prestigious research scholarship, went to Cambridge and by 1930 was a fellow of Christ's College.

After a short time, however, Snow concluded that his main vocation was as a novelist rather than in science. His most famous work, the eleven novels that comprise the 'Strangers and Brothers' series, was written between 1935 and 1970. These novels follow the life of the central character Lewis Eliot, and two of them, *Strangers and Brothers* (later published as *George Passant*) and *Time of Hope*, are largely set in a Midlands town clearly based on Leicester. The novels were highly successful and brought Snow acclaim nationally and internationally.

During the Second World War, Snow was responsible for recruiting scientists to the government radar programme, and in the post-war years he continued recruitment work as a civil service commissioner. In 1964, under the Wilson government, he was appointed Parliamentary Secretary to the Minister of Technology.

Snow is also associated with the phrase 'The Two Cultures', first used in an article in the *New Statesman* in 1956 and then in his Rede Lecture of 1959: 'The Two Cultures and the Scientific Revolution'. The two cultures referred to were those inhabited respectively by arts and science intellectuals. Snow perceived there to be an unhealthy gap between the two groups that prevented them from contributing as much as they could to the wider society. He particularly lamented the lack of even basic scientific knowledge among many of those prominent in the arts. The opinions Snow expressed were controversial, and led to considerable and sometimes acrimonious debate.

During his life, Snow received formal honours for his work, receiving a CBE in 1943 and a knighthood in 1957. When he accepted a life peerage in 1966 he became known as Baron Snow of the City of Leicester.

## Sources

D. Shusterman, *C.P. Snow* (Boston, 1975); E. Snow and P. Snow, *C.P. Snow, Lord Snow of Leicester 1905–1980* (Leicester, 1984); P. Snow, *Strangers and Brothers* (London, 1982); S. Weintraub, 'Snow, Charles Percy, Baron Snow (1905–1980) in *Oxford Dictionary of National Biography* (Oxford, 2004), www.oxforddnb.com/view/article/31698, accessed 28 October 2012; J. Simmons, *Leicester Past and Present vol.2 Modern City, 1860–1974* (1974), pp.78–80

was made in a *Leicester Daily Post* editorial that the university college could be dedicated as a memorial to those who had died in the war, the idea caught the imagination of the public and donations started to flood in.[5] University College opened in 1921 with the motto *'ut vitam habeant'* – 'so that they might live'. The new college was soon licensed to award University of London degrees and started out with a total of eleven students. A second memorial, the Leicester Arch of Remembrance, designed for Leicester by Sir Edward Lutyens and completed in 1926, was sited close by the college in Victoria Park.

Civic pride in Leicester during the interwar years was also underpinned by an increasingly productive and confident local economy. This had gained impetus during the First World War, and afterwards Leicester consolidated an international reputation as a major centre for both

LEICESTER, LEICESTERSHIRE AND RUTLAND UNIVERSITY COLLEGE

# BAZAAR & FÊTE HANDBOOK

MAY 15 to 20, 1922

JUNIOR TRAINING HALLS AYLESTONE ROAD, LEICESTER EACH DAY 2—10 P.M.

Handbook for the University College Bazaar, 1922. This image is reproduced courtesy of the University of Leicester Archive.

footwear and knitted goods. The city was also becoming the home to a wide variety of smaller trades, including food processing, the production of office supplies and various new areas of light engineering, such as the manufacture of optical and electrical goods. This diversification of trade and industry brought stability and prosperity, prosperity that was relatively well sustained despite the depression of the 1930s. This was not true for all sections of the population, of course: there was still poverty arising from unemployment, with the numbers out of work fluctuating and rising to a high of around 1,600 in the early 1930s. In comparison to many cities, though, Leicester was doing well, and in 1936 statistics issued by the League of Nations declared it to be the second most prosperous city in Europe.[6]

The number of clubs, societies and other voluntary organisations continued to increase in the interwar years, as did the range of social events reported in the local press. Organised social life in Leicester was energetic, something that the new press photography vividly conveyed. In the 1930s,

A dance display by Leicester University College students, around 1929. Women's sport and dance was increasingly popular in the interwar years. This image is reproduced courtesy of the University of Leicester Archive.

the *Leicester Evening Mail* ran a daily feature called 'Camera News', a whole page of photographs recording many events of local interest, including a wide range of social functions. From September onwards the page was loaded with photographs of dances and socials, and between January and March this became particularly intense – with three of Leicester's leading venues, the Palais de Danse, the Bell Hotel and the Grand Hotel, constantly booked. One innovation was that many firms now held an annual dance for their staff, with the occasion often organised by the firm's sports and social club, suggesting an ongoing and regular social life within the business. Other events were organised by independent trade and employees associations, and frequently by local sports clubs, though there were also groups of an entirely different type that followed the same pattern. These included the Leicester Peace Council, which in November 1938 held a dance at the Leicester Palais for its members, and later in the same month the congregation of St Saviour's church also went to the Palais for their annual parish dance.[7] By the end of the 1930s an event like this was clearly the vogue for that special annual party.

*Right* A flower seller at the market. This image is reproduced courtesy of the Record Office for Leicestershire, Leicester and Rutland.

*Below* Wolsey underwear shop display. This image is reproduced courtesy of the Record Office for Leicestershire, Leicester and Rutland.

The photographs reinforce Leicester's reputation at the time as a prosperous city. It has been observed that the popular view of the 1930s as a time of 'unbroken deprivation and decay' has often been overstated, and that old photographs of the time 'suggest a people, even a working class, better dressed than their parents and grandparents before the first war'.[8] Obviously, the press photographers looked for shots that would convey a positive impression, but, although at some events such as parish socials and works' parties people were dressed quite plainly, they were well enough attired not to look out of place at a hotel or dance hall. The style of photography frequently emphasised the large numbers of people participating in the functions. Crowd shots were popular, for instance a sea of upturned faces shot over the balustrade of the Grand Hotel. Photographs were also used to convey a sense of community and comradeship: for example, guests were photographed dancing the Palais Glide or performing actions to 'Under the Spreading Chestnut Tree'. The impression given was of a unified and prosperous local society.

## Local Democracy and Citizenship

In the post-war years, Britain finally became a democracy. The 1918 Representation of the People Act gave all working-class men and women aged 30 and over the right to vote, and this was extended to younger women in 1928. Society was officially more inclusive.

Universal suffrage led the way to the rise of the Labour Party in Leicester, both in national and municipal politics, and as the Labour Party captured the working-class vote, the Liberals, dominant for so long, went into decline. During the interwar decades a powerful Labour following emerged in two of the city's three Parliamentary constituencies, Leicester East and Leicester West. This success did not go unopposed, of course. In the third constituency, Leicester South, the Conservatives dominated. Local politics had been reconfigured: whereas before the war there had been a long-standing alliance between the Liberals and Labour, the Conservatives now allied with the Liberals in an effort to constrain the increasing power of the Labour Party.[9]

Leicester's new working-class politicians emerged from the working-class organisations of the town, including trade unions, the Labour Club, the Labour churches and the Cooperative movement. In the immediate post-war years the

The Fielding and Johnson Bond Street spinning mill. This image is reproduced courtesy of the Record Office for Leicestershire, Leicester and Rutland.

town council installed its first working-class mayors, first Jabez Chaplin and then a few years later Amos Sherriff, both of them veterans of the shoemakers' march to London. Another well-known working-class mayor from this period was Harry Hand, who took office in 1928. He was a prominent trade unionist and founder member of the Leicester Labour Party, and his memory is preserved today by the name Hand Avenue in Braunstone. Labour mayors and councillors highlighted the problems that were facing working-class people, such as poor housing and unemployment. They criticised the harshness of the Poor Law Guardians, and in the 1930s they challenged the means testing that was imposed on unemployed men who applied for National Assistance.[10]

While politics divided social classes and interest groups, working for the common good of the city also brought them together. Leicester townspeople who made a civic contribution during the interwar years were from a wide variety of social backgrounds. The middle-class elite, manufacturers and other businessmen who had been instrumental in developing the town and its industries, continued to participate in local public life. The number of local

A presentation to an employee at the J. Pick and Sons knitwear firm, late 1930s. This image is reproduced courtesy of the Record Office for Leicestershire, Leicester and Rutland.

businessmen serving on the city council was reduced, but during the interwar years they still composed about a third of the councillors.[11] Many also took part in associational life, travelling in from the suburbs to attend meetings of the Lit and Phil, a society that continued to demonstrate civic commitment by supporting educational initiatives in Leicester, from the university college to adult schools.[12] Another leading middle-class group, the Kyrle Society, which in the late nineteenth century had dedicated itself to improving the town environment, was relaunched in 1928 and made its commitment to the city more overt through its new name: the Leicester Civic Society.[13] Membership of these societies became less exclusive over the years, and broadened to include more individuals from a lower middle-class background. This wider social mix was also found at the newly established Leicester Rotary Club, which soon made its name for promoting citizenship and headlining issues that were important to the town as a whole.[14]

Working-class people also supported the city by helping local charitable causes. This support was now publicly acknowledged, with local newspapers reporting on it, and representing working people as full participants in a democratic society; citizens whom the community relied on. One example is the coverage given to Leicester's working men's clubs. In the 1920s and 1930s there was an extensive network of working men's clubs in Leicester and its suburbs, so active that the *Leicester Evening Mail* dedicated a special column to their activities every Saturday. These clubs regularly raised money for local good causes through concerts and other events, the infirmary, which had been renamed the Leicester Royal Infirmary in 1912, being a particular favourite.

Voluntary societies that helped people with disabilities also enjoyed widespread public support. Many soldiers returned from war with serious injuries, and no doubt this promoted a particular public interest. Popular societies included the Wycliffe Society for Helping the Blind, the Leicester Guild of the Crippled and the Leicester and County Mission for the Deaf and Dumb.

The Wycliffe Society provides a good illustration of how local charities of this type were identified with community spirit and civic pride during the interwar years.[15] The society was originally founded in 1893 and was associated with the Wycliffe Congregational Church; it became well known in Leicester for organising regular social events for local blind people, including an annual summer outing. After the war it gained a still higher local profile, and worked in partnership with the city council. Leicester people from every social background gave Wycliffe their support. Sir Jonathan North was a life member of the society, as was another ex-mayor, the well-known architect Arthur Wakerley. North and Wakerley were prominent members of Leicester society, but there were key members of Wycliffe, as well as many helpers, who came from a more middle of the road background. Ordinary working people made a significant financial contribution. Donations were made by trade unions, the Cooperative Society, adult schools, churches, sports clubs and working men's clubs, and regular collections were made in workplaces and pubs. Throughout the year the society ran a regular social programme, with parties hosted by all types of businesses, individuals and groups. The highlight of the year was the annual outing, which was staged with considerable ritual. Typical was the 1922 event, when the press reported that crowds gathered in the Municipal Square to wave off ten charabancs, which drove in a triumphant procession through the city

An outing for local blind people. Both these images are reproduced courtesy of the Record Office for Leicestershire, Leicester and Rutland

before leaving for the big day out. The occasion aroused enough community spirit to draw similarly enthusiastic crowds every year, and the choice of the Municipal Square as a place of departure and the participation of councillors gave the occasion a civic edge.

In addition to supporting the work of voluntary associations, the local council made direct interventions to support health and welfare. Since the early twentieth century the need for more state-supported welfare had become accepted, and in Leicester, as in other towns, improvements were made. These included important changes to hospital care available. In 1929 the workhouse was finally closed and the old Poor Law Infirmary, situated on Gwendolen Road, became the City General Hospital, coming under the control of the council. In 1938 the City General opened a maternity ward for the first time. This was a real breakthrough for women in the city, as Leicester Royal Infirmary had only provided maternity services in exceptional circumstances. There was a voluntarily run maternity hospital, but despite this provision in the city had been woefully inadequate.[16]

## Social Housing and Home Ownership

Housing was also a major issue during the interwar years, both in terms of social housing and home ownership opportunities for the middle classes. The war stimulated a 'homes for heroes' campaign, and the 1919 Housing Act required local councils to expand their social housing, with the help of government subsidies. In Leicester the Coleman Road estate was built in the immediate post-war period, and this was followed in the mid-1920s first by development of the Saffron Lane estate (or Park estate as it was originally known) and then by the Braunstone estate. As Rodger explains, in terms of architectural design considerable efforts were made to make these new estates attractive places to live in.[17] Garden city principles were applied, which meant that there were open spaces, green verges, curved roads and a variety of detailing on the houses to provide interest. Despite these advantages the new estates were sorely lacking in even basic facilities, including essential shops. On the Park estate some residents took to hoarding and selling groceries from their houses, which breached their contracts of residence. Inadequate transport links were also a problem, and there was a complete lack of pubs or any other form

Calais Hill, one of the streets picked for slum clearance. This image is reproduced courtesy of the Record Office for Leicestershire, Leicester and Rutland.

of entertainment. Living in this kind of environment discouraged community feeling, as well as isolating residents from the rest of the town. Slum clearance, including the demolition of many old houses in the Wharf Street and St Margaret's areas, followed, and more new estates were built, including Tailby, North Braunstone, Northfields and Freak's Ground. Although the new houses were more cramped than those in Saffron Lane and Braunstone, they were of far better quality than those that the new occupants had moved from. Again there were drawbacks, however, not least that during the rehousing operation tenants were stigmatised as slum dwellers, a label that stuck and helped create a distance between the estates and other Leicester residents.[18]

While these council housing projects were being developed a great many houses were also built in the city for private ownership. Building programmes offered semi-detached houses at prices that a non-manual worker on a modest wage could aspire to, and the availability of mortgages at low interest rates during the 1930s meant that many lower middle-class families grasped this opportunity.[19]

The spread of anonymous middle-class suburbia in Britain during the interwar years has been associated with problems of social isolation, particularly among women, who sometimes found themselves exiled into a dull and entirely private life. Not everyone was dissatisfied with suburban living, though: it was the lifestyle of choice, and a proud badge of class identity and respectability for at least some lower middle-class women. This is illustrated by A.F.C. Harrison's account *Scholarship Boy* of family life in a semi-detached house in Byway Road during the interwar years. This was a newly built semi, which the Harrison family bought in 1936 after moving from a Victorian terraced house in Lynton Street in Highfields. His mother, as was the custom, did not work, did not know her neighbours and in his memory would 'happily spend her mornings, washing, dusting, polishing and vacuum cleaning'. One reason, however, why she seems to have survived this ordeal so cheerfully is because she ensured that the family did not move very far away from the older and more Victorian suburb in which she had previously lived. This meant she was able to attend the same church, St Philip's, and continue to take an active part in all the social activities that were organised around it.[20]

## Women as Citizens

Now that women had the vote a milestone had been passed, and an important aspect of the interwar years in Leicester was the increased participation of women in the public life of the town, and the recognition of this by the civic authorities and local newspapers. The founding of the new university college provided an early opportunity to showcase this trend: in 1922 a highly publicised 'ladies' bazaar raised over £15,000 to equip and furnish it. The bazaar was held in mid-May and was publicised as 'the social event of the year'. Lady Diana Cooper opened it, giving the occasion a dash of celebrity, and the bazaar continued for six days, opening daily from early in the morning to late in the evening. As well as a large number of stalls, there were drama performances, musical entertainment and dancing, and the week culminated in a grand ball.[21]

The bazaar was packaged from the beginning as a women's project. In the summer of 1921 a large number of middle-class women were invited to the Town Hall for a meeting: they included members of the local branch of the National Council of Women, wives of local employers, ex-mayoresses and women who had served as Poor Law Guardians.[22] A bazaar committee was elected, and encouraged individuals and organisations into providing stalls, help, funds and entertainment. The bazaar was supported by a wide range of organisations, including schools and churches, and professional, recreational and women's associations. Wealthier groups sponsored a bazaar stall, and if the organisation was male-dominated it was arranged that members' wives and daughters would front it. Voluntary associations with fewer financial resources played a supporting role: these included the women of the adult school network who agreed to sell entrance tickets, and the Girl Guides, who volunteered to sell tickets for the special attractions. Reporter Mary Maitland, writing in the *Leicester Mail*, highlighted the amount of time and effort involved in the preparation. She wrote of her sympathy for any local mother who had children at more than one school, because all schools would ask for her help with the bazaar effort. In addition, a woman would find her church asking for help, together with 'some society or organisation or possibly a friend responsible for a stall imploring harder than any of them'.[23] This intensive preparation and coordination paid off, however. The local newspapers declared the bazaar a triumph and congratulated the women of Leicester for their contribution to the city.[24]

The success of this bazaar demonstrated the willingness of a large number of local women to spend time and effort on a civic project, and reflected the goals of the National Council of Women, which was very active in the city and sought to promote the position of women by embracing opportunities to demonstrate citizenship. This approach was sustained throughout the interwar years, and in Leicester it prompted the city council to publicly acknowledge the importance of women's voluntary work to local society.

One occasion on which this public acknowledgement was given was in 1935, when the annual conference of the National Council of Women was held in Leicester.[25] Nearly 1,000 delegates came from all over Britain to the five day event, which was held in the De Montfort Hall. The women were given a civic welcome and entertained by the corporation with a programme that included a reception in the Lord Mayor's Parlour, a dedicated service at the cathedral attended by the lord mayor and mayoress, and a special performance by Leicester Drama Society. An editorial in the *Leicester Mercury* on 16 October 1935 commented: 'The women of Britain are now in the position of a victorious army consolidating their gains to the great advantage of the whole community ... their contribution is found to be of supreme value and importance.'[26]

One reporter who covered the events was a local journalist named Suzanne Harrison. She wrote a daily column entitled 'Woman's World' for the *Leicester Evening Mail*, which highlighted the new perception of women as active citizens. There had long been women's columns in the local press, but in the late nineteenth and early twentieth centuries these had not conveyed much sense of the welfare work women did for the town. Earlier columnists included one with the pen-name 'Penelope', who in the 1880s wrote a 'ladies column' in the *Leicester Chronicle and Leicestershire Mercury*. This concerned itself with domestic matters, fashion and London events. In the 1890s and early 1900s a column in the *Leicester Daily Post* penned under the name 'Aurora' continued in much the same vein, adding to the repertoire some commentary on the doings of British and continental royalty. During the pre-war period the seeds of change were evident, when *Leicester Mail* columnist Kitty Clive began to comment in a limited way on local clubs and associations. It was, however, in the interwar years that the character of the women's column showed real change. In the 1920s Mary Maitland in the *Leicester Mercury* and a journalist in the *Evening Mail* known as 'L'Estrienne' wrote daily columns that covered women's meetings and events on a regular basis; and from these grew the more fully developed model such as that written by Suzanne Harrison in the 1930s.

The content of Suzanne Harrison's column did not in any way seek to undermine women's traditional domestic role; indeed much space was given to the art of homemaking as well as to beauty and fashion. However, the message conveyed was that women should and did combine a domestic life and a more public role as citizens, and much space was devoted to reporting the involvement of women in local associational life. This echoed a 'citizenship for homemakers' approach, which branches of the Women's Institute and Townswomen's Guild adopted in the interwar years, as well as the belief, expressed by the first editor of *Woman* magazine in 1937, that content directed by the media at women readers ought to deal with social problems as well as flower arrangements.[27] While this approach was dropped in national weeklies such as *Woman*, with editors soon returning to purely domestic, fashion and beauty content, it was maintained on a daily basis throughout the 1930s by Suzanne Harrison in the *Leicester Evening Mail*.

Unlike the Leicester newspapers of the mid- to late Victorian and Edwardian period, the main pages of the 1930s local press were not organised in a way that drew attention to the regular annual cycle of events. Lengthy columns recording almost verbatim the exact procedure of annual meetings, dinners and other social occasions had been replaced by a more disparate presentation, with shorter pieces on local and international news, reports of crime, accidents, social functions and other incidents all mixed together. Within the paper, the daily block of text that was Suzanne Harrison's column stood out, giving insight into a vibrant strand of local society, written from a woman's perspective but of communal interest. This daily chronicle of events provided a diary that encouraged women in Leicester to identify with and take part in local society, and reported on their efforts to do so.

Suzanne Harrison's column illustrated that many of the rhythms of Leicester's calendar had not changed since the late Victorian period.[28] September remained the real beginning of the yearly cycle, just as it had been pre-war. In early September 1938 Harrison noted that associational life was getting back into gear after the summer break. She observed: 'By this time of year secretaries of various associations all over Leicester are busily preparing for the winter season … there is definitely an autumnal feeling in the air and this is proved by the large post that I am getting every morning, with invitations to social events which always mark the season.'

The municipal elections were still held in November, and in the weeks leading up to them Harrison reported on ward meetings held by political party associations, in which women now played a significant role. The autumn months continued to be a time for lecture programmes, and the Lit and Phil lectures, as well as the free lectures at the museum, remained central. Harrison's column drew attention to various newer lecture series put on by women's organisations during the autumn and winter, including those organised by the Leicester Personal Health Association, the Leicester Women's Luncheon Club and the Soroptimists. The subject matter of these lectures was far from the literary and historical concerns of the Leicester Ladies Reading Society: favoured topics were social policy and other public affairs, with lecture titles such as 'Women Police' and 'Health in Industry'. Lectures like this provided a women's alternative to those put on by the Rotary Club, a branch of which had been launched in Leicester immediately post-war.

October to December was the season for church bazaars, and reporting on these gave Harrison an opportunity to highlight women's ability as efficient fundraisers. However, by the 1930s women's fundraising far exceeded the occasional bazaar. Many clubs and societies had women's committees, which were often given the task of raising funds. From September to June there was a fairly constant stream of fundraising whist and bridge drives reported by Harrison. There was also, predictably, an emphasis on raising money for good causes, such as the Leicester Royal Infirmary, local boys' clubs and the Wycliffe Society. Typical of this was Daisy Day in May, a flag day organised in aid of the blind that generated a host of activities, including whist drives, a garden fête and an annual ball. After the Christmas and New Year festivities another programme of social events began. In 1939 one of these was a civic reception exclusively for women, hosted by the lady mayoress at Leicester Museum and echoing the civic receptions given for leading citizens each January by the mayor, a tradition that had been established at the turn of the century. In the New Year this was soon followed by another important civic and social event, the Maternity Hospital dance, which was attended by both the lord and lady mayoress. This hospital had been established as a result of campaigning by the National Council of Women and was a symbol of what women's associations could achieve.

In addition to a continuing round of social activities, there were still many annual meetings in the first six months of the year, and those that Harrison emphasised were the meetings of women's organisations such as the Women's International League, the St Mary's Home for Girls, and the YWCA.[29]

Easter still signalled the start of an outdoor season in the city, with summer sports, including those for women, beginning at this time. In addition to swimming and tennis, cricket was a popular sport for women, and the opening of the women's cricket season was heralded by the annual meeting of the Leicester Ladies' Cricket Club in April. Another sport that received a great deal of attention was women's bowls. The summer opening of the ladies' bowling clubs was reported extensively, and their activities were constantly referred to during the following months. However, despite the seasonal emphasis on sporting activities there was no relaxation in good works; on the contrary, some sports clubs made a point of demonstrating their civic awareness. One annual summer occasion for each ladies' bowling club was a 'cot day', in which a hospital bed, bought from club members' contributions, was donated to the Leicester Royal Infirmary; a ceremony was held at the hospital to mark the occasion.

June and July were months in which Harrison highlighted some of the activities of girls' schools, and thus gave them a higher profile in the city.

With the end of term in sight, the column also made a point of representing girls as future members of the workforce, with advice to girl school-leavers on the correct approach and clothes for job interviews. Finally, in July, there were the end of year speech days, where guidance was often offered to girls and on how to view their future. Typical of these was a speech day at Moat Girls School, where the headmistress emphasised the role of women as citizens. To reinforce the message Harrison summarised the main points of the speech in her column the next day, underlining its importance for Leicester as a whole.[30]

The summer months remained a time for group excursions as well as garden fêtes and parties hosted by churches, voluntary associations and municipal institutions. By late July the holiday season was under way, and in August the round of Leicester flower shows began; some of these also provided material for Harrison's column. In August 1939 the Highfields and District Horticultural Show was opened by Elisabeth Frisby, one of Leicester's first women councillors and a member of the National Council of Women. By reporting on this Harrison was able to showcase Councillor Frisby as a role model for women in the city.[31] As the holiday season drew to a close so did the end of an annual cycle.

The events that packed Suzanne Harrison's 'Women's World' column illustrated the variety and density of women's activities in Leicester at this time, and the emphasis placed on citizenship and working for the common good of the city. The column kept a record of the activities of associations and institutions that specifically focused on women and girls, as well as bringing to light the many other areas of associational life in which women were involved, demonstrating their work as active political campaigners and energetic fundraisers for a wide variety of causes. From Harrison's column it is possible to trace the local calendar within which women's activities had become largely integrated. This local calendar had become more complex, but despite this the basic rhythm of the Victorian year was still recognisable, the calendar had grown and developed rather than radically changing.

## Young People: the Citizens of the Future

In 1935 about 2,000 Leicester Girl Guides gathered in Abbey Park to celebrate the jubilee of King George V and Queen Mary, and to present to the city an ornamental birdbath for the park. The design decorating the birdbath, 'a lead figure of Peter Pan, symbolising Youth, the hope of the future', conveyed the new public role attributed to young people at this time. The gift, draped in the Union Jack, was unveiled by the Bishop of Leicester and accepted on behalf of the city by Lord Mayor Alderman E. Grimsley.[32]

Youth organisations that emphasised citizenship, such as the Boy Scouts and Girl Guides, became very popular in the 1920s and 1930s, and offered young people a new place in the spotlight, representing them as citizens of the future. The Scouts and Guides were primarily patriotic organisations, but civic loyalty was also highlighted, promoting a positive view of cooperation between the local and the national. The birdbath ceremony in Abbey Park was a special occasion, but there was also a regular calendar of parades and displays throughout the year, frequently attended by the mayor.

Scout troops and Guide companies were rooted in neighbourhoods, where they were based at schools and churches, and gave many children the opportunity to bond in groups, making local friends. Both Scouts and Guides had city centre offices that coordinated the network of groups in Leicester, allowing them to come together for activities, and giving members the chance to make wider social contacts. Scouting and Guiding also offered previously unavailable activities such as camping, which for girls in particular presented new opportunities for independence from home. As well as offering children a chance to have fun and take part in different activities, the role of apprentice citizen brought with it a certain public status. Scouts and Guides were not just seen as passive recipients of adult instruction or charity, a role that voluntary organisations had often allocated to

Lady Baden Powell visits Leicester Girl Guides. This image is reproduced courtesy of the Record Office for Leicestershire, Leicester and Rutland.

the young, but also as the rising generation, on which the future of the country and the empire depended.

The Boy Scouts organisation was launched in 1908 and was a model for the Girl Guide Association, officially established in 1920. Initially the movement reflected the public concerns that were at the forefront during the Edwardian period: imperialism, national efficiency and a belief in the spiritual and health benefits of outdoor activity. After the war the leadership skilfully reacted to widespread anti-militarism by associating the movement with a peace-seeking internationalist approach, similar to that of the League of Nations.[33] The London headquarters, under Baden-Powell, decided policy, but there were also autonomous local associations that oversaw Guiding and Scouting in their own area. The local prestige of the movement was boosted in Leicester when, from an early stage, leading citizens took up the opportunity to involve themselves in the movement. By 1913 both the mayor and the bishop were vice-presidents of the Leicester Scout Association, while many other well-known names from the Leicester world of business and professions, including Corah, Bennet, Astley Clarke and Gee, appeared in the list of members. During the interwar years the annual meeting of the Leicester Boy Scout Association was held in the Council Chamber at the Town Hall, demonstrating the level of civic support for the movement.[34] The activities of both the Scout and Guide associations were covered regularly in the local newspaper, helping to give young people a higher profile in the city than they had ever had before.

## The Leicester Pageant of 1932

Thirteen years after the soldiers returned from the Front, Leicester staged the most ambitious civic event in its history, the 1932 Leicester Pageant. This was a ten-day spectacle of historical enactments and public ceremony organised by the corporation and local voluntary associations, in partnership with the county. Over 4,000 local people actively participated in the pageant, while many more took part in related events. An amphitheatre was put up in Abbey Park and was filled to capacity every night, with audiences eager to see the history of Leicester acted out by the pageant players. Crowds of locals and visitors thronged to watch the civic and industrial processions.[35]

The Leicester Pageant of 1932 reflected two major themes of the interwar years: a civic pride based on a prosperous local economy and the perception of Leicester as a modern democratic city in which everybody as a citizen had the right to participate in local public life. Other provincial towns, including neighbouring Northampton, had already staged pageants, which had proved successful in raising these towns' profile. To the corporation a civic celebration seemed the perfect opportunity to promote Leicester business, as well as emphasising local unity and downplaying differences and disagreements. A historical pageant also gave the chance to advertise modern Leicester, while using local history to add both gravitas and glamour to its image.[36]

Serious planning for the pageant started in December 1931, with a public meeting at the Town Hall. The *Leicester Evening Mail* described this as 'a meeting of the citizens of Leicester attended by representatives of almost every social, industrial and religious movement in the city and the county'.[37] The gathering ensured access to the numerous social networks in the city, making it possible to mobilise large numbers of townspeople. Further meetings followed, and soon the organisers managed to secure the services of Frank Lascelles, one of the best-known professional pageant masters in the country. Among his previous successes were events in London, Oxford, Bath, Bristol, Carlisle, Stoke, Bradford and Rochester, as well as extravaganzas in Quebec, Cape Town and Calcutta.

The pageant consisted of seven episodes that traced the history of Leicester, from the arrival of the Romans to the 1882 opening of Abbey Park just fifty years earlier. The actors in the pageant were the townspeople, and the episodes were delegated to groups of organisations to prepare at grassroots level. In April 1932, for example, it was reported that plans for episode one were underway: the organisations providing the actors were the Catholic parishes of Leicester, the British United (shoe company) Drama League, the Glen Parva Army Barracks and the Leicester Women's Athletic Club. A subcommittee was put in place to coordinate this, the secretary being the headmistress of Sacred Heart Catholic School.[38]

In the months before the pageant, the 4,000 people taking part put in a great deal of hard work. Not only were there regular rehearsals to attend but actors were also responsible for making their own costumes, to approved designs provided by the organisers. While this was going on, momentum was built up in a variety of other ways. A series of public lectures was held on the pageant,

Actors in costume for an episode of the Leicester Pageant, 1932. This image is reproduced courtesy of the Record Office for Leicestershire, Leicester and Rutland.

and newspapers referred constantly to the preparations, updating the public on progress made. A pageant song competition was held, and when the winning song had been chosen it was taught to children in all the local schools.

The pageant week, scheduled for June, at last arrived, and every evening a pageant performance was given before a packed audience in Abbey Park. Every evening, local newspapers gave extensive photographic coverage to actors and audience alike, no doubt boosting sales as readers bought papers looking for themselves and their friends. The performances were so popular that it was decided to extend the pageant week, so that more people had the opportunity to see it. In addition to the pageant itself a wide variety of additional events were put on, arranged in a series of themed days: Civic Day, Day of Industry, County Day, Day of the British Empire, Pageant Sunday, Shops Display Day and Children's Day. The most outstanding of these events were the industrial exhibition, the trade procession and the civic procession.

The industrial exhibition was held at De Montfort Hall and was opened on the Day of Industry by Viscountess Snowdon, wife of the former Labour chancellor Philip Snowdon. Fifty firms from the county and city contributed to the display, which was kept open throughout the pageant period.

The trade procession, which took place on the same day, provided an even more comprehensive display of local industry. Drawing great crowds of spectators, it included tableaux from at least ninety local firms as well as marching contingents of trade union and trade association members. National trade union leaders, representatives of the TUC and leaders of various other workers' organisations had been invited to the event, and also to a civic dinner at the museum. Many speeches were made, and much was made of the diversity of the local economy and the prosperity this was bringing to the city, when other towns were suffering badly from the effects of the depression. As well as showcasing Leicester's trade and industry, these events sought to convey the message that the civic leaders and workers' organisations were joined in partnership to promote the interests of the city.

Civic Day was the day on which Charles Street was opened, and a civic procession was organised to celebrate the occasion. In addition to Leicester's civic leaders, the mayors of thirteen other provincial towns took part in the procession, and the Lord Mayor of London was invited to cut the cord and open the new thoroughfare. It was an elaborate occasion: full ceremonial dress was worn by all the mayors, the 400-year-old Leicester mace was on show and the Lord Mayor of London was carried in his ceremonial coach. Behind this paraded the 4,000 performers in costume, making a line almost half a mile long. A half day's public holiday had been given in honour of the event, and the streets were densely packed with spectators. After Charles Street had been opened, all returned to Abbey Park, where the lord mayor circled the auditorium in his coach before a special afternoon performance of the pageant was given.

The civic procession and the cheering crowds were reminiscent of the royal visit and the opening of Abbey Park, but the pageant of 1932 was a more inclusive and far more complex event. What was particularly remarkable was not just the number and variety of people involved but also the level of commitment that they showed, going to meetings, forming committees and attending rehearsals for six months. It was genuinely a display of mass participation. This was underpinned by the still increasing associational life of the town. Local clubs, societies, charities and church congregations continued to bring townspeople regularly together, and formed an efficient social network. The city's newspapers continued to represent this network as a coherent and shared local culture.

The pageant was a financial and popular success, and the prosperity that it reflected was to continue throughout the decade. It seemed that the city had recovered from the traumas of the First World War, but as the 1930s drew to a close the international situation grew more ominous. In September 1938 there was relief when Neville Chamberlain seemed to bring a reprieve back from Berlin, and on 2 October, when the British Legion held a parade at Leicester Cathedral, crowds of people took to the streets to mark their gratitude to Chamberlain for apparently making a pact with Hitler. The elation was short lived. Hitler had deceived Chamberlain, and in September 1939 war broke out again.

*eight*

# THE SECOND WORLD WAR AND THE DECADES THAT FOLLOWED

## The Second World War

When war was declared on 3 September 1939 conscription was introduced immediately, while preparations for the defence of the civilian population – which had been going on for several years – accelerated. Systems to protect citizens from aerial attack, including the blackout of street lighting and the provision of air-raid shelters, first-aid centres and extra accommodation for casualties, all shifted into gear. The relative inactivity of the early months of the war, the so-called phoney war, gave time for the city to organise itself.[1]

In order for these systems to work, the corporation team overseeing the project had to rely heavily on local people to volunteer their help, as recruits were needed for a wide range of jobs, such as air-raid wardens, first aiders, ambulance drivers and auxiliaries to the police and fire brigade. Full-time volunteers were paid but part-time workers were not; nevertheless, within a few months of the onset of war over 6,000 part-time volunteers had been recruited. One leading member of the team in charge of the operation was Councillor Charles Gillot, a driving force behind the Leicester Pageant of 1932. Here he was involved in the organisation of large networks of volunteers once again, albeit for a more sombre purpose. Protection of supplies as well as people became an immediate priority, and during the first year of the war rationing was gradually introduced; this started with petrol and eventually extended to almost all food and clothing.

When the air raids finally arrived there was significant loss of life and extensive damage. In comparison with cities such as London or nearby Coventry, Leicester escaped lightly. Nevertheless, 122 Leicester people died in air raids during 1940 and 1941, many others were injured, and approximately 6,000 buildings were damaged or destroyed. The first air raid took place on the morning of 21 August 1940, when a series of bombs from a single plane hit Cavendish Street in the Saffron Lane area, killing six people. The specific reason for the bombing was uncertain, but it has been suggested that the plane was just 'reconnoitring the Midlands'.[2] A few weeks later a similar attack occurred, and Essex Road near Gypsy Lane was hit, leaving four dead and five injured. A lull of nearly three months followed until 14 November, when another lone plane bombed the west side of the city, with hits including Fosse, Hinckley and King Richard's Road. This was the same night as the famous raid on Coventry, which claimed many lives and destroyed Coventry Cathedral; it is thought that the Leicester bombs could have been originally meant for Coventry.[3] A few days later a much more serious and clearly targeted attack on Leicester came on the night of 19/20 November; this sustained raid by a group of bombers lasted about six hours. A souvenir booklet written to commemorate the night tried to recreate the fear and apprehension felt by people in the city when the raid started:

> In the early darkness of a mid-winter evening it became obvious that there was something in the air. To the familiar bright ribbons of searchlights probing the sky was added a new and ominous glare, the all revealing, weird white brightness of enemy flares. The banshee wail of the sirens quickened the pulse; there was the dread expectancy that this was not just another false alarm. Despite that few people had sought shelter when the thuds of the first H.Es [high explosives] crashed across the residential south east of the city. From then on the story is not one of incident but of thousands of personal experiences, each of the hundreds of H.Es and innumerable incendiaries bringing fates and reactions to the people in or near the five thousand homes and factories damaged in varying degrees during the six hours of the raid.[4]

This description contrasted with the more restrained headline of the *Leicester Mercury* that appeared the morning after the raid: 'Fires Guide Midland Raiders – Firemen's Heroic Work as Bombs Fall'. In the news report that followed the name of the town raided was not identified, but it was recorded that most people had arrived at work that morning and after clearing up had 'got on with their job'.[5] The destruction on the night of 19 November included

Bomb damage: Sparkenhoe Street and Saxby Street, Highfields, 1940. This image is reproduced courtesy of the Record Office for Leicestershire, Leicester and Rutland.

Bomb damage: the Victoria Park Pavilion, 1940. This image is reproduced courtesy of the Record Office for Leicestershire, Leicester and Rutland.

the premises of two prominent local employers, Freeman Hardy and Willis in Rutland Street and Faire brothers in Wimbledon Street. A bomb also went through the roof of the Town Hall, though it failed to explode. The residential area that suffered the most intense bombing was Highfields, in particular South Highfields. These streets suffered a lengthy attack that lasted several hours, an episode later dubbed the Highfields Blitz. It was here that there was the most concentrated loss of life: a bomb that hit a hostel on the corner of Tichborne Street killed forty-one people. As an epilogue to the raid, a single bomber passed over Leicester the following night and dropped two landmines, one of which hit an iconic local landmark, the pavilion on Victoria Park.

In 1941 there were a further three air attacks on Leicester, and though these were minor in comparison with the onslaught of November 1940, eight people were killed. In April 1941, on the night of another raid on Coventry, Leicester received hits in Ash Street and Humberstone Road, and a month later a bomb was dropped on the Braunstone estate during the same night as a major attack on Nuneaton. Finally, in July, London Road station in Leicester was targeted, and although the bomber missed the station, nearby Conduit Street and Guthlaxton Street were hit. These would be the last raids on Leicester, although air-raid warnings continued to frighten residents until 1945.

## Council Housing and Slum Clearance

The city faced an urgent demand for housing in the years that followed the war. This was not so much because of bomb damage, which was significant rather than overwhelming, but because population growth had long put pressure on existing housing stock. By the early 1950s a national strategy of slum clearance was also under way, and long-term plans to demolish thousands of local houses considered unfit for habitation brought still more pressure.[6]

Local authorities responded to the housing demand by planning and building a series of housing estates on the perimeter of the city: the New Parks estate was the leading housing project of the immediate post-war years. Building work began in spring 1946, and while there were some temporary prefabs put up, most of the new houses were permanent structures. The work progressed rapidly, with many houses occupied by the end of 1948. Building continued into the early 1950s, when blocks of flats were added, and later a school, shops and a church. Other important housing projects of the earlier post-war years included the Scraptoft Valley Scheme, an extension of the Braunstone estate, Thurnby Lodge, Goodwood, Stocking Farm, Eyres Monsell and Netherhall.

The Leicester slum clearance operation rolled into action in 1954, with the first demolition of houses in the Wharf Street district of the city; while a decade later houses were earmarked for demolition in Highfields. Demolition, new construction and rehousing proved a lengthy business, but eventually the St Matthew's estate, situated in the old Wharf Street area, was

Rowletts Hill flats under construction, 1965. This image is reproduced courtesy of the Record Office for Leicestershire, Leicester and Rutland.

completed; it was fully occupied by 1966. In Highfields, building of the new St Peter's Estate was started in 1967, and after a series of setbacks that dogged the construction process it was finally ready for tenants in 1973. Residential tower blocks had been introduced for the first time in Leicester when the Rowletts Hill estate was built in 1958, and these were also a feature of the St Matthew's and St Peter's estates.

While the house-building schemes of the post-war years rehoused thousands of city residents, not all the tenants were uncritical about their new accommodation. BBC Radio Leicester, launched in November 1967, gave those who were less than happy a chance to air their views. The tower blocks on St Peter's estate came in for particular criticism, and a programme broadcast in May 1977 featured tenants complaining bitterly about vandalism, lack of security and social isolation.[7]

By the mid-1970s the scene was set for a change in approach to inner-city housing. In 1976 the city council launched a housing programme to renovate a large number of houses in Leicester. This programme proved popular and successful, and by the early 1980s a conflict had emerged between planners committed to house clearance and rebuilding and the supporters of the renovation of old houses. Those who backed renewal got the upper hand, with the number of houses earmarked for clearance dramatically reduced and the trend for renovation rather than demolition becoming more thoroughly established.[8]

# JOE ORTON

The playwright Joe Orton (1933–67), whose successes included *Entertaining Mr Sloane* and *Loot*, was a native of Leicester. He was born John Kingsley Orton, the eldest child of William Orton, a gardener, and his wife Elsie, a machinist. The family lived on the Saffron Lane Estate, and at the age of 11 the young Orton was sent to a commercial school called Clark's College. This, in his teens, led to a series of office jobs, which he found highly frustrating.

In his free time, Orton liked reading and listening to music, but his passion above all was drama. He involved himself in various local drama groups, including the Vaughan Players and the Leicester Drama Society – a group that had fostered the talents of the young Richard Attenborough. He kept a diary of his activities, which records his joy at receiving a small part in a production of *The Tempest* by the Vaughan Players and the pleasure he got from the rehearsals and performance. Soon after this he started elocution lessons, and with the help of his teacher won a place at the Royal Academy of Dramatic Art (RADA).

It was at RADA that Orton met his partner Kenneth Halliwell. Neither Orton nor Halliwell stayed with acting after drama school but instead took up writing. Of the two it was only Orton who was successful in his work, and his success was outstanding. By the mid-1960s he was the toast of the London theatre scene, with *Loot* receiving the *Evening Standard* Best Play award in 1966. There was a proposal at one point that Orton might provide a screenplay for a Beatles film; this was written but never produced.

Orton's life came to an abrupt end in August 1967 when he was murdered by Halliwell in his Islington flat. The story of Joe Orton has been fully recorded in a biography by John Lahr, and a street in Leicester has been called Orton Square to recall and celebrate his talent.

## *Sources*

M .Arditti, 'Orton, John Kingsley (1933–1967)' in *Oxford Dictionary of National Biography* (Oxford, 2004), www.oxforddnb.com/view/archive/35334, accessed 28 October 2012; J. Lahr, *Prick Up Your Ears* (New York, 2002); J. Lahr (Ed.), *The Orton Diaries* (London, 1986); M. Charney, *Joe Orton* (London and Basingstoke, 1984); University of Leicester Library Orton Collection, MS 237: personal papers and memorabilia, 1/1-1/7.

# Accommodating the Car

It is sometimes said that while wartime bombing did not destroy much of historical Leicester, the town planners of the post-war period did. When this criticism is made it often refers to the damage done to the Roman and medieval heart of the town when a new road, Vaughan Way, was cut through the area in the 1960s.[9]

The new road system was built in a drive to relieve the city of traffic congestion. By the 1930s it was clear that the old streets could not cope with the increasing number of cars on the road, and post-war the situation was made more urgent by a planned extension of the M1 motorway through Leicestershire. The traffic plan created by the corporation under the direction of John Beckett, the city engineer and surveyor, involved the construction of three concentric ring roads. These were designed to siphon off traffic from the main roads leading into the city, reducing congestion in central Leicester. A publicity pamphlet of the time promoted the plan, proclaiming: 'Towns in general have creaked along in the van of the progress of the motor vehicle; the only solution to choked central streets is bold forward planning such as this.'[10] Construction of the M1 extension began in 1959, and work on the Leicester ring roads started a year later in 1960. The traffic plan was completed in 1970 and, as expected, reduced congestion. Sadly, however, it was at a cost to the city's heritage and upset all those who liked to be visually reminded of Leicester's long history.

The problem resulted from the route of the central ring road and from the construction of the Southgates underpass. The southern part of Highcross Street and old roads around St Nicholas church were demolished, and a new roundabout, St Nicholas Circle, was created. The roads destroyed the sense of unity and place by carving up the area, and by separating Leicester's most important historical monuments, the Jewry Wall and St Nicholas, St Mary de Castro, Leicester Castle, the Guildhall and the Magazine Gateway. The Magazine was sited in a particularly unfortunate way, stranded on a road island surrounded by lanes of traffic. Professor Jack Simmons of Leicester University, writing in 1974, concluded that 'the old town of Leicester had almost been entirely destroyed' by these developments.[11]

This damage can never be completely undone, but forty years later there is hope for improvement. A step forward was made in the first decade of

The building of the underpass: Vaughan Way, 1967. This image is reproduced courtesy of the Record Office for Leicestershire, Leicester and Rutland.

The building of the underpass: Castle Street and Southgate, 1967. This image is reproduced courtesy of the Record Office for Leicestershire, Leicester and Rutland.

the twenty-first century when De Montfort University, as part of its own development plan, supported a reconfiguration of Oxford Street. This rescued the Magazine Gateway from its traffic island, leaving it in a more harmonious position on the edge of the De Montfort campus. More recently a proposal by the civic authorities for a pedestrian way that would reconnect the cathedral and Guildhall has also been floated.[12]

A key figure in Leicester's post-war planning history was John Beckett's successor Konrad Smigielski, who was appointed to the new post of Chief Planning Officer in 1962. Before the war, Smigielski had been a town planner in the historic Polish town of Krakow, and after settling in England post-war he held senior academic positions in London and Leeds.[13] He was a professional, and therefore of some prestige, but as far as his career in Leicester is concerned he was and still is considered a controversial figure. From the beginning, Smigielski's emphasis was on change and on a grand plan to modernise Leicester, adapting it to the era of the motor car. His plan *Leicester Today and Tomorrow*, published in 1964, proposed an ultra-modern design for the city centre, a design that is probably best remembered for proposing an elevated monorail as a method of public transport.[14] Much of this plan, including the monorail, did not materialise, but overall Smigielski's projects had a strong impact. These schemes included the redesign and refurbishment of Leicester Market, the development of the Haymarket Centre, including shopping areas and a theatre, and the transformation of Gallowtree Gate into a pedestrian precinct.

Despite this emphasis on modernisation and change, there was also some conservation work. New Walk, the Crescent in King's Street and Town Hall Square were smartened up, and four conservation areas were established. However, old buildings that were judged to be of no value by the planning office were liable to be demolished in the name of progress. This provoked considerable anger among those members of the public who disagreed with the 'experts' on what should and should not be preserved. One plan that met with particular public outrage, and eventually proved too unpopular to carry out, was a proposal to demolish the Loseby Lane area and build a multi-storey car park on the site. Local protests provoked by council planning policy resulted in the revival of the Leicester Civic Society. This group gave a voice to local people who believed that that the planners were placing too much emphasis on the car and failing to appreciate the damage done to the environment when old buildings were demolished.[15]

A milk cart in Groby, 1961. This image is reproduced courtesy of the Record Office for Leicestershire, Leicester and Rutland.

Konrad Smigielski resigned in 1972, and after he left office various other unpopular plans were dropped. These included a plan to drive an 'inner motorway' thorough the eastern part of Leicester from Belgrave to London Road, and a proposal to build a forty-four-storey office block in the city centre.

## The Local Economy

For at least twenty-five years after the Second World War Leicester's economy prospered. The three industries of footwear, knitting and engineering continued to be at the heart of local economic life, and alongside these there was an expanding service sector. Jobs were plentiful, and this created a sense of security. There were, however, early signs that there was a time limit on this happy situation. From the 1950s onwards the growing influx of cheap imported goods became a more obvious challenge to local manufacture.[16]

The boot and shoe industry was the first to show signs of strain. The threat from overseas competition, especially from Italy and the Middle East, became increasingly apparent, and by the late 1960s it was clear that the industry was in serious difficulty. The situation deteriorated further, and by the mid-1970s the number of local people employed in boot and shoe manufacture was less than half what it had been in the late 1940s. Takeovers and mergers also changed the character of the industry. A feature of pre-war Leicester had been its family firms, and while many of these continued in business after the war, a new economic climate made them vulnerable to takeover by larger operations with no historical connection to the area. This threat became a reality when in the early 1960s many shoe companies, including Freeman Hardy and Willis, lost their independence after a takeover led by the financier Charles Clore, who amalgamated them into a giant enterprise called the British Shoe Corporation.

Leicester's knitting industry also had to face the challenge of cheap imported goods, although it withstood the pressure longer and in the early 1970s was still doing relatively well. Another concern, however, was the control that some of the more prominent retailers gained over local knitwear firms. These retailers offered regular and substantial orders, but in return the manufacturer had to conform strictly to their demands – trading independence for security.

Engineering expanded in the post-war decades, with a variety of successful light engineering concerns including instrument engineering and, a particularly

The British Shoe Corporation. This image is reproduced courtesy of the Record Office for Leicestershire, Leicester and Rutland.

A social for employees at J. Pick and Sons knitwear firm. This image is reproduced courtesy of the Record Office for Leicestershire, Leicester and Rutland.

important area of growth, electrical and electronic engineering. The production of machines for the boot and shoe and knitting industries also remained important, but here again overseas competition became a problem. Smaller firms supplying the footwear factories were the first to suffer, and as these either went out of business or were taken over the field became dominated by one large firm, British United Shoe Machinery. Although the manufacture of knitting machinery remained relatively buoyant through the 1950s and 1960s, a similar pattern occurred as smaller local firms came under the control of the bigger Leicester players.

By the late 1960s the British economy was looking increasingly fragile, and after the oil crisis of 1973 it became obvious that the post-war boom had come to an end. National employment numbers began to rise and Leicester, which had enjoyed almost full employment in the two previous decades, was no exception. The closure of some prominent leading firms sent shockwaves through the city. One of these was George Stibbe and Co., a leading knitting machine company with staff numbers running into the thousands. The decline of the footwear industry was intensified by the recession, and twenty years later boot and shoe manufacture was no longer a key sector of the local economy. In 1996 the British Shoe Corporation was broken up, and after holding out for thirteen more years Equity Shoes, the last major shoe factory in Leicester, closed in 2009.[17]

The knitting industry also began to deteriorate in the 1970s, and soon even leading firms were struggling. A Radio Leicester series spotlighting local industry broadcast a programme about Corah's in 1980. The firm still maintained the family atmosphere it had nurtured for nearly a century, with a thriving sports and social club; highlights of the year including the annual Christmas dinner as well as free Christmas hampers for all the staff. Although the firm hoped for a positive future, ominous mention was made of difficult business conditions, and the problem of competing with clothing imported from the Far East.[18] During the 1980s the situation worsened. In 1989, Corah's was taken over by another company, Charterhall, and shortly afterwards was broken up.[19] In the years that followed, the knitting industry was greatly reduced, and the situation worsened after 1999 when Marks and Spencer broke a long relationship with local firms in favour of overseas partners. A further blow came in 2004 when the international agreement known as the Multi Fibre Arrangement expired, removing the last protection against foreign imports in the field and leaving the limited activity that remained in Leicester industry narrowly focused on highly specialised markets.

Engineering has remained a contributor to the Leicester economy, but those firms that supplied the footwear and knitting industries struggled; as the old industries faded so did the engineering firms that supplied them. One long-standing survivor was the British United Shoe Company, which finally became insolvent in 2000 and closed, with an accompanying collapse of its pension fund that caused a public outcry.[20]

Recent changes to the economy in Leicester have broken a long-standing link with the past. Knitting and shoe manufacture were the heart of the Victorian industrial town, and the importance of these traditional industries to local life continued late into the twentieth century. Light engineering is still part of the city's economy, and in the 2001 census Leicester still had more manufacturing jobs than the national average. Nevertheless, most local employment is now found in various branches of the service industry, such as retail, catering and educational administration.

# The Universities

Leicester University College received state funding for the first time in 1945, funding that enabled it to enter a period of growth. In the year after the war there were still only approximately a hundred students, and the Fielding Johnson remained the only major building on the campus. Numbers grew rapidly, and by the mid-1950s there were more than 800 students. To accommodate growth the Fielding Johnson was extended, and the first new building on the campus, the Astley Clarke, was opened in 1951. The name of the new building was a reminder of the origins of the university: it was Dr Astley Clarke who had formally revived the idea of a local university at a meeting of the Lit and Phil, and who had worked with other local leading citizens, most notably Thomas Fielding Johnson, to achieve this.[21]

University College gained its independence in 1957, becoming a full university in its own right. During the celebrations that marked this event the city council demonstrated its support with a civic banquet and gifts. Both city and university remained keen to retain a close relationship, even though the university was no longer the intensely local institution it had been before the war. The majority of students enrolled came from other parts of the country, a result of the post-war policy which allowed university students a maintenance grant that was not tied to their place of residence.

The growth in student numbers continued into the 1960s, as did the building programme. At the same time the university consolidated its research reputation. By the early 1970s there were more than 3,000 students, and there was further expansion in 1975 when the medical school was launched. The achievements of the 1970s, however, took place against the increasingly gloomy national economic backdrop, and stringent government cuts to funding did not auger well. This led to a serious funding crisis in the 1980s, and the university was forced to close some departments. Student numbers were static for a while, but by the end of the decade they were growing again, rising to more than 5,000 in 1988. The upward trend continued into the 1990s and accelerated as the percentage of young people entering higher education and the numbers of overseas students increased.

Leicester became a two university town in 1992, when De Montfort University was established. The new university originated with the municipal Colleges of Art and Technology, housed in the Hawthorn building (near the castle) since 1897. In 1966 the campus was extended when the Fletcher building was opened, and in 1969 the colleges were renamed Leicester Polytechnic. When the polytechnic was awarded university status in the early 1990s a period of expansion began.[22]

The Victorian colleges at the heart of De Montfort University were founded to enhance Leicester commerce and industry by providing training and developing local talent.[23] Even though the traditional local industries have almost disappeared, the memory of the city's manufacturing past is perpetuated in the clothing and shoe design programmes offered by the De Montfort University School of Fashion and Textiles.[24]

In the first decade of the twenty-first century, student numbers rose to over 20,000 across both of Leicester's universities. By this time the institutions had become significant local employers, with staff running into thousands.[25]

## A Multicultural City

Leicester, centrally situated at the heart of a road network, has always attracted visitors, and nineteenth-century industrialisation brought still more people to the town in search of employment and commercial opportunities. Many came from Leicestershire and the surrounding counties, but there were also some, including Irish migrants, who came from further afield in the British Isles. By the interwar years there were a range of associations in the city with names such as the Caledonian Society, the Welsh Society and the Yorkshire Society.[26]

There was also a long-standing Jewish community, with the origins of the Leicester Hebrew Congregation dating back to at least the 1870s. Israel Hart, partner in the local tailoring firm of Hart and Levy and four times Mayor of Leicester in the 1880s and 1890s, was a leading member of this congregation.[27] In the 1890s, in the wake of antisemitic pogroms in Russia, the number of Jewish migrants to Britain grew, and some settled in Leicester. In the twentieth century local numbers were significantly increased by migrants escaping Nazi persecution.

In the years immediately after the Second World War the number of foreign nationals resident in the city rose: the upheaval of war left many Europeans displaced and often unwilling to return to their country of origin. Those who settled in Leicester included Germans who had been prisoners of war, some of whom married local women and elected to stay.[28] Other Europeans who stayed in or came to Leicester at this time included Latvians, Lithuanians, Serbs, Ukrainians, Italians and Poles. Among these the Poles and Ukrainians in particular formed enduring and close-knit city communities.[29]

Rebuilding Leicester industry was a priority post-war, and there was a need to expand the workforce in local factories. This provided work for a lot of the European migrants, as well as Irish workers and new arrivals from the Caribbean. During this period many of the newcomers, largely single men, found cheap accommodation in lodging houses, often in the Highfields area, and from that time the district began to develop a more ethnically mixed character.

There were also migrants from the Indian subcontinent in Leicester. The 1951 census recorded that there were over 600 people of Indian and Pakistani descent living in Leicester, a number that steadily rose during the 1950s as further new arrivals, mostly from Gujerat and the Punjab, came to the city in search of employment. When the British government signalled its intention to impose greater restrictions on immigration from the Commonwealth from 1962, the number of migrants further increased. By the early 1960s the profile of the Asian migrant community in Leicester had changed, as many of the single men who had originally settled in the city chose to bring wives, children and other family members to join them. There was still a concentration of migrants in the Highfields area, but the era of lodging houses was past and families commonly lived in rented terraced houses.

The late 1960s heralded a more intense wave of immigration from East Africa. This came as a result of the Africanisation policies in the newly independent colonies, policies that disadvantaged the local Asian populations. In 1972 a large number of Ugandan Asians came to Leicester, after suffering persecution and then expulsion at the hands of Idi Amin's regime. The incoming Ugandan Asians unfortunately faced many problems on arrival in the city. Not only had they been stripped of their assets by the Ugandan government, but their arrival in the city set off a wave of hostility in some sections of the local population. More positively, however, the commercial skills that this group brought were impressive, which enabled many to rapidly set up as traders.

In the early 1970s the city council was ill equipped to deal with the new challenges, and it was not until 1976 when the Race Relations Act was passed that the way forward became a little clearer. This created the Commission for

Racial Equality at national level, and at local level gave the council statutory powers to create race relations policies that would help manage the more diverse Leicester. By the 1980s the situation had improved, with a greater tolerance and more productive approaches to local governance. As had been the case earlier in the century, voluntary associations proved a useful tool in bringing excluded groups into the mainstream of town life. A range of new associations emerged to give a voice to ethnic minority groups, and individuals who were active in these groups found a platform from which to enter local politics. A number of Asian councillors were elected to office in both the 1983 and 1987 local elections, in 1988 Ghordan Parmar became the first Asian mayor, and in 1987 Keith Vaz was elected MP for Leicester East. Asian women also took part in public life, and in 2009 Manjula Sood was the first Asian woman to become Mayor of Leicester.

The 1990s and early twenty-first century have brought other newcomers to the city, including Bosnian Muslims, Kosovans, Zimbabweans, Portuguese, Poles, Slovaks and Somalis. Leicester has been enriched culturally by its ethnic minorities, and is now seen widely as a successful model of multicultural practice.

## The Present and the Past

The official motto of Leicester, 'semper eadem', means 'always the same' – but a city is always changing, and Leicester is no exception. The decades since the Second World War have been a time of particular change, and a few of the more outstanding aspects, the construction of the post-war council estates and slum clearance, adaptation to accommodate modern levels of traffic, the decline of the knitting and boot and shoe industries and the emergence of a multicultural city, have been highlighted here. To this list perhaps should be added, at least briefly, some of the more overt changes to the city leadership. Leicester's corporation was reborn as the Leicester City Council in 1974, and became a unitary authority in 1997. Since 2011 the city has had a directly elected mayor.

Changes there may have been, but there are also threads of continuity to the past. Victorian and early twentieth-century Leicester was a place with a busy social life. Relatively compact and easy to get around, it had a wealth of clubs and societies and a regular annual calendar of events. In the later twentieth century associational life in British towns and cities famously declined, and Leicester was no exception. Nevertheless, in the twenty-first century it continues to be a busy and sociable city. In addition to theatres, cinemas, pubs and shopping centres, there are still many voluntary groups that bring people together: sports teams, choirs, gardening clubs, walking clubs, lunch clubs, book groups, political groups, historical societies, faith and interfaith groups, tenants' associations and associations run by ethnic minority groups. As well as these, some of the larger societies prominent in the nineteenth century still survive. The Leicester Literary and Philosophical Society, the Leicestershire Archaeological Society and the Leicester Secular Society all provide a direct link to the Victorian past. There is also still a Leicester calendar that is punctuated by a succession of regular festivals and events. Some of the most prominent are now the Diwali celebrations in October, the Abbey Park bonfire and fireworks display in November, and in the summer the Belgrave Mela, the Summer Sundae festival and the Caribbean Carnival. All of these attract not only Leicester residents but also many visitors.[30]

The most obvious continuity between Leicester and its past still lies in the buildings of the city. Although so many Victorian buildings were pulled down in the 1960s and 1970s many survived, and red-brick schools, branch libraries and terraces, converted factories, the railway station, Town Hall Square and the Clock Tower are all reminders of the Victorian past, though also part of life today. Although it is Victorian Leicester that is most widely represented in the modern city environment, there are memories too of the more distant past. The New Walk promenade takes us back to the eighteenth century, and the Magazine Gateway, where the citizens stored their arms, reminds us of the years of civil war and the storming of Leicester. The Elizabethan Grammar School is a memory of a Leicester that was dominated by the Puritan Earl of Huntingdon, while the Guildhall and St Mary de Castro remind us of Leicester's medieval splendour. Looking further back still, there are traces of Saxon Leicester in St Nicholas church, while the Jewry Wall is a reminder that on the site of Leicester there was once another city called Ratae.

# NOTES

## Chapter One

### Ratae Corieltavorum: the Town at the Crossroads

1 J. Giles (ed.), *Six Old English Chronicles* (London, 1848), pp.114–16.
2 M. Morris, R. Buckley and M. Codd, *Visions of Ancient Leicester* (Leicester, 2011); A. Connor, *Roman and Medieval Occupation in Causeway Lane Leicester: Excavations 1980 and 1981* (Leicester, 1999), N.J. Cooper and R. Buckley, 'New Light on Roman Leicester' in P. Wilson (ed.), *The Archaeology of Roman Towns, Studies in Honour of John Wacher* (Oxford, 2003), pp.31–43. These three sources have been an invaluable source in writing this first chapter, as have the exhibitions and information given at Jewry Wall Museum.
3 The information about Ratae and wider information about Roman Britain given in this section is based on information derived from A.E. Brown, 'Roman Leicester' in A.E. Brown (ed.), *The Growth of Leicester* (Leicester, 1972), pp.11–18; M. Hebditch, 'Roman Leicester' in C. Ellis, *History in Leicester* (second edition, Leicester, 1969), pp.13–22; J. Mellor, 'Roman Leicester' in C. Ellis, *History in Leicester* (third edition, Leicester, 1976), pp.16–21; Morris, Buckley and Codd, *Visions of Ancient Leicester* (Leicester, 2011); J. Simmons, *Leicester Past and Present*, vol.1, *Ancient Borough* (London, 1974); P. Salway, *Roman Britain* (Oxford, 1981); M. Todd, *The Coritani* (second edition, Oxford, 1991); J. Wacher, *Towns of Roman Britain* (third edition, London, 1995); J. Wacher, *Roman Britain* (third edition, Stroud, 1999). Many of these sources are also drawn on in the second and third sections.
4 This derivation is given in Wacher, *Towns of Roman Britain*, p.343.

### Romano-British Town

5 The information given on the buildings of Ratae in this section is largely derived from Wacher, *Roman Towns of Britain*, pp.343–62; Todd, *The Coritani*, pp.47–67; Morris, Buckley and Codd, *Visions of Ancient Leicester*, pp.17–39 and information given at the Jewry Wall Museum, Leicester.

6 O.D. Harris, 'Jews, Jurats and the Jewry Wall: a name in context', *Transactions of the Leicestershire Archaeological and Historical Society*, vol.82 (2008), pp.113–23.

7 Todd, *The Coritani*, p.63.

8 Morris, Buckley and Codd, *Visions of Ancient Leicester*, p.33.

9 Mellor, 'Roman Leicester', p.21.

## The People of Ratae

10 Wacher, *Roman Towns*, p.359.

11 *Ibid.*, Simmons, *Leicester Past and Present*, pp.7–8.

12 Cooper and Buckley, 'New light on Roman Leicester' pp.31–43; O'Connor, *Roman and Medieval Occupation in Causeway Lane Leicester: Excavations 1980 and 1981*, pp.55–6; Morris, Buckley and Codd, *Visions of Ancient Leicester*, p.25.

13 O'Connor, *Roman and Medieval Occupation in Causeway Lane Leicester: Excavations 1980 and 1981*, pp.57–8.

14 Hebditch, 'Roman Britain', pp.17; Mellor, 'Roman Britain', p.21.

15 Cooper and Buckley, 'New Light on Roman Leicester', pp.40–1; Wacher, *Roman Towns*, p.362.

16 Wacher, *Roman Towns*, 1998, p.409.

## Saxon and Danish Leicester

17 Giles, *Six Old English Chronicles*, pp.299–314.

18 Sources used in the third section of the chapter include J. Campbell, E. John and P. Wormald, *The Anglo-Saxons* (London, 1991); C. Ellis, *History in Leicester* (Leicester, 1976), 25–34; Simmons, *Leicester Past and Present*, pp.11–18; B. Yorke, *The Anglo Saxons* (Stroud, 1999); J.D. Richards, *Viking Age England* (London, 1991).

19 Morris, Buckley and Codd, *Visions of Ancient Leicester*, p.39.

20 This description is based on information given at the Jewry Wall Museum in Leicester.

21 Simmons, *Leicester Past and Present*, p.11.

22 *Ibid.*, p.12.

23 B. Cox, *The Place Names of Leicestershire, part 1, The Borough of Leicester* (Nottingham, 1998), p.2. This volume is published by the English Place Name Society.

24 *Ibid.*, Simmons, *Leicester Past and Present*, p.12.

# Chapter Two

1 L. Fox, 'Leicester Castle' in A.E. Brown (ed.), *The Growth of Leicester* (Leicester, 1972), pp.19–25.

2 J. Simmons, *Leicester Past and Present*, vol.1; *Ancient Borough* (London, 1974); C.J. Billson, *Medieval Leicester* (Leicester, 1920).

# Power and Ambition: the Castle and the Medieval Overlords of Leicester

### The Grandsmesnils and the Beaumonts

3   The main sources for this section are C. Ellis, *History in Leicester, 55 BC–1976 AD*, third edition (Leicester, 1976); Simmons, *Leicester, Past and Present*, pp.19–56; A.M. Erskine 'The city of Leicester: political and administrative history 1066–1509' in R.A. McKinley (ed.), *A History of the County of Leicester*, vol.4, in R.B. Pugh (ed.), *The Victoria History of the Counties of England* (London, 1958), pp.1–30; Fox, 'Leicester Castle', pp.19–25; A.H. Thompson, *The Abbey of St Mary in the Meadows* (Leicester, 1949).

4   A.H. Thompson, *The Abbey of St Mary in the Meadows*.

5   A. (Mrs T.) Fielding Johnson, *Glimpses of Ancient Leicester* (London and Leicester, 1891), p.56.

6   Simmons, *Leicester Past and Present*, p.24; J. Throsby, *The History and Antiquities of the Ancient Town of Leicester* (Leicester, 1791, Milton Keynes, 2010, eighteenth-century collections online, print edition) pp.32–3.

### The Montforts

7   The main source of information on Simon de Montfort used here is J.A. Maddicott, *Simon de Montfort* (Cambridge, 1994).

8   *Ibid.*, p.1. This quote is taken from a fragment of autobiography left by Montfort.

### John of Gaunt

9   The main source of information on John of Gaunt used here is A. Goodman, *John of Gaunt: the Exercise of Princely Power in Fourteenth-Century Europe* (Harlow, 1992).

10   A. Seton, *Katherine* (London, 1954).

11   Simmons, *Leicester Past and Present*, p.53.

### The Fifteenth Century: the Castle and the Wars of the Roses

12   *Ibid.*, p.53; Fox, 'Leicester Castle', p.24.

13   Source for following three paragraphs A.M. Erskine, 'The city of Leicester: political and administrative history 1066–1509', pp.6–7; Simmons, *Leicester Past and Present*, pp.53–4.

14   J. Gairdner (ed.), 'Gregory's Chronicle: 1420–1426', *The Historical Collections of a Citizen of London in the Fifteenth Century* (1876) pp.126–161. www.british-history.ac.uk, accessed 10 August 2012.

15   J. Thompson, *The History of Leicester* (1879), p.88.

16   Simmons, *Leicester Past and Present*, p.54.

### Richard III

17   L. Fox, 'Leicester Castle', p.24.

18   The main source for the information on Richard III in the next two paragraphs is C. Ross, *Richard III* (London, 1981–1983).

19   C. Billson, *Medieval Leicester* (Leicester, 1920), pp.178–86.

20  *Ibid.*, p.182.

21  D. Baldwin, 'King Richard's Grave', *Transactions of the Leicester Archaeological and Historical Society*, vol.60 (1986), pp.20–4.

22  C. Ross, *Richard III* (London, 1981–1983).

## The Medieval Town and its People

23  Billson, *Medieval Leicester*, pp.1–11.

24  G.M. Martin (ed.), *Knighton's Chronicle, 1337–1396* (Oxford, 1995), p.99.

25  The main sources for the remainder of this section are M.K. Dale, 'The city of Leicester: social and economic history 1066–1509' in R.A. McKinley (ed.), *A History of the County of Leicester*, vol.4, in R.B. Pugh (ed.), *The Victoria History of the Counties of England* (London, 1958) pp.31–54; Ellis, *History in Leicester, 55 BC–1976 AD* (Leicester, 1976); Simmons, *Leicester Past and Present*, pp.19–56; Erskine, 'The city of Leicester: political and administrative history 1066–1509', pp.1–30.

26  Billson, *Medieval Leicester*, pp.127–37. Billson gives a detailed study of the baking trade here.

27  Simmons, *Leicester Past and Present*, p.37.

28  Dale, 'The city of Leicester: social and economic history 1066–1509', p.38.

29  *Ibid.*, p.38.

30  *Ibid.*, pp.39–40; Simmons, *Leicester Past and Present*, p.41.

31  Dale, 'The city of Leicester: social and economic history 1066–1509', pp.40–1; Simmons, *Leicester Past and Present*, pp.50–1; and Leicester City Council website, roll of mayors, www.leicester.gov.uk, accessed 10 August 2010.

32  Simmons, *Leicester Past and Present*, p.40.

33  Billson, *Medieval Leicester*, pp.149–50.

34  The sources of information for markets and fairs are Billson, *Medieval Leicester*, pp.112–22; Dale, 'The city of Leicester: social and economic history 1066–1509', pp.46–9; S.E. Green and J. Wilshere, *Leicester Markets and Fairs* (Leicester, 1973).

35  Green and Wilshere, *Leicester Markets and Fairs*, p.8.

36  Simmons, *Leicester Past and Present*, p.38.

37  Main sources of information about development of early local government are: Ellis, *History in Leicester*, pp.42–5; Erskine, 'The city of Leicester: political and administrative history 1066–1509', pp.19–26; Simmons, *Leicester Past and Present*, pp.55–6.

## Religious Life

38  The main sources of information in this section are: Dale, 'The city of Leicester: social and economic history 1066–1509', pp.49–51; G.H. Martin, 'Church life in Medieval Leicester' in A.E Brown (ed.), *The Growth of Leicester* (Leicester, 1972), pp.27–37; G.H. Martin (ed.), *Knighton's Chronicle, 1337–1396* (Oxford, 1995); Simmons, *Leicester Past and Present*, pp.42–7; A.H.Thompson, *The Abbey of St Mary in the Meadows* (Leicester, 1949).

39  Martin, *Knighton's Chronicle*, pp.199–203.

## Religious Dissent

40  The main sources of information relating to religious dissent are: J. Crompton, 'Leicestershire Lollards' in *Transactions of the Leicestershire Archaeological Society*, vol.44 (1968–9), pp.11–14; Martin, 'Church life in Medieval Leicester', pp.27–37; Martin, *Knighton's Chronicle*; Simmons, *Leicester Past and Present*, pp.47–9. Relating to religious guilds: Simmons, *Leicester Past and Present*, p.51; J. Wilshere, *The Religious Gilds of Medieval Leicester* (1979).

41  Martin, *Knighton's Chronicle*, pp.367–25.

42  Simmons, *Leicester Past and Present*, p.49.

43  Simmons, *Leicester Past and Present*, p.50.

# Chapter Three

1  The account of Wolsey's last days in this section is based on the witness account of George Cavendish reproduced in G.H.M. Simpson (ed.), *The Life of Cardinal Wolsey* (London, 1901), www.archive.org, accessed 30 October 2012. Further background information on Wolsey is mostly derived from R. Bucholz and N. Key, *Early Modern England 1485–1714* (Oxford, 2004); D. MacCulloch, 'The consolidation of England 1485–1603' in J. Morrill (ed.), *The Oxford Illustrated History of Tudor and Stuart Britain* (Oxford, 1996), pp.41–4; S. Schama, *A History of Britain, vol.1 At the Edge of the World? 3000 BC–AD 1603* (London, 2009), pp.300–2.

2  Bucholz and Key, *Early Modern England*, p.56.

3  *See* note 1.

## Religious Revolution and the Birth of Protestant Leicester

4  A.H. Thompson, *The Abbey of St Mary in the Meadows Leicester* (Leicester, 1949), p.232; T.Y. Cocks, 'The Last Abbot of Leicester', *Transactions of the Leicestershire Archaeological Society*, vol.58 (1982–3), pp.6–19.

5  J. Simmons, *Leicester Past and Present*, vol.1, p.59, also pp.57–93 have been used extensively as a source of information this chapter.

6  J. Chandler, *John Leland's Itinerary: Travels in Tudor England* (Stroud, 1993), pp.277–9.

7  Cocks, 'The Last Abbot of Leicester', p.13.

8  C. Billson, *Medieval Leicester* (Leicester, 1920), p.202.

9  Chandler, *John Leland's Itinerary*, pp.277–9; Billson, *Medieval Leicester*, pp.200–1; Simmons, *Leicester Past and Present*, p.58.

10  Simmons, *Leicester Past and Present*, p.61; T. North, *A Chronicle of the Church of St. Martin in Leicester During the Reigns of Henry VIII, Edward IV, Mary and Elizabeth, With Some Account of Its Minor Altars and Major Guilds* (London, 1886) pp.104–5.

## Lady Jane Grey, Mary Tudor and the Aftermath

11  The background information here about Lady Jane Grey and the conflict with Mary Tudor is largely based on information in Bucholz and Key, *Early Modern England 1485–1714*, pp.101–6; A. Squires, *The Greys a Long and Noble Line* (Hale, 2002).

12  R. Ascham, *The Scholemaster* (1570), quoted at www.tudorplace.com.ar/aboutJaneGrey, accessed 20 Apr. 2010.

13  Battista Spinola is quoted in A. Squires, *The Greys a Long and Noble Line*, p.51.

14  D. Slatter, 'The City of Leicester: Political and Administrative History, 1509–1660' in R.A. McKinley (ed.), *A History of the County of Leicester*, vol.4 in R.B. Pugh (ed.), *The Victoria History of the Counties of England* (London, 1958), pp.55–75.

15  *Ibid.*

16  www.tudorplace.com.ar/Bios/Thomas White, edited from L. Stephens and S. Lee (eds), *Dictionary of National Biography* (London, 1891), accessed 14 May 2011.

17  Simmons, *Leicester Past and Present*, p.61.

## Living in and Managing the Tudor Town

18  W. Hoskins, 'An Elizabethan Provincial Town: Leicester' in J.H. Plumb (ed.), *Studies in Social History* (London, 1955), pp.33–67.

19  The information in this section is largely a synthesis of the information given in Hoskins, 'An Elizabethan Provincial Town: Leicester', pp.36–67; Simmons, *Leicester Past and Present*,.pp.67–76; Slatter, 'The City of Leicester: Political and Administrative History, 1509–1660', pp.55–75.

20  Hoskins, 'An Elizabethan Provincial Town: Leicester', pp.53–9.

21  P. Slack, *The English Poor Law 1531–1782* (Basingstoke, 1995).

## The Earl of Huntingdon and the Leicester Free Grammar School

22  The powers of the corporation are described in detail in Slatter, 'The city of Leicester: political and administrative history, 1509–1660', pp.55–75.

23  The greater part of this section about the Earl of Huntingdon and his relationship is derived from three sources all by Claire Cross: M.C. Cross, *The Free Grammar School of Leicester* (Leicester, 1953); M.C. Cross, 'The Third Earl of Huntingdon and Elizabethan Leicestershire', *Transactions of the Leicestershire Archaeological Society*, vol.36 (1960), pp.6–21; M.C. Cross, *The Puritan Earl* (London, 1966).

24  *See* note 24.

25  P. Collinson, *The Elizabethan Puritan Movement* (London, 1967), p.50.

26  M.C. Cross, 'The Third Earl of Huntingdon and Elizabethan Leicestershire', p.17.

27  While the majority of this is summarised from M.C. Cross, *The Free Grammar School of Leicester*, pp.5–34, there is also input from G. Cowie, *The History of Wyggeston's Hospital, the Hospital Schools and the Old Free Grammar School* (Leicester and London, 1893).

28 A.G.R. Smith, *The Emergence of a Nation State: the Commonwealth of England, 1529–1660* (London, 1984), p.195.

29 The story of Nicholas Harwar, John Pott and Anthony Faunt given here is a slightly summarised version of the story told in Cross, *The Free Grammar School of Leicester*, 11–12. Although Sampson gained a legal settlement over the money that was allegedly misused it seems that the financial accusations were primarily driven by a desire to get rid of Pott, for, as Cross points out, shortly after Pott's departure the hospital statutes were amended to make the financial practices that Harwar and Pott were denounced for officially permitted.

30 Cross, *The Leicester Free Grammar School*, p.12.

31 M. Bateson, *Records of the Borough of Leicester*, vol.3, 1509-1603 (London, 1905), p.139.

32 Cross, *The Leicester Free Grammar School*, p.14.

33 Cross, 'The Third Earl of Huntingdon and Elizabethan Leicestershire', pp.15–16.

34 Simmons, *Leicester Past and Present*, pp.82–5.

35 Simmons, *Leicester Past and Present*, p.82; J. Simon, 'The Two John Angels', *Transactions of the Leicestershire Archaeological Society*, vol.31 (1955), pp.35–50.

## Catastrophe: Civil War and the Storming of Leicester

36 S. Schama, *A History of Britain: the British Wars 1603–1776*, (London, 2009) p.15.

37 J. Miller, *A Brief History of The English Civil Wars* (London, 2009).

38 A. Everitt, *The Local Community and The Great Rebellion*, London, 1969; J. Wilshire and S. Green., *The Siege of Leicester – 1645* (London, 1984), p.18.

39 The description here on events as they played out in Leicester is for the most part based on the accounts given in J.H. Plumb, 'Political history 1530–1885' in W.H. Hoskins (ed.) assisted by R.A. McKinley, *A History of Leicestershire*, vol.2, in R.B. Pugh (ed.), *The Victoria History of the Counties of England* (London, 1954); pp.102–34; P.A. Scaysbrook, *The Civil War in Leicestershire and Rutland* (Oxford, 1977); Simmons, *Leicester Past and Present*, pp.86–92; J. Wilshere and S. Green, *The Siege of Leicester – 1645* (Leicester, 1984).

40 Simmons, *Leicester Past and Present*, p.86.

41 Simmons, *Leicester Past and Present*, pp.89–90.

## Chapter Four

1 W. Bray (ed.), *The Diary of John Evelyn* (London, 1901), p.332.

2 R.W. Greaves, 'Parliamentary history, 1660–1835' in R.A. McKinley (ed.), *A History of the County of Leicester*, vol.4, R.B. Pugh (ed.), *The Victoria History of the Counties of England* (London, 1958), pp.110–52.

3 J. Throsby, *The History and Antiquities of the Ancient Town of Leicester* (1791, Milton Keynes, 2010, eighteenth century collections online, print edition), p.130.

4   Bray, *The Diary of John Evelyn*, pp.293–5.
5   C. Morris (ed.), *The Illustrated Journeys of Celia Fiennes 1685–1712* (Far-Thrupp, 1995), pp.1–31.
6   *Ibid.*, pp.143–46.
7   J. Simmons, *Leicester Past and Present*, vol. 1, pp.99–101; A Temple Patterson, *Radical Leicester: a History 1780–1850* (Leicester, 1954), pp.2–8.
8   W.A. Jenkins and C.T. Smith, 'Social and administrative history, 1660–1835' in R.A. McKinley (ed.), *A History of the County of Leicester*, vol.4, in R.B. Pugh (ed.), *The Victoria History of the Counties of England* (London, 1958), pp.153–200.
9   Temple Patterson, *Radical Leicester*, pp.2–3.
10  Jenkins and Smith, 'Social and administrative history, 1660–1835', pp.165–6.
11  *Ibid.*, p.166.
12  Simmons, *Leicester Past and Present*, pp.110–11.
13  D. Defoe, *A Tour Through The Whole Island of Great Britain*, Everyman revised edition (1723–7, London, 1962).
14  *Ibid.*, p.89.
15  Simmons, *Leicester Past and Present*, p.110.

## The Beginning and Growth of the Hosiery Industry

16  Defoe, *A Tour of the Whole Island of Great Britain*, p.88
17  The information in the following paragraphs concerning the hosiery industry is derived from G.A. Chinnery, 'Eighteenth century Leicester' in A.E. Brown (ed.), *The Growth of Leicester* (Leicester, 1972) pp.47–53; Jenkins and Smith, 'Social and administrative history, 1660–1835', pp.168–78; A.N. Newman, 'The evolution of Leicester, 1066–1835: Stuart and Hanoverian' in N. Pye (ed.), *Leicester and its Region* (Leicester, 1972), pp.280–7; Simmons, *Leicester Past and Present*, pp.112–14.
18  *Leicester and Nottingham Journal*, 20 March 1773.

## The Development of Roads, Canals and the Railway

19  F. O'Gorman, *The Long Eighteenth Century: British and Social History 1688–1832* (London, 1997), pp.322–3. The information in the following paragraphs concerning the development of roads and canals in Leicestershire is derived from Chinnery, 'Eighteenth century Leicester', pp.47–63; Newman, 'The evolution of Leicester, 1660–1835: Stuart and Hanoverian', pp.280–7; Simmons, *Leicester Past and Present*, pp.130–4; P.A Stevens, *The Leicester and Melton Mowbray Navigations* (Far-Thrupp, 1975).
20  Simmons, *Leicester Past and Present*, pp.155–9.

## Politics and Religion

21 Greaves, 'Parliamentary history 1660–1835', pp.110–19; Simmons, *Leicester Past and Present*, p.102.

22 Information concerning Leicester dissenters in the following section is derived from H. Thomas, *A History of the Great Meeting, Leicester and its Congregation* (Leicester, 1908); R.A. McKinley and J.D. Martin, 'Protestant Nonconformity' in R.A. McKinley (ed.), *A History of the County of Leicester*, vol.4, in R.B. Pugh (ed.), *The Victoria History of the Counties of England* (London, 1958), pp.390–4.

23 The background information here concerning the Glorious Revolution is derived from S. Schama, *A History of Britain: the British Wars, 1603–1776* (London, 2009), pp.238–64; O'Gorman, *The Long Eighteenth Century*, pp.29–36.

24 W. Gardiner, *Music and Friends or Pleasant Recollections of a Dillettante*, vols 1–3 (London and Leicester, 1838).

25 *Ibid.*, vol.2, pp.609–10.

26 N. Curnock (ed.), *The Journal of the Rev John Wesley, A.M.* vol. 4 (London, 1909–16).

27 O'Gorman, *The Long Eighteenth Century*, pp.32–4.

28 Simmons, *Leicester Past and Present*, p.103.

29 J. Thompson, *The History of Leicester in the Eighteenth Century* (Leicester, 1871), pp.60–75.

30 *Ibid.*, pp.60–75.

31 Throsby, *The History and Antiquities of the Ancient Town of Leicester*, p.151–2.

32 Simmons, *Leicester Past and Present*, p.104.

33 *Ibid.*, p.104.

## Town Improvements and Social Life

34 P. Borsay, 'The English urban renaissance: the development of provincial urban culture 1680–c.1760' in P. Borsay (ed.), *The Eighteenth Century Town* (London, 1990), pp.159–87.

35 Simmons, *Leicester Past and Present*, pp.110–11.

36 *Ibid.*, pp.119 and 140.

37 G.A. Potts, 'The development of New Walk and the King Street area' in A.E. Brown (ed.), *The Growth of Leicester*, (Leicester, pp.55–61.

38 Simmons, *Leicester Past and Present*, pp.138–40.

39 A. Temple Patterson, *Radical Leicester*: p.14.

40 *Ibid.*, p.13.

41 *Ibid.*, p.122.

42 *Ibid.*, p.7.

43 *Ibid.*, p.7.

44 *Ibid.*, pp.9–10.

45 E. Frizelle and J.D. Martin, *The Leicester Royal Infirmary 1771–1971* (Leicester, 1971), pp.1–77.

46 This and the other paragraphs in this section are mostly based on information in A. Temple Patterson, *Radical Leicester*, pp.64–78; Simmons, *Leicester Past and Present*, p.143.

47 *Leicester Herald*, May 1972, exact date uncertain.

## Schools

48 Gardiner, *Music and Friends*, p.75.

49 Except where indicated the information in this and the following three paragraphs is from J. Martin, 'Primary and secondary education' in R.A. McKinley (ed.), *A History of the County of Leicester*, vol.4, in R.B. Pugh (ed.), *The Victoria History of the Counties of England* (London, 1958), pp.328–31.

50 R.W. Greaves, 'The origins and early history of Alderman Newton's Foundation' in *Leicestershire and Archaeological and Historical Society Transactions*, vol.19, part 2 (1936–7), pp.347–76.

51 Martin, 'Primary and secondary education', pp.328–31; Simmons, *Leicester Past and Present*, pp.172–6.

52 C. Grewcock,' The Leicester Mechanics Institute' (1833–70), in D. Williams (ed.), *The Adaptation of Change* (Leicester, 1980), pp.13–31.

## The Reform of the Leicester Corporation

53 The main sources in this section are: Simmons, *Leicester Past and Present*, pp.143–53; Temple Patterson, *Radical Leicester*, pp.146–215; R.W. Greaves, *The Corporation of Leicester* (Leicester, 1970).

## Chartism

54 T. Cooper, *The Life of Thomas Cooper* (London, 1897), chapter 13, 'Wretchedness of stockingers', unnumbered pages online at www.gerald-massey.org.uk.

55 *Ibid.*, chapter 20, 'Chartist life continued: my first trial and acquittal, 1842', unnumbered pages.

# Chapter Five

## Hosiery

1 The account of the hosiery industry given in this section is largely based on the information given in C. Ashworth, 'Hosiery manufacture', in R.A. McKinley (ed.), *A History of the County of Leicester*, vol.4, in R.B. Pugh (ed.), *The Victoria History of the Counties of England* (London, 1958), pp.303–14; F.A. Wells, *The British Hosiery and Knitwear Industry: its History and Organisation*, (Newton Abbot, 1972).

2 C.W. Webb, *An Historical Record of N. Corah and Sons Ltd* (Leicester,1940-1949), p.20.

3  *Leicester Chronicle and Leicestershire Mercury*, 22 April 1871.

4  F.A.Wells, *The British Hosiery and Knitwear Industry: its History and Organisation*, p.129.

5  Webb, *An Historical Record*, p.39.

## Boots and Shoes

6  The account of the boot and shoe industry given in this section is largely based on information given in V.W. Hogg, 'Footwear manufacture' in R.A. McKinley (ed.), *A History of the County of Leicester*, vol.4, in R.B. Pugh (ed.), *The Victoria History of the Counties of England* (London, 1958), pp.315–27; B. Lancaster, *Radicalism, Cooperation and Socialism: Leicester Working Class Politics 1860–1906* (Lancaster, 1987); J. Simmons, *Leicester Past and Present*, vol.2: *Modern City* (London, 1974), pp.2–4; J.D. Welding, *The Leicestershire Boot and Shoe Industry* (Leicester, 1985).

7  Hogg, 'Footwear manufacture', p.314.

8  Hogg, 'Footwear manufacture', p.316.

9  The census statistics in this paragraph are taken from Simmons, *Leicester Past and Present*, vol.2, p.151.

## Public Health: Disease, Sanitation and Water

10  J. Simmons, *Leicester Past and Present, vol.1: Ancient Borough* (London, 1974) p.184.

11  E.R. Frizelle and J.D. Martin, *Leicester Royal Infirmary, 1771–1971* (Leicester, 1971), p.101.

12  Simmons, *Leicester Past and Present*, vol. 2, pp.17–19

13  R.A. McKinley and C.T. Smith, 'Social and administrative history since 1835' in R.A. McKinley (ed.), *A History of the County of Leicester*, vol.4, in R.B. Pugh (ed.), *The Victoria History of the Counties of England* (London, 1958), pp.263–5.

14  *See* McKinley and Smith 'Social and administrative history', pp.267–9; Simmons, *Leicester Past and Present*, vol.2, pp.13–14.

## Suburbanisation

15  The information in this section is mostly sourced from C. Jordan, *Leicester Mercury: the Illustrated History of Leicester's Suburbs* (Derby, 2003); R.H. Evans, 'The expansion of Leicester in the nineteenth century' in A.E. Brown (ed.), *The Growth of Leicester* (Leicester, 1972), pp.63–70; McKinley and Smith, 'Social and administrative history', pp.290–2; Simmons, *Past and Present*, vol.2, pp.6–10.

16  Simmons, *Leicester Past and Present*, vol.2, p.151.

17  J. Farquhar, *Arthur Wakerley 1862-1931* (Leicester, 1984), pp.28-46; Simmons, *Past and Present*, vol. 2, pp.121-22; M.Taylor, *The Quality of Leicester*, 2nd edn (1997), pp. 129–131.

18  R. Read, *Modern Leicester* (London, 1880), p.285.

19  R. Rodger, 'The built environment', in D. Nash and D. Reeder (eds), *Leicester in the Twentieth Century* (1993), pp.10–13.

20  G. Davison, 'The suburban idea and its enemies', *Journal of Urban History* vol. 39: 5, (2013) pp. 829–49.

## Civic Participation and Civic Pride

21  E.P. Hennock, *Fit and Proper Persons* (London, 1973), p.17.

22  J. Garrard, *Leadership and Power in Victorian Industrial Towns 1830–1880* (Manchester, 1983), pp.13–23.

23  A. Briggs, *Victorian Cities* (third edition, London, 1990), pp.195–201; Hennock, *Fit and Proper Persons*, pp.61–79.

24  Briggs, *Victorian Cities*, p.196.

25  This is based on information about societies and the town council given in *The Leicestershire Trade Protection Society: Street, Alphabetical and Trade Directory of Leicester*, 1870, especially pp.5–11; details given about attendance at Leicester Infirmary AGM in the *Leicester Chronicle and Leicestershire Mercury*, 15 April 1871 and membership lists of the John of Gaunt (Masonic) Lodge in A.J.S. Cannon, *The History of John of Gaunt Lodge No 523: One Hundred Years 1846–1946* (Leicester, 1946).

26  F.B. Lott, *The Centenary Book of the Leicester Literary and Philosophical Society* (Leicester, 1935).

27  *Ibid.*, pp.32–3.

28  *Ibid.*, p.37.

29  A. Newman, 'Sir Israel Hart', *Transactions of Leicestershire Archaeological and Historical Society*, vol.49, (1975) pp.43–56; Simmons, *Leicester Past and Present*, vol.2, pp.31–3.

30  R.J. Morris and R. Rodger, 'An introduction to British Urban History 1820–1914' in R.J. Morris and R. Rodger (eds), *The Victorian City: a Reader in Britain Urban History, 1820–1914* (London, 1993), p.8.

31  Simmons, *Leicester Past and Present*, vol.2, pp.48–9.

32  J. and T. Spencer (firm), *Spencers' New Guide to Leicester* (1888).

33  *Ibid.*, p.115.

34  *Ibid.*, pp.128–31.

35  *Ibid.*, p.152.

36  *Ibid.*, p.135.

37  *Ibid.*, p.136.

38  *Ibid.*, p.140.

## The Opening of Abbey Park

39  Briggs, *Victorian Cities*, p.135.

40  J.S. Phipps, *Leicester in Parliament* (Leicester, 1988), p.96.

41  *Leicester Daily Post*, 14 January 1882.

42  The descriptions given here of the opening of Abbey Park in Leicester are based

on contemporary accounts in the *Leicester Daily Post*, 3 June 1882 and the *Leicester Daily Mercury*, 3 June 1882.

## Chapter Six

1   Information based on end of year chronologies published in the *Leicester Chronicle and Leicestershire Mercury (LCLM)*, chronology for 1874 published 7 January 1875 and chronology for 1875 published on 8 January 1876.
2   J. Simmons, *Leicester Past and Present*, vol.2: Modern City (London, 1974), p.30.

### The Leicester Calendar in the 1870s and 1880s

3   The information in this paragraph is derived from *the Leicestershire Trade Protection Society: Alphabetical and Trade Directory of Leicester*, 1870; J. Simmons, *Leicester Past and Present*, vol. 2, p.30.
4   J. Crump, 'The Great Carnival of the Year: the Leicester Races in the 19th Century', *Transactions of the Leicestershire Archaeological Society'*, vol.58 (1982–3), pp.58–74; R. Read, *Modern Leicester* (London, 1981), pp.206–7.
5   S.E. Green and J. Wilshere, *Leicester Markets and Fairs* (Leicester, 1973).
6   *LCLM*, 14 October 1871.
7   Simmons, *Leicester Past and Present*, vol. 2, p.58.
8   *LCLM*, 1 November 1884.
9   *LCLM*, 22 November 1884.
10  www.the phil.org.uk/history, accessed 10 August 2011.
11  *LCLM*, 8 Jan 1876, chronology for 1875.
12  *Ibid.*
13  *LCLM*, 7 October 1871.
14  *LCLM*, 8 January 1876, chronology for 1875.
15  *LCLM*, 7 January 1871.
16  Both the Ragged School dinner and the outing for workhouse children are recorded in *LCLM*, 21 January 1871.
17  *LCLM*, 18 February 1871.
18  *LCLM*, 4 March 1871.
19  *LCLM*, 6 May 1971.
20  Simmons, *Leicester Past and Present*, vol. 2, p.36.
21  The information on amateur cricket clubs given in this and the following paragraph is derived from *Wright's Directory of Leicester*, 1882.
22  *LCLM*, 16 February 1884.
23  *Leicester Daily Mercury (LDM)*, 31 June 1882; *Wright's Directory of Leicester*, 1882.
24  The Abbey Park Flower Show was reported annually in the local press. For example, *Leicester Daily Post (LDP)*, 9 August 1893. The format was sustained with minor changes until the 1930s.
25  *LCLM*, 21 June 1881.
26  The All Saints' Discussion Group organised an annual summer walk throughout the early 1870s and 1890s. One such trip is described in *LCLM*, 5 August 1871.

27  G.A. Steppler, *Britons to Arms! The Story of the British Volunteer Soldier* (Stroud, 1992).

## Social Networks

28  J.F.C. Harrison, *Learning and Living, 1790–1960: a Study in the History of the English Adult Education Movement* (London, 1961), p.4. Harrison, himself a native of Leicester, was not in fact referring to Leicester here, but his descriptions also fit the Leicester context.

29  *Report of the Council of the Leicester Literary and Philosophical Society* (1871), pp.1–7.

30  The sources used for information about Leicester Working Men's College are: A.J. Allaway, *Vaughan College Leicester 1862–1962* (Leicester, 1962); E. Atkins, *The Vaughan Working Men's College, Leicester 1862–1912: its History and Work for Fifty Years* (Leicester, 1912).

31  *Leicester Literary and Philosophical Society: Reports 1871–1880* (1871–80).

32  This viewpoint was argued in a paper by F.D. Maurice that was read by the Revd T.W. Barlow at a Lit and Phil meeting in 1862. *LCLM*, 25 February 1862.

33  *LCLM*, 21 January 1871.

34  Harrison, *Learning and Living, 1790–1960*, p.91.

35  Record Office for Leicester, Leicestershire and Rutland (ROLLR), 10 D 68/17. F.J. Gould, *History of the Secular Society* (Leicester, 1900), p.8.

36  ROLLR, L288, *The Leicester Domestic Mission Annual Reports* (1872).

37  *LCLM*, 21 January 1871.

38  ROLLR, CRO pamphlets, 45, G. Robson, *The Twentieth Walkout of All Saints Discussion Group and Other Poems* (Leicester, c.1972).

39  B. Lancaster, *Radicalism, Cooperation and Socialism: Leicester Working Class Politics, 1860–1906* (1987) pp.86–7.

40  ROLLR, 10 D 68/17, Records of the Secular Society, F. Gould, *The History of the Secular Society* (1900), p.12; Simmons, *Leicester Past and Present*, vol.2, pp.34–5.

41  *The Freethinker*, April 1890, cuttings in ROLLR 10/D 68/6, Records of the Secular Society, scrapbook concerning the society, 1873–1908.

42  The source for information given here on Tom Barclay is Lancaster, *Radicalism, Cooperation and Socialism*, pp.86–92 and III–15.

43  Simmons, *Leicester Past and Present*, vol.2, pp.34–5.

44  J. Harris, *Public Lives, Public Spirit* (London, 1993), p.23.

45  G. Ellis, *The Leicester Ladies Reading Society* (Leicester, 1930). All the information included here about this society comes from Ellis's account.

## 1890–1914: New Influences, New Organisations and a Growing Social Calendar

46  *Ibid.*, p.9.

47  *LDP,* 8 December 1893.

48  *Wright's Directory of Leicester*, 1894.

49  ROLLR, DE 2838/3811 a book of correspondence belonging to the Mayor Charles Lakin.

50  *Wright's Directory of Leicester*, 1894.

51  A. Fox., *A History of the National Union of Boot and Shoe Operatives, 1874–1957* (Oxford, 1958), pp.147–8, 177–8 and 219–20.

52  R. Evans, 'Parliamentary history since 1835', in R.A. McKinley (ed.), *A History of the County of Leicester*, vol.4, in R.B. Pugh (ed.), *The Victoria History of the Counties of England* (London, 1958), pp.224–41.

53  Lancaster, *Radicalism, Cooperation and Socialism*, pp.174–5.

54  The description and quotations in the following paragraphs are taken from the description given in the *LDP*, 5 June 1905.

55  Lancaster, *Radicalism, Cooperation and Socialism*, pp.177–82.

## Chapter Seven

### The First World War

1  The main source of information in this and the next five paragraphs is B. Beazley, *Four Years Remembered: Leicester During the Great War* (Derby, 1999).

2  Beazley, *Four Years Remembered*, p.17.

### The Interwar Years: Civic Pride, Economic Success and Social Activity

3  J. Harris, *Public Lives, Public Spirit: Britain 1870–1914* (London, 1994), pp.17–23.

4  S. Gunn, *The Public Culture of the Victorian Middle Class: Ritual and Authority in the English Industrial City, 1840–1914* (Manchester, 2000), pp.163–86.

5  F.B. Lott, *The Centenary Book of the Leicester Literary and Philosophical Society* (Leicester, 1935).

6  The major source for this and the previous paragraph is D. Reeder and C. Harrison, 'The Local Economy' in D. Nash and D. Reeder (eds), *Leicester in the Twentieth Century* (Stroud, 1993), pp.49–90.

7  *Leicester Evening Mail (LEM)*, 1 November 1938 and 24 November 1938.

8  H. Cunningham, 'Leisure and culture' in F.M.L. Thompson (ed.), *The Cambridge Social History of Britain 1750–1950*, vol.2 (Cambridge, 1990), pp.330 and 305.

### Local Democracy and Citizenship

9  P. Jones, 'Politics' in D. Nash and D. Reeder (eds), *Leicester in the Twentieth Century* (Stroud, 1993), pp.90–120.

10  *Ibid*.

11  *Ibid*.

12  Record Office of Leicester, Leicestershire and Rutland (ROLLR); Records of the Leicester Literary and Philosophical Society, 14 D 55 and University of Leicester Library, *Transactions of the Literary and Philosophical Society* (1881–1937).

13  ROLLR, Records of the Kyrle Society/Civic Society 17 D 51.

14  ROLLR, Records of Leicester Rotary Club 21 D 69.

15  This section on the Wycliffe Society for Helping the Blind is mostly based on ROLLR, DE 2730/106 and DE 122. Reference was also made to D. Seaton, *Light Amid the Shadows* (1994).

16  D. Reeder and C. Brown, 'Municipal provision: education, health and housing', in Nash and Reeder, *Leicester in the Twentieth Century*, pp.121–57.

## Social Housing and Home Ownership

17  R. Rodger, 'The built environment' in Nash and Reeder, *Leicester in the Twentieth Century*, pp.1–48.

18  *Ibid.*

19  J.F.C. Harrison, *Scholarship Boy: a Personal History of the Mid-Twentieth Century* (London, 1995), p.50.

20  *Leicester Mercury (LM)*, 21 January 1930.

## Women as Citizens

21  University of Leicester archives AD/B3/1. Copy of letter sent out by V. Astley Clarke and Jonathan North. *LM* 1 July 1921 has reports of the meeting.

22  *LM*, 22 April 1922 records the involvement of adult school members and *LM, 16* May 1922 records the involvement of the Girl Guides.

23  *LM*, 5 July 1921.

24  ROLLR, 16 D 58/8. Scrapbook of news cuttings programmes and photographs recording the conference of the National Council of Women in Leicester in 1935.

25  C.L. White, *Women's Magazines 1693–1968* (London, 1976), referred to in M. Pugh, *Women and the Women's Movement in Britain, 1914–1959* (Basingstoke, 1993).

26  *LEM*, 22 September 1938.

27  These titles are taken from the programme of the Leicester Personal Health Association, reported on by Suzanne Harrison in *LEM*, 7 September 1938.

28  *LEM*, 7 December 1938.

29  *LEM*, 11 May 1939, St Mary's Home for Girls and 17 May 1939, Maternity Hospital and YMCA.

30  *LEM*, 4 July 1939, Moat Girls' School Sports Day.

31  *LEM*, 21 August 1939.

## Young People: the Citizens of the Future

32  ROLLR L369.443 booklet entitled *History of the Girl Guide Movement in Leicester and County over the Past 50 years.* No author or date given but the fifty years covered are 1912–62.

33  R.J. Morris, 'Clubs, societies and associations ' in F.M.L. Thompson (ed.), *The Cambridge Social History of Britain*: 175–1950, vol.3 (Cambridge, 1990), p.423.

34  See ROLLR, DE 4283/49, records of the Boy Scout Council and Leicester District Boy Scouts Association, 1909–88, register of the Leicester District Local Association, 1913–15.

## The Leicester Pageant of 1932

35 The information here is based on *Leicester Evening Mail* reports during June 1932.

36 The account of the Leicester Pageant given here is based on reports in the *LEM*, 1931–2.

37 *LEM*, 15 December 1931.

38 *LEM*, 15 April 1932.


# Chapter Eight

## The Second World War

1 The main sources of information for this section on the Second World War are B. Beazley, *Wartime Leicester* (Stroud, 2004), pp.80–1, J. Simmons, *Leicester Past and Present, vol.2: Modern City 1860-1974* (London, 1974) and *Leicester Blitz Souvenir* produced by Wright Process Engraving Co. Ltd (undated).

2 Beazley, *Wartime Leicester*, p.54.

3 *Ibid.*, pp.56–58.

4 *Leicester Blitz Souvenir.*

5 *Leicester Mercury*, 20 November 1940.

## Council Housing and Slum Clearance

6 The main sources for this section on housing are B. Beazley, *Post-War Leicester*; R. Rodger, 'The built environment' in D. Nash and D. Reeder (eds), *Leicester in the Twentieth Century* (Stroud, 1993), pp.1–48.

7 My Leicestershire digital archive, myleicestershire.wordpress.com. BBC Radio Leicester, 'High rise hell', series title *In Perspective*, transmission date 11 May 1977, accessed 1 August 2012.

8 See Roger, 'The built environment', p.29 for full story.

## Accommodating the Car

9 The main sources for this section are: J. Simmons, *Leicester Past and Present*, pp.82–93; Beazley, *Post-War Leicester*, pp.1–48.

10 *Leicester of the Future* issued by the Authority of the Leicester Publicity and Development Committees (undated), p.59.

11 Simmons, *Leicester Past and Present* (1974), p.86.

12 Leicester mayor's bid to change city layout, 5 December 2011. www.thisisLeicestershire.co.uk, accessed 1 August 2012.

13 B. Beazley, *Post-War Leicester*, p.113.

14 K. Smigielski, *Leicester Traffic Plan* (Leicester, 1964).

15 My Leicestershire digital archive, myleicestershire.wordpress.com. BBC Radio Leicester, 'Conservation', series title *In Perspective*, Transmission date 23 May 1972 and BBC Radio Leicester, 'Konrad Smigielski', series title, *In Perspective*, transmission date 2 December 1972, accessed 1 August 2010.

## The Local Economy: Changes Since the Second World War

16  Main sources of information in this section on the local economy are: D. Reeder and C. Harrison, 'The local economy' in D. Nash and D. Reeder (eds), *Leicester in the Twentieth Century* (Stroud, 1993), pp.49–90; Beazley, *Post-War Leicester*, pp. 72–83 and pp.117–31.

17  Beazley, *Post-War Leicester*, p.133.

18  'County's last major shoe factory to shut', 9 January 2009, www.thisisleicestershire.co.uk, accessed 1 August 2010.

19  Corah Plc, www.knittingtogether.org.uk, accessed 1 August 2010.

20  P. Atherton, 'Government agrees to BUSM pension inquiry', *Daily Telegraph*, 25 July 2005, www.telegraph.co.uk, accessed 1 August 2012.

## The Universities

21  The sources of information used here for the history of the University of Leicester since the war are: B. Burch, *The University of Leicester, a History, 1921–1996* (Leicester, 1996); J. Simmons, *New University* (Leicester, 1958).

22  www.dmu.ac.uk, accessed 1 August 2012.

23  Simmons, *Leicester Past and Present*, p.25.

24  www.dmu.ac.uk, accessed 1 August 2012.

25  www.dmu.ac.uk and www.le.ac.uk, accessed 1 August 2012.

## Multicultural Leicester

26  The main sources of information here are P. Winstone, 'Managing a multi-ethnic and multi-cultural city in Europe: *Leicester in International Social Science Journal*, 48 (1996), pp.33–41; D. Nash, 'Organisational and associational life' in D. Nash and D. Reeder (eds), *Leicester in the Twentieth Century* (Stroud, 1993), pp.158–93; J. Martin and G. Singh, *Asian Leicester*.

27  A. Newman, 'Sir Israel Hart of Leicester', *Transactions of the Leicester Archaeological and Historical Society*, vol.49 (1975), pp.43–51.

28  Beazley, *Postwar Leicester*, p.23.

29  Nash, 'Organisational and Associational life', pp.158–93.

## The Present and the Past

30  *Leicester Link*, 2011–12.

# BIBLIOGRAPHY

## Books

Allaway, A.J., *Vaughan College, Leicester 1862–1962* (Leicester, 1962)

Ascham, R., The Scholemaster (1570) quoted at www. tudorplace.com, accessed 20 Apr. 2012

Ashworth, C., 'Hosiery manufacture' in (ed.), R.A. McKinley, *A History of the County of Leicester*, vol.4 in *The Victoria History of the Counties of England* (ed.) R. B. Pugh, (London, 1958)

Atkins, E., *The Vaughan Working Men's College, Leicester 1862–1912: its History and Work for Fifty Years* (Leicester, 1912)

Aucott, S., *Mothercraft and Maternity: Leicester's Maternity and Infant Welfare Services 1900 to 1948* (Leicester, 1997)

Baldwin, D., 'King Richard's grave in Leicester', *Transactions of Leicestershire Archaeological Society*, vol.60 (1986), pp.21–24

Bateson, M. (ed.), *Records of the Borough of Leicester, vol. 1, 1103–1327* (London, 1899)

Bateson, M. (ed.), *Records of the Borough of Leicester, vol. 2, 1327–1509* (London, 1904)

Bateson, M. (ed.), *Records of the Borough of Leicester, vol. 3, 1509–1603* (Cambridge, 1905)

Beazley, B., *Four Years Remembered: Leicester During the Great War* (Derby, 1999)

Beazley, B., *Wartime Leicester* (Stroud, 2004)

Beazley, B., *Post-War Leicester* (Stroud, 2006)

Billson, C.J., *Medieval Leicester* (Leicester, 1920)

Borsay, P., (ed.), *The Eighteenth Century Town* (London, 1990)

Bray, W. (ed.), *The Diary of John Evelyn* (London, 1901)

Brown, A.E., 'Roman Leicester' in A.E. Brown (ed.), *The Growth of Leicester* (1972), pp.11–18.

Briggs, A., *Victorian Cities* (third edition, London, 1990)

Bucholz, R. and Key, N., *Early Modern England 1485–1714* (Oxford, 2004)

Burch, B., *The University of Leicester, a History, 1921–1996* (Leicester, 1996)

Campbell, J., John, E. and Wormald, P., *The Anglo Saxons* (London, 1991)

Cannon, A.J.S., *The History of John of Gaunt Lodge No 523: One Hundred Years 1846–1946*, Masonic pamphlet (Leicester, 1946)

Carswell, J., *Ours to Defend. Leicestershire People Remember World War II* (Leicester, 1989)

Chandler, J., *John Leland's Itinerary: Travels in Tudor England* (Stroud, 1993)

Charman, D., 'Wealth and trade in Leicester in the early sixteenth century', *Transactions of the Leicestershire Archaeological Society*, vol.25 (1949), pp.69–97

Chinnery, G.A., 'Eighteenth century Leicester' in A.E. Brown (ed.), *The Growth of Leicester* (Leicester, 1972) pp.47–53

Cocks, T.Y., 'The last abbot of Leicester', *Transactions of the Leicestershire Archaeological Society*, vol.58 (London, 1982–3), pp.6–19

Cooper, T., *The Life of Thomas Cooper* (1897) www.geraldmassey-org.uk, accessed 1 August 2012

Collis, H., Hurll, F. and Hazlewood, R., *Official History of the Boy Scouts Association* (London, 1961)

Connor, A., *Roman and Medieval Occupation in Causeway Lane Leicester: Excavations 1980 and 1981* (Leicester, 1999)

Collinson, P., *The Elizabethan Puritan Movement* (London, 1967)

Cowie, G., *The History of Wyggeston's Hospital, the Hospital Schools and the Old Free Grammar School,* Leicester (Leicester and London, 1893)

Cox, B., *The Place Names of Leicestershire, Part 1, The Borough of Leicester* (Nottingham, 1998)

Crompton, J., 'Leicestershire Lollards', *Transactions of the Leicestershire Archaeological Society*, vol.44 (1968–9), pp.11–44

Cross, M.C., *The Free Grammar School of Leicester* (Leicester, 1953)

Cross M.C., 'The Third Earl of Huntingdon and Elizabethan Leicestershire', *Transactions of the Leicestershire Archaeological Society*, vol.36 (1960), pp.6–21

Cross, M.C., *The Puritan Earl* (1966)

Crump, J., 'The Great Carnival of the Year': the Leicester Races in the 19th century', *Transactions of the Leicestershire Archaeological Society*, vol.58, 1982–3 (1955), pp.58–74

Cunningham, H., 'Leisure and culture' in FML Thompson (ed.), *The Cambridge Social History of Britain 1750–1950,* vol. 2 (Cambridge, 199), pp.305, 330.

Dale, M.K., 'The city of Leicester: social and economic history 1066–1509' in *The Victoria History of the Counties of England* (ed.) R. B. Pugh, (London, 1958) pp.31–54

Davison, G., 'The suburban idea and its enemies' (Journal of Urban History, vol.39:5, pp.829–849)

De Beer, E.S. (ed.), *The Diary of John Evelyn* (Oxford, 1955)

Defoe, D., *A Tour Through The Whole Island of Great Britain,* (1724–6, London, 1962)

Ellis, C. (ed.), *History in Leicester,* third edition (Leicester, 1976)

Elliot, M., *Victorian Leicester* (London, 1979)

Ellis, G., *The Leicester Ladies Reading Society* (Leicester, 1930)

Ellis, I.C., *Records of Nineteenth Century Leicester* (Guernsey, 1935)

Erskine, A.M., 'The city of Leicester: political, administrative history 1066–1509' in (ed.), R.A. McKinley, *A History of the County of Leicester,* vol.4 in *The Victoria History of the Counties of England* (ed.) R. B. Pugh, (London, 1958) pp.1–30

Evans, R.H., 'The expansion of Leicester in the nineteenth century' in (ed.), A.E. Brown, *The Growth of Leicester* (Leicester, 1972), pp.63–70

Evans, R.H., 'Parliamentary history since 1835' in (ed.), R.A. McKinley, *A History of the County of Leicester,* vol.4 in *The Victoria History of the Counties of England* (ed.) R. B. Pugh, (London, 1958), pp.224–41

Everitt, A.M., *The Local Community and the Great Rebellion* (London, 1969)

Farquhar, J, *Arthur Wakerley, 1862–1931* (Leicester, 1984)

Fielding Johnson, A. (Mrs T.), *Glimpses of Ancient Leicester* (London, first edition, 1891)

Fleming, R., *Britain after Rome: the Fall and Rise, 400–1070* (London, 2010)

Fox, A., *A History of the National Union of Boot and Shoe Operatives, 1874–1957* (Oxford, 1958)

Frizelle, E.R. and Martin, J.D., *The Leicester Royal Infirmary 1771–1971* (Leicester, 1971)

Gardiner, W., *Music and Friends or Pleasant Recollections of a Dilettante*, vols 1–3 (London and Leicester, 1838)

Garrard, J., *Leadership and Power in Victorian Industrial Towns 1830–1880* (Manchester, 1983)

Giles, J., *Six Old Chronicles* (London, 1848)

Goodman, A., *John of Gaunt: The Exercise of Princely Power in Fourteenth Century Europe* (Harlow, 1992)

Gould, F.J., *History of the Secular Society* (Leicester, 1900) p. 8

Greaves, R.W., *The Corporation of Leicester* (Leicester, 1970)

Greaves, R.W., 'The origins and early history of Alderman Newton's Foundation' in the *Leicestershire Archaeological and Historical Society Transactions*, vol.19, part 2, pp.347–76

Green, S.E., and Wilshire, J., *Leicester Markets and Fairs* (Leicester, 1974)

*Gregory's Chronicle: 1420–1426, The Historical Collections of a Citizen of London in the Fifteenth Century* (1876), pp.126–61, www. british-history.ac.uk, accessed 10 August 2012

Grewcock, C., 'The Leicester Mechanics Institute', 1833–70 in D. Williams (ed.), *The Adaptation of Change* (Leicester, 1980), pp.13–31

Gunn, S., *The Public Culture of the Victorian Middle Class: Ritual and Authority in the English Industrial City 1840–1914* (Manchester, 2000)

Haigh, Christopher, *English Reformations: Religion, Politics and Society Under the Tudors* (Oxford, 1993)

Harrison, J.F.C., *Scholarship Boy: a Personal History of the Mid-Twentieth Century* (London, 1995)

Harris, J., *Public Lives, Public Spirit: Britain 1870–1914* (London, 1994)

Harris, O.D., 'Jews, Jurats and the Jewry Wall: a name in context', *Transactions of the Leicestershire Archaeological and Historical Society*, vol.82 (2008), pp.113–23

Harrison, J.F.C., *Learning and Living, 1750–1960: a Study in the History of the English Adult Education Movement* (London, 1961)

Haynes, B., *Working-Class Life in Victorian Leicester: the Joseph Dare Reports* (Leicester, 1991)

Hebditch, M., 'Roman Leicester' in C. Ellis, *History in Leicester*, (second edition, Leicester, 1969) pp.13–22

Hennock, E.P., *Fit and Proper Persons* (London, 1973)

Herne, F.S. (ed.), *The Historical Pageant of Leicester: Official Souvenir* (Leicester, 1932)

Hogg, V.W. 'Footwear manufacture' in (ed.), R.A. McKinley, *A History of the County of Leicester*, vol.4 in *The Victoria History of the Counties of England* (ed.) R. B. Pugh, (London, 1958), pp.315–27

Hoskins, W.H. and McKinley, R.A. (eds), *A History of Leicestershire*, vol.2 in R.B. Pugh (ed.), *The Victoria History of the Counties of England* (London, 1954)

Howie, I., *Serving the Shoemaker for 100 Years. The Official Centenary History of British United Shoe Machinery* (Leicester, 1999)

Jenkins, W.A. and C.T. Smith, 'Social and administrative history, 1660–1835' in (ed.), R.A. McKinley, *A History of the County of Leicester*, vol.4 in *The Victoria History of the Counties of England* (ed.) R. B. Pugh, (London, 1958)

Jones, P., 'Politics' in D. Nash and D. Reeder (eds), *Leicester in the Twentieth Century* (Stroud, 1972), pp.90–120

Jordan, C., *Leicester Mercury: the Illustrated History of Leicester's Suburbs* (Derby, 2003)

Kearney, H, *The British Isles: a History of Four Nations* (Cambridge, 1989)

Lancaster, B., *Radicalism, Cooperation and Socialism: Leicester Working Class Politics, 1860–1906* (Leicester, 1987)

Lott, F.B., *The Centenary Book of the Leicester Literary and Philosophical Society* (Leicester, 1935)

Maddicott, J.R., *Simon de Montfort* (Cambridge, 1994)

Marrett, V., *Immigrants Settling in the City* (Leicester, 1989)

Martin, G.H., 'Church life in Medieval Leicester' in A.E. Brown (ed.), *The Growth of Leicester* (Leicester, 1927), pp.27–37

Martin, G.H. (ed.), *Knighton's Chronicle, 1337–1396* (Oxford, 1995)

Martin, J., 'Primary and secondary education' in (ed.), R.A. McKinley, *A History of the County of Leicester*, vol.4 in *The Victoria History of the Counties of England* (ed.) R. B. Pugh, (London, 1958), pp.328–31

Martin, J. D., 'Protestant Nonconformity' in (ed.), R.A. McKinley, *A History of the County of Leicester*, vol.4 in *The Victoria History of the Counties of England* (ed.) R. B. Pugh, (London, 1958), pp.390–94

Martin, J., and Singh, G., *Asian Leicester* (Stroud, 2002)

McKinley, R.A. and C.T. Smith, 'Social and adminstrative history since 1835' in (ed.), R.A. McKinley, *A History of the County of Leicester*, vol.4 in *The Victoria History of the Counties of England* (ed.) R. B. Pugh, (London, 1958), pp.263–65

McKinley, R.A. and Martin, J.D. 'Protestant Nonconformity' in (ed.), R.A. McKinley, *A History of the County of Leicester*, vol.4 in *The Victoria History of the Counties of England* (ed.) R. B. Pugh, (London, 1958) pp.390–94

Mellor, J., 'Roman Leicester' in C. Ellis, *History in Leicester* (third edition, Leicester, 1976)

Miller, J., *A Brief History of the English Civil Wars* (London, 2009)

Millward, R., *A History of Leicestershire and Rutland* (Chichester, 1985)

Morrill, J. (ed.), *The Oxford Illustrated History of Tudor and Stuart Britain* (Oxford, 1996)

Morris, M., Buckley, R. and Codd, M., *Visions of Ancient Leicester* (Leicester, 2011)

Morris, C., *The Illustrated Journeys of Celia Fiennes 1685–1712* (Far-Thrupp, 1995)

Morris, R.J., and Rodger, R. (eds), *Victorian City: a Reader in Britain Urban History 1820–1914* (London, 1993)

Nash, D. and Reeder, D. (eds), *Leicester in the Twentieth Century* (Stroud, 1993)

Newman, A., 'Sir Israel Hart of Leicester', *Transactions of Leicestershire Archaeological and Historical Society*, vol.49 (1975), pp.43–51

Newitt, N., *A People's History of Leicester* (Derby, 2008)

Nichols, J., *History and Antiquities of the County of Leicester*, vol.1, part 2 ([London, 1815] Wakefield, 1971)

North, T., *A Chronicle of the Church of St Martin in Leicester During the Reigns of Henry VIII, Edward VI, Mary and Elizabeth, with some account of its minor altars and ancient guilds* (London, 1866)

O' Gorman, F., *The Long Eighteenth Century: British and Social History 1688–1832* (London, 1997)

Paget, G. and Irvine, L., *Leicestershire* (London, 1950)

Patterson, A. Temple, *Radical Leicester: A History of Leicester 1780–1850* (Leicester, 1954)

Phipps, J., *Leicester in Parliament* (Leicester, 1988), p.96

Platt, C., *Medieval England: a Social History and Archaeology from the Conquest to 1600 AD* (London, 1997)

Plumb, J.H. (ed.), *Studies in Social History* (London, 1955), pp.33–67

Potts, G.A., 'The development of New Walk and the King Street area' in A.E. Brown (ed.), *The Growth of Leicester* (Leicester, 1971), pp.55–61.

Proctor, T.M., 'Uniforming Youth: Girl Guides and Boy Scouts in Britain, 1908–1939', *History Workshop Journal*, vol.45 (1998), pp.103–44

Pugh, M., *Women and the Women's Movement in Britain, 1914–1959* (Basingstoke, 1993)

Purkiss, D., *The English Civil War: Papists, Gentlewomen and Witchfinders in the Birth of Modern Britain* (Boulder, 2006)

Pye, N. (ed.), *Leicester and its Region* (Leicester, 1972)

Read, R., *Modern Leicester* (London, 1881)

Reeder, D. and C. Harrison, 'The Local Economy' in D. Nash and D. Reeder (eds) *Leicester in the Twentieth Century* (Stroud, 1993), pp.49–90

Reeder, D. and C. Brown, 'Municipal provision: education, health and housing' in D. Nash and D. Reeder (eds) *Leicester in the Twentieth Century* (Stroud, 1993), pp.121–57

Richards, J.D., *Viking Age England* (London, 1991)

Robson, G., *The Twentieth Walkout of All Saints Open Discussion Class and Other Poems* (Leicester, *c*.1972)

Rodger, R., 'The built environment' in D. Nash and D. Reeder (eds) *Leicester in the Twentieth Century* (Stroud, 1993) pp.1–48

Ross, C., *Richard III* (London, 1981–1983)

Royle, E., *Modern Britain: A Social History 1750–1997* (second edition, London, 1997)

Royle, T., *Civil War: the Wars of the Three Kingdoms 1638–1660* (London, 2010)

Salway, P., *Roman Britain* (Oxford, 1981)

Scaysbrook, P.A., *The Civil War in Leicestershire and Rutland* (Banbury, 1977)

Schama, S., *A History of Britain, vol.1. At the Edge of the World? 3000 BC–AD 1608* (London, 2009)

Schama, S., *A History of Britain: the British Wars 1603–1776* (London, 2009)

Seaton, D., *Light Amid the Shadows* (Leicester, 1994)

Seton, A., *Katherine* (London, 1954)

Simmons, J., *Leicester Past and Present, vol.1: Ancient Borough* (London, 1974)

Simmons, J., *Leicester Past and Present, vol.2: Modern City* (London, 1974)

Simmons, J., *New University* (Leicester, 1958)

Simon, J., 'The two John Angels', *Transactions of the Leicestershire Archaeological Society*, vol.31 (1955), pp.35–50

Simpson, H.M. (ed.), *The Life of Cardinal Wolsey* (London, 1901), www. archive.org, accessed 30 October 2012

Slack, P., *The English Poor Law 1531–1782* (Basingstoke, 1995)

Slatter, D., 'The city of Leicester: political and adminstrative history, 1509–1660' in (ed.), R.A. McKinley, *A History of the County of Leicester, vol.4* in *The Victoria History of the Counties of England* (ed.) R. B. Pugh, (London, 1958) pp.55–75

Smith, A.G.R., *The Emergence of a Nation State: the Commonwealth of England* (London, 1984)

Squires, A., *The Greys: A Long and Noble Line* (Hale, 2002)

Simmons, J., *New University* (Leicester, 1958)

Smigielski, K., *Leicester Traffic Plan* (Leicester, 1964)

Smigielski, K., *Leicester Today and Tomorrow* (Leicester, 1968)

Spencer J. and T. (Firm), *Spencer's Guide to Leicester* (Leicester, 1888)

Stephens, L. and Lee, S. (eds), *Dictionary of National Biography* (London, 1891)

Steppler, G.A., *Britons to Arms! The Story of the Volunteer Soldier* (Stroud, 1992)

Stevens, Philip A., *The Leicester and Melton Mowbray Navigations* (Far-Thrupp, 1975)

Stevenson, J., *Leicester through the Ages* (Newton Linford, 1995)

Story, J., Bourne, J. and Buckley, R. (eds), *Leicester Abbey: Medieval History, Archaeology and Manuscript Studies* (Leicester, 2006)

Sweet, R., *The English Town, 1680–1840: Government, Society and Culture* (New York, 1999)

Taylor, M., *The Quality of Leicester* (second edition, Leicester, 1997)

Thomas, H., *A History of the Great Meeting, Leicester and its Congregation* (Leciester, 1908)

Todd, M., *The Coritani* (second edition, Stroud, 1991)

Todd, M., *Roman Britain* (third edition, Oxford, 1999)

Thompson, A.H., *The Abbey of St. Mary in the Meadows Leicester* (Leicester, 1949)

Thompson, F.M.L. (ed.), *The Cambridge Social History of Britain 1750–1950*, vol.2 (Cambridge, 1990)

Thompson J., *The History of Leicester* (second edition, Leicester, 1879)

Thompson. J., *The History of Leicester in the Eighteenth Century* (Leicester, 1871)

Throsby, J., *The History and Antiquities of the Ancient Town of Leicester* (Leicester, 1791)

Wacher, J., *Roman Britain* (Stroud, 1998)

Wacher, J., *Towns of Roman Britain* (second edition, London, 1995)

Webb, C.W., *An Historical Record of N. Corah and Sons Ltd* (Leicester, between 1940–1949)

Wells, F.A., *The British Hosiery and Knitwear Industry: its History and Organisation* (Newton Abbot, 1972)

Welding, J.D., *The Leicestershire Boot and Shoe Industry: from its Origins to the Present Day* (Leicester, 1985)

White, C.L., *Women's Magazines, 1693–1968* (London, 1970)

Whitmore, R., Alice Hawkins and the Suffragette Movement in Edwardian Leicester (Derby, 2007)

Wilshere, J. and Green, S., *The Siege of Leicester – 1645* (Leicester, 1984)

Wilshere, J., *The Religious Gilds of Medieval Leicester* (Leicester, 1979)

Wilson, P. (ed.), *The Archaeology of Roman Towns, Studies in Honour of John Wacher* (Oxford, 2003)

Winstone, P., 'Managing a multi-ethnic and multi-cultural city in Europe: Leicester', *International Social Science Journal*, vol.48 (1996), pp.33–41

Yorke, B., *The Anglo Saxons* (Stroud, 1999)

# Newspapers

*Leicester and Nottingham Journal*
*Leicester Chronicle and Leicestershire Mercury*
*Leicester Daily Mercury*
*Leicester Daily Post*
*Leicester Evening Mail*
*Leicester Link*
*Leicester Mercury*
*Leicester Pioneer*

# Directories

*The Leicestershire Trade Protection Society: Street, Alphabetical and Trade Directory of Leicester, 1870*
*Wright's Directory of Leicester, 1882*
*Wright's Directory of Leicester, 1894*
*Wright's Directory of Leicester, 1904*
*Wright's Directory of Leicester, 1914*
*Kelly's Directory of Leicester, 1938*

# INDEX